INTIMATE VIOLENCE AND ABUSE IN FAMILIES

Intimate Violence and Abuse in Families

FOURTH EDITION

Richard J. Gelles

OXFORD
UNIVERSITY PRESS

Oxford University Press is a department of the University of Oxford. It furthers
the University's objective of excellence in research, scholarship, and education
by publishing worldwide. Oxford is a registered trade mark of Oxford University
Press in the UK and certain other countries.

Published in the United States of America by Oxford University Press
198 Madison Avenue, New York, NY 10016, United States of America.

© Oxford University Press 2017

First Edition published in 1985
Second Edition published in 1990
Third Edition published in 1997
Fourth Edition published in 2017

Library of Congress Cataloging-in-Publication Data
Names: Gelles, Richard J., author.
Title: Intimate violence and abuse in families / Richard J. Gelles.
Other titles: Intimate violence in families
Description: Fourth edition. | Oxford ; New York : Oxford University Press,
[2017] | Includes bibliographical references and index.
Identifiers: LCCN 2016010563 | ISBN 9780195381733 (alk. paper)
Subjects: LCSH: Family violence—United States.
Classification: LCC HV6626.2 .G45 2017 | DDC 362.82/92—dc23
LC record available at https://lccn.loc.gov/2016010563

9 8 7 6 5 4 3 2 1

Printed by WebCom, Inc., Canada

Contents

Preface

IN THE EARLY FALL OF 1971, I dropped by Murray Straus's office at the University of New Hampshire. I was a second-year doctoral student in the Department of Sociology and Murray was a full professor. I was making the rounds of the faculty trying to decide on a topic for my doctoral dissertation and trying to match a topic to the proper advisor.

Frankly, I had low expectations when I asked Murray if he would have lunch with me. Murray was an established scholar in the field of family sociology with a specialty in quantitative measurement. I saw myself as a qualitative researcher and had done a participant-observation study of television news for my master's thesis.

I had enough knowledge of Murray's work to know that his most recent project was a laboratory study of family decision making. As much as I respected Murray as a teacher and scholar, I could not see how our interests could possibly align.

Lunch produced short-term and long-term unexpected results. First, Murray described his new research project on "family violence." He was co-editing a book on violence in the family with Suzanne Steinmetz (Steinmetz & Straus, 1974). In addition, he was distributing questionnaires to college students seeking responses to questions about their experience with, and observations of, violence in their homes.

I was fascinated by the challenge of actually trying to conduct research on violence between family members. Here was a scholar who was willing to ask the question, "Have you stopped beating your wife?" On the other hand, I was not much of a fan of quantitative research. I opined that, as much as I admired Murray's approach of surveying college students, I had concerns that the field of "the sociology of the family" was actually "the sociology of the family of American college students."

Murray tolerated my youthful impudence and was intrigued by the possibility of someone being willing to carry out research in the community through in-depth interviews. So, I left lunch with a dissertation topic and a major professor.

What I did not realize is that I left lunch with a career. Thinking only short-term, I just assumed I had a dissertation topic and that was it. But like so many others who came into the field of intimate violence and abuse, I discovered that the topic begins to own you. The emotional aspects of seeing and talking to victims of intimate violence is heartbreaking. The challenges of trying to find meaningful help for victims and offenders is frustrating. The indifference of policy-makers to the tragedies that befall victims was, and often continues to be, infuriating. Lastly, conducting quality and useful research continues to be challenging.

It took a bit longer to come face to face with the next unexpected outcome of my lunch. Our program of research evolved into the design and carrying out of the First National Family Violence Survey in 1976. After we collected data from a nationally representative sample of 2,146 individuals, Murray, Suzanne Steinmetz, and I set out to prepare presentations and publications based on our data. I worked on violence against children, Murray analyzed the data on violence between intimate partners, and Suzanne examined the sibling violence data. Things were relatively quiet at my end, although a goodly number of scholars were taken aback by our conclusions that nearly 2 million parents used abusive physical violence toward their children each year.

The reactions to Murray and Suzanne's work were considerably more heated. Murray presented a paper and then published that same paper on intimate partner violence. The paper presented data that showed that slightly more *women* struck their male intimate partners than men struck women. For each form of severe violence, with the exception of "using a gun or knife," the frequency of female-to-male violence exceeded the rate of male-to-female violence. In the very same journal where Murray published his statistical data (1977), Suzanne published her article, "The Battered Husband Syndrome" (1977a). Suzanne's paper was considered so controversial that the editors commissioned a critique of the paper that was published in the same issue.

Perhaps I was a bit young and naïve, but I was surprised by the controversy stirred up by the data on female-to-male violence. These were the data. We did not make the data up; this is what our respondents had told us. There was no malice in our research, no hidden agenda. So why the uproar?

Well, I quickly learned that there are fault lines that exist between research, practice, policy, and advocacy. Advocates, struggling to have their voices heard by policy makers, embraced the data on violence toward women, but believed the data on violence towards men severely undercut their claims that violence against women deserved a special place on the social policy agenda and deserved funding from federal and state sources.

Over the years, I discovered that such fault lines and controversies are not confined to the field of intimate partner violence. When I first published my critique of intensive family-preservation programs, I ran into a buzz saw of controversy. What was the problem? I asked. The answer was that funding for family preservation programs was a critical resource practitioners depended on as they worked to preserve families in which child maltreatment occurs. Well, I countered, maybe some families are not worth preserving. That set off another explosion: "Don't you realize that minority families are dispro-portionately affected by child welfare policies?" The families I thought were not "worth" preserving were likely to be disproportionately minority and low-income families. Clearly, gender and race are at the core of controver-sies regarding many social problems, and intimate violence and abuse are no exception.

In this, the fourth edition of *Intimate Violence and Abuse*, I do not avoid the controversies. My goal is to be inclusive of all the disciplines and constituencies involved in the efforts to explain, predict, understand, and prevent intimate vio-lence and abuse. I try to be respectful of all points of view and present the differ-ent points of view that surround some of the key contentious issues in the field on intimate violence and abuse. If I am guilty of a bias, it is that I draw upon the best available research and data to settle a controversy.

This volume is designed to be a core text for students examining intimate violence and abuse. As a core text, the book serves as a launching pad for stu-dents who wish to explore one or more aspects of intimate partner violence at a deeper level.

In the 40 years since I sat down for lunch with Murray Straus, the field of intimate violence and abuse has become a rich and exciting field of endeavor for scholars, teachers, advocates, practitioners, and policy-makers. While we still clash politely, and sometimes not so politely, those of us in the field can take some satisfaction that our collective efforts have not just contributed to a larger knowledge base, but, as you will read in the chapters that follow, we have actually contributed to a reduction in the level of intimate violence and abuse.

Richard J. Gelles, Ph.D.
October, 2015

INTIMATE VIOLENCE AND ABUSE IN FAMILIES

1 Introduction to Intimate Violence and Abuse in Families

TWENTY OR THIRTY YEARS AGO, a book on the topic of intimate or family violence would always begin with introduction that made the case that, while violence and abuse between intimates has occurred across time and cultures, such behavior is generally not thought of as a major social problem. Such an introduction is no longer necessary. News and social media accounts about some form of family violence are common, and hardly a day goes by without one or more cases coming to public attention. For intimate partner violence, the media accounts focus chiefly on reporting on violence perpetrated by public celebrities or sports figures. After Ray Rice, a star player with the National Football League's (NFL) Baltimore Ravens, was arrested for assaulting his fiancée, the National Football League instituted a new policy that called for a six-game suspension for any professional football player found to have perpetrated domestic violence against a partner. The six-game suspension is for the first offense. A player with a second offense will be banished for life—with the right to appeal after one year. The policy, which is a component of the NFL's personal conduct policy, was implemented by the NFL Commissioner Roger Goodell after he was widely criticized for imposing only a two-game suspension penalty on Rice, who was shown on a video dragging his unconscious fiancée (and later wife) out of an elevator in Atlantic City. Three days after the commissioner instituted the new policy, a San Francisco 49ers player was arrested on suspicion of felony domestic violence. When a second video emerged in September 2014 showing Rice punching his fiancée and her falling to the floor of the elevator unconscious, the commissioner banned Rice from playing, and the Ravens released Rice.

Domestic violence receives considerable attention on the sports pages of papers and websites, as it does on entertainment pages when celebrities are involved. Olympic sprinter Oscar Pistorius was tried for killing his girlfriend, Reeva Steenkamp. Pistorius was acquitted of premeditated murder but convicted of "culpable homicide." Others charged with some form of domestic violence include actor Charlie Sheen and rapper/producer Chris Brown. Celebrity victims have included actresses Halle Berry and Pamela Anderson, television personality Meredith Viera, and singers Rihanna and Tina Turner.

The public portrayal of child maltreatment—both physical abuse and neglect—comes largely in the form of news reports of horrific cases. Most news reports of child maltreatment are local stories that involve newborns or infants killed by caregivers.[1] When older children are victims, the news reports tend to portray victims of cruel torture or starvation. The public reporting of child maltreatment cases heavily over-represents minority families living in poverty.

A second form of child-maltreatment reporting involves the same poor and minority families, but concentrates on the failure or inadequacies of the local or statewide child welfare system. The *Miami Herald* published a horrifically graphic series titled "Innocents Lost" that detailed the cases of numerous children who died after they and their families became involved in the Florida child welfare system. Similar series have appeared in the *Washington Post, Philadelphia Inquirer, New York Times*, and *Arizona Republic*. The Public Broadcasting Service (PBS) show *Frontline* broadcast a multi-part series of the functioning of the Maine child welfare system. The show began with the case of a child killed by her foster mother, who was an employee of the Maine child protective service system.

While a book on intimate violence and abuse probably does not have to make the case that child maltreatment and intimate partner violence are important social problems, it seems obvious that some of the media presentations of intimate violence tend to over-represent one segment of the problem. Celebrities are neither the only perpetrators nor the only victims of intimate partner violence, and child maltreatment is not confined to poor and minority families. In addition, important forms of intimate violence and abuse are almost completely overlooked. Violence between siblings, abuse of the elderly, child-to-parent violence, and violence among gays, lesbians, and transgendered couples are nowhere to be found in public media.

When the topic of sexual abuse is presented in the news media or film, perpetrators are typically the clergy, daycare providers, or choir or scout troop leaders. Family members, who make up the vast majority of sexual abuse perpetrators, are rarely covered or portrayed in movies.

While it is not new or news that intimates can be violent or abusive, there is considerable material to cover on the topic—beyond making the case that intimate violence is a problem that calls for public, policy, and practice attention. This book is designed to provide a basic overview of the subject of intimate violence and abuse. Many books look at only one aspect of violence and maltreatment in the home. Typically, an author will focus on only intimate partner violence, child abuse and neglect, sexual abuse and victimization, or elder abuse (there are very few books on sibling violence or child-to-parent violence).

The single focus is also found in professional journals. There are journals with the titles of *Child Maltreatment; Child Abuse and Neglect: The International Journal; Violence Toward Women; Partner Abuse;* and the *Journal of Elder Abuse and Neglect*. A few journals, such as *Journal of Intimate Violence, Journal of Family Violence*, and *Violence and Victims*, among others, do publish articles on a full range of intimate violence.

Policy and advocacy also tend to be developed around single aspects of intimate violence. Enactment and oversight of the federal Violence Against Women Act (Public Law 103-322) is located with the Senate and House of Representatives judiciary committees. The Senate Finance Committee and the House Committee on Ways and Means oversee the major child welfare legislation that funds child welfare services (Title IV-E of the Social Security Act of 1935). Each form of intimate violence has its own advocacy organizations—for example, the Family Violence Prevention Fund (now titled Futures Without Violence) for intimate partner violence, and the Child Welfare League of America for child maltreatment.

Finally, practice dealing with such abuses is also compartmentalized. The Children's Hospital of Boston developed separate teams to assess and respond to specific forms of child maltreatment. There was a Trauma X team for physical child abuse, a Failure to Thrive team for suspected neglect, and a Sexual Abuse team. Social service agencies also tend to "silo" or compartmentalize programs and interventions for specific categories of violence, abuse, and maltreatment.

The compartmentalization of research, policy, practice, and advocacy may function well for the goals of each group, but it artificially segments the reality of what goes on among intimates and families. Moreover, the compartmentalization may obscure the entire picture and hinder better and more effective prevention and treatment approaches.

An example of the problems produced by narrowly focusing on just one form of violence and abuse is illustrated by the experience of one hospital's emergency room staff. The physicians and nurses in an inner-city children's hospital treated a two-year-old boy for bruises and a possible concussion. The case came into stark focus when the examining physician realized that the bruise on the boy's face was in the form of the outline of a hand, and that there was a clear indication of an injury caused by a ring on one of the fingers. The physician approached the mother of the boy, who was also in the waiting room, and asked her to hold out her hand. The ring on the mother's finger matched the injury on the little boy's face. The physician began to raise his voice to the mother, accusing her of inflicting the injury and telling her in no uncertain terms that he would report the case to Child Protective Services and hold the child in the hospital rather than release the boy to the clearly abusive mother. One of the nurse practitioners stepped forward and pulled the physician away. She asked the doctor whether he noticed that the mother also had bruises on her face and around her eyes. While there was little doubt that the mother had injured the child, there was also the likelihood that the mother was a victim of some sort of violence—perhaps inflicted by an intimate partner. While the suspected abuse of the child would have to be reported, the victimization of the mother should also be a concern for the emergency room staff.

Research does in fact find that one form of intimate violence is often related to another. There is a considerable correlation between the abuse of children and intimate partner violence (Edleson & Graham-Bermann, 2001; Gelles & Straus, 1988; Renner & Slack, 2006). There is less clarity in terms of what the appropriate interventions and policies should be when there are multiple victimizations in a home.

An example of social policies' being at cross-purposes arose in a lawsuit filed in New York City. The case, *Nicholson v. Scopetta,* arose in 1999 when Sharwline Nicholson ended her relationship with the father of her child. Her former partner assaulted Ms. Nicholson, and the resulting injuries required her to be hospitalized. Ms. Nicholson provided the child protective workers from the New York City Administration for Children's Services (ACS) with names of relatives who could care for the children, but the ACS decided to seek legal custody of the children because they were in imminent danger. The argument was that Ms. Nicholson could not protect herself or her children. The children were placed in foster care. Later, Ms. Nicholson and others filed a class-action suit against ACS, claiming that taking her children from her when she had done no harm to them violated her constitutional rights. Advocates for battered women, as well as advocates for parents, lined up on the side of Ms. Nicholson and the other plaintiffs in the lawsuit. Others worried that, even though Ms. Nicholson had not hurt her children, they were in a dangerous environment, and returning them to Ms. Nicholson could have compromised their safety. In the end, the New York Court of Appeals ruled that a mother's inability to protect her child was not, in and of itself, "neglect" and could not be the sole factor leading to a removal.

And so, at every level—research, social services, and policy, forms of family violence, perpetrators, and victims intersect.

Myths and Controversies That Hinder the Understanding of Intimate Violence and Abuse

ADVOCACY STATISTICS

As we will discuss in Chapter 2, intimates and family members have been violent and abusive toward one another across time and cultures. But for most time periods and most cultures, the problem of intimate violence and the abuse of children occurred in private and was very much what sociologist C. Wright Mills (1959) called a "private trouble." Many victims were too young or dependent to seek help, while other victims were too scared or incapacitated to reach out for assistance. The threat of victim-blaming kept many other victims silent. One of the necessary steps that must occur before a "private trouble" becomes a social issue is for there to be some kind of public recognition that the private trouble affects a significant number of individuals. Secondly, the private trouble must generate significant negative consequences for individuals and society.

Child advocates, feminists, and women's rights advocates played the lead roles in identifying intimate violence and abuse as social issues and important social problems. To make the case about the harm violence and abuse caused, advocates relied on graphic and horrific case examples, often accompanied by photographs. But advocates faced a major roadblock in establishing the case that intimate violence and abuse were widespread. Until the mid-1970s, there was no research at all on the extent of child abuse, sexual abuse, intimate partner violence, or elder abuse. In the mid-1970s, as a result of the Child Abuse Prevention and Treatment Act of 1974 (Public Law 93-247), Congress mandated that the states keep track of child abuse and neglect reports. The mandate was a requirement that had to be fulfilled in order to receive federal funds, but not all states initially complied with the mandate. The same law called for a national survey of the incidence of child maltreatment. The incidence study would not be completed and published until 1979. There was a scattering of statistics on intimate partner violence. An analysis of the U.S. Department of Justice's Uniform Crime Reports could be used to determine how many homicides involved a family member as a perpetrator against another family member. The Justice Department's National Crime Victimization Survey, however, would not include specific questions on intimate partner violence until 1992 (Gelles, 2000).

In the absence of official statistics or high-quality epidemiological research, advocates stitched together anecdotes, case studies, and small-scale surveys to make the case that intimate violence was a significant social problem. Some of the estimates were little more that pulling a number from thin air. Others were extrapolations from limited studies. Whatever the source, the advocates' statistics took on a reality and a life that endured for decades. Some of the statistical claims have faded, while others have enjoyed a long life on the web and social media. A few of the enduring advocacy statistics and claims include:

- More women are treated in emergency rooms for battering injuries than for muggings, rapes, and traffic accidents combined.
- The March of Dimes reports that battering during pregnancy is the leading cause of birth defects and infant mortality.
- According to the Federal Bureau of Investigation (FBI), a women is battered every 15 seconds.

Each of these claims appeared on a web page in 2015, and each is incorrect to one degree or another. The first claim, about emergency rooms, is based on a small local study in New Haven, Connecticut, and has never been replicated on a larger level. The March of Dimes statement is simply made up. The claim about battering every 15 seconds was never based on FBI data, but was derived from the First National Family Violence Survey (Straus, Gelles, & Steinmetz, 1980).

The rise in concern about the problem of sexual assault on campus revived the statistic that one in five college women is a victim of sexual assault. President Obama embraced this statistic when he announced the creation of a White House Task Force to Protect Students from Sexual Assault. The "one in five" statistic is derived from the "Campus Sexual Assault Study" commissioned by the National Institute of Justice and carried out between 2005 and 2007 (Krebs et al., 2007). The survey was carried out at two large four-year universities—clearly not a representative sample—and had a large non-response rate. A second problem with the Campus Sexual Assault Study, and its predecessor carried out by *Ms. Magazine* and psychologist Mary Koss and her colleagues (1987), is concerns about the overly broad definition of what constitutes "sexual assault" and "rape." The Koss survey concluded that one in four campus women were victims of "sexual assault" (Koss, Gidycz, & Wisniewski, 1987).

The American Association of Universities (AAU) commissioned their own survey of sexual assault on member campuses.[2] The AAU Campus Climate Survey on Sexual Assault and Sexual Misconduct contacted students on 27 campuses (16 AAU members). Representative samples of students were contacted by email on each campus. The survey headline echoed previous campus sexual assault surveys:

"More Than 1 in 5 Female Undergrads at Top Schools Suffer Sexual Attacks."[3]

But the AAU survey suffered from the same methodological problems as prior studies. First, the overall response rate across the 27 universities was only 19.3%. Second, the top-line headline of "1 in 5 Female Undergrads" combined all forms of sexual assault and exploitation, ranging from forced penetration to unwanted kissing.

Are we being overly picky when we point out the methodological weaknesses and flaws in advocates' and advocacy groups' statistics? After all, isn't one victim enough? Well, first and foremost, the reality is that "one victim is *not* enough." Many illnesses and social problems bid for public attention, resources, and policy solutions. It really is important to know how many individuals and families are victimized and what is the nature of the harm caused by the problem. Second, bad data can produce harmful reactions, policies, and programs. Many parents react emotionally when they hear about advocacy statistics claiming that hundreds of thousands of children are abducted by strangers. Parents line up to have their children fingerprinted and impress upon their children the need to be wary of any stranger. In reality, nearly all of the hundreds of thousands of missing children are involved in parental or relative kidnapping. The number of children kidnapped and actually killed by strangers is less than 100 per year (Gelles, 2011). Why terrify children about a problem they are less likely to experience than almost any other physical threat?

CONTROVERSIES

Myths and advocacy statistics can mostly be managed by sound research and appropriate methodological critiques. Controversies, on the other hand, arise from deep-seated beliefs and values about the way the world should be and are not so easily dismissed or countered. This section examines some of the major controversies that continue to influence the ways in which we understand and respond to the problems of intimate violence and abuse.

Is it a psychological or a social problem? At first glance, it is easy to understand why many people assume that abusers are mentally ill and suffer from some kind of psychopathy. Given the media, newspaper accounts, photos, and now Internet videos of cases of abuse, the nearly obvious takeaway is that no one who is mentally stable would do such a thing. The earliest writings on child maltreatment and wife abuse all came to the same conclusion—mental illness is the cause of intimate and family violence. But all the early studies were case studies of a very small number of victims or offenders who were seen by mental health or medical professionals. And all the diagnoses were carried out *after the offense occurred.* Larger, more representative studies undermined the case that mental illness or psychopathy is the sole cause of abusive acts. Researchers identify social factors that are correlated with child maltreatment and intimate partner violence. Both surveys and case study data indicated that intimate violence rates are higher in low-income families and among individuals who were unemployed or underemployed. Social stressors and social isolation also are correlated with high rates of abuse. Some forms of intimate victimization, however, such as sexual abuse of children, are not correlated with social factors at all. Later chapters in this book will delve deeper into the psychological and social factors that increase the risk of intimate violence and abuse. For this discussion, we can conclude with some general findings. Child maltreatment, intimate partner abuse, and other forms of intimate violence can be found among all social and demographic groups. But the distribution is not even. The risk of intimate violence is greater in some social groups and lower in others—even when factoring in that some social characteristics increase the risk of being reported for or identified for engaging in some form of intimate violence. Yet, in some cases, psychological factors are the most salient explanatory variables. While reducing poverty would certainly lower the overall rate of child abuse and neglect, some abuse and neglect is going to occur independently of the economic resources available to caregivers.

It is the drink and the drugs. The second most common explanation for intimate violence and abuse is that it is the result of "demon rum" and "damned drugs." The common-sense link between alcohol, drugs, and violence is not without support. Research indicates that as many as half the instances of violence and abuse in families involve some alcohol or drugs (Flanzer, 2005). This is a very strong association. But do drugs and/or alcohol *cause* people to become violent? Are drugs and alcohol dis-inhibitors that unleash violent behavior? And would solving the drug or drinking problem eliminate the violence? Common sense frequently says "yes" to these questions. Empirically sound research, however, generally argues "no" (Gelles & Cavanaugh, 2005).

GLOBAL PERSPECTIVES BOX 1.1
ALCOHOL AND VIOLENCE: CULTURAL EXPECTATIONS AND TIME-OUT

"Only when he was drinking would he do that. When he was sober, he was a totally different man."

One of the most consistent findings from studies of intimate violence and abuse is the link between alcohol and violence. Time and again, victims and observers would point out that perpetrators would only be violent when under the influence of alcohol. Alcohol, it seems, is some kind of superego solvent that dissolves inhibitions and releases violent and other suppressed behaviors.

Anthropologists Craig MacAndrew and Robert Edgerton (1969) explode the myth of alcohol as a superego solvent in their cross-cultural examination of alcohol and behavior. How people behave when drunk, MacAndrew and Edgerton point out, is very much dependent on the local culture's view of alcohol and acceptable behavior. Among the Camba, a population of some 80,000 in eastern Bolivia, alcohol beverages are consumed regularly and in large quantities. Yet, when drinking, the Camba rarely express physical or verbal aggression. An early twentieth-century ethnography of the Papago, who lived in what is now southern Arizona, describe instances when Papago men consumed so much alcohol that they were literally falling down drunk; yet, there was little quarreling and few fights.

The bottom line of MacAndrew and Edgerton's analysis is that cultural expectations, rather than the chemical properties of alcohol, greatly influence how people behave when they drink or drink heavily.

So why is there a link between drinking and violence in the United States and so many other countries and cultures? MacAndrew and Edgerton (1969, p. 90) explain that in those countries where drinking leads to what appears to be "out-of-character" behavior, cultural norms create a "time-out" from everyday rules and norms. Knowing they will not be held accountable for their behavior when drinking is much more of a superego solvent than the actual alcohol.

Source: MacAndrew, C., & Edgerton, R. B. (1969). *Drunken Comportment: A Social Explanation*. Chicago: Aldine.

There is little scientific evidence to support the theory that alcohol and drugs, such as cocaine, have chemical and pharmacological properties that *directly* produce violent and abusive behavior. Evidence from cross-cultural research, laboratory studies, blood tests of men arrested for partner abuse, and survey research all indicate that, although alcohol use may be *associated* with intimate violence, alcohol is *not a primary cause* of the intimate partner violence (Caetano, Schafer, & Cunradi, 2001; O'Farrell, Van Hutton, & Murphy, 1999; MacAndrew & Edgerton, 1969). It is probable that some individuals may even consciously use alcohol and/or drugs as an excuse for their violent behavior.

In some cultures, people drink and become violent; in others, people drink and are passive (See Global Perspectives Box 1.1). What explains the difference? The difference is due to what people in those societies believe about alcohol. If they believe alcohol or drugs are disinhibitors, people become disinhibited. If they believe that alcohol is a depressant, people become depressed. Because our society believes that alcohol and drugs release violent tendencies, people are given a "time-out" from the acceptable rules of social behavior when they drink or when people believe they are drunk. Combine the time-out with the desire to cover up instances of family violence, and one has the perfect excuse: "I didn't know what I was doing: I was drunk." Or, from the victim's perspective, "My partner is a Dr. Jekyll and Mr. Hyde—when he drinks, he is violent; when he is sober, there is no problem." In the end, violent partners and parents learn that if they do not want to be held responsible for their violence, they should either drink before they hit, or at least say they were drunk.

One drug does stand out, however, as a possible cause of violent behavior—amphetamine. Amphetamine use is associated with increased crime and violence. In fact, if used frequently, it is more closely related to violent behavior than any other psychoactive drugs. Amphetamines raise excitability and muscle tension, and this may lead to impulsive behavior. The behavior that follows from amphetamine use is related to both the dosage and the pre-use personality of the user. Frequent users who already have aggressive personalities are likely to become more aggressive when using this drug (Kosten & Singha, 1999).

Except for the evidence that appears to link amphetamine use to violence, the picture of the alcohol- and drug-crazed partner or parent who impulsively and violently abuses a family member is a distortion. If alcohol and other drugs are linked to violence at all, it is through a complicated set of individual, situational, and social factors (Gelles & Cavanaugh, 2005).

Only men are violent; if women strike their partners, it is only in self-defense. It would be fair to say that the most enduring and heated controversy in the study of intimate partner violence is the question of female-to-male violence. More than 40 years ago, when I published my first book on domestic violence and initiated the scholarly conversation about intimate partner violence (Gelles, 1974), the initial reaction to my data on female-to-male violence was that such violence simply does not occur (Dobash & Dobash, 1979). A few years later, when Suzanne Steinmetz published her journal article "The Battered Husband Syndrome" (1977), she was severely criticized for making up an issue based on case studies and cartoon representations of female-to-male violence (Pleck, Pleck, Grossman, & Bart, 1977). Shortly thereafter, Murray Straus and his colleagues (Straus, 1977; Straus, Gelles, & Steinmetz, 1980) published the results of the First National

Family Violence Survey. The survey, based on in-person interviews with a nationally representative sample of 2,147 households, found that the rates of female-to-male violence—both minor and severe violence—were equivalent to the rates of male-to-female violence. To say this finding set off a firestorm of protest in the academic and advocacy arenas would be an understatement. Straus and his colleagues actually received death threats. Straus himself was accused of using his research to cover up his own wife battering. When the *ad hominem* attacks quieted down, critics focused on the methodology—specifically the way intimate partner violence was measured using the Conflict Tactics Scales (Loseke & Kurz, 2005). Straus consistently rebutted each of the methodological critiques (Straus, 2005, 2011; Straus & Ramirez, 2007). Chapters 4 and 5 of this book look more deeply into the various statistics and studies of intimate partner violence and what has come to be known as the "gender symmetry" controversy. Suffice it to say, the controversy burns as brightly today as it did in 1977.

Violence always gets worse. A less volatile, but persistent, belief among those who work with victims of violence and abuse is that, left unchecked, violence will always escalate. In fact, some researchers suggest that minor assaults of any type are likely to lead to more serious attacks (Feld & Straus, 1989; Pagelow, 1981). But Feld and Straus (1989) also found that couples reported that from one year to the next, 33% of couples said that there was no violence in the year following a year in which violence occurred. This provides evidence of desistence. Secondly, research finds that, instead of violence escalating, there are various types of offenders, and that certain types of offenders never escalate their violence above a certain threshold. A recent review of the literature on violence typologies reveals that male batterers can be classified into three categories—low-, moderate-, and high-risk offenders (Cavanaugh & Gelles, 2005). The three types of offenders can be further subtyped according to the dimensions of severity and frequency of violence, criminal history, and level of psychopathology (see Table 1.1).

The specific characteristics, particular to both the type of offender and the individual within that type, create a threshold at which the offender either will or will not escalate in violence. This is not to say that this threshold can never be crossed; only that it is unlikely that an offender will "move" from one particular type to another. This observation refutes previous claims among researchers and advocates that battering always escalates in frequency and intensity over time.

Is the answer compassion or control? Forty years ago, the prevailing response to intimate partner violence was indifference, unless a severe injury occurred. The police in Washington, D.C., applied an informal "stitch rule" that meant that, unless an injury required a specific number of surgical sutures, the perpetrator would not be arrested (Gelles, 1974). In response to this and other similarly

TABLE 1.1

Synthesis of Batterer Typologies

Low-Risk Batterer	Moderate-Risk Batterer	High-Risk Batterer
Gondolf (1988) Type III—typical	Gottman et al. (1995)—Type II pit bull	Gondolf (1988) Types I & II
Hamberger, Lohr, Bonge & Tolin (1996)—nonpathological	Holtzworth-Munroe & Stuart (1994)—dysphoric—borderline	Gottman at al. (1995)—Type I cobra
Holtzworth-Munroe & Stuart (1994)—family only		Hamberger et al. (1996)—antisocial
Johnson (1995)—common couple violence	Hamberger et al. (1996)—passive aggressive—dependent	Holtzworth-Munroe & Stuart (1994)—generally violent—antisocial
		Johnson (1995)—intimate terrorist
Low severity of violence	Moderate severity of violence	High severity of violence
Low frequency of violence	Moderate frequency of violence	High frequency of violence
Little or no psychopathology	Moderate to high psychopathology	High levels of psychopathology
Usually no criminal history		Usually have criminal history

Source: Cavanaugh, M. M., & Gelles, R. J. (2005). The utility of male domestic violence offender typologies: New directions for research, policy, and practice. *Journal of Interpersonal Violence*, 20, 163.

Reproduced with permission, Sage Publications.

informal practices, women's groups across the county brought class-action lawsuits seeking to insure that domestic violence would be responded to like other assaults. Eventually, and with the support of research findings (Sherman & Berk, 1984), police departments instituted mandatory arrest policies, and prosecutors were more consistent and punitive in their charges. In short, the response to intimate partner violence evolved into one that favored a strategy of formal social control. Nonetheless, not all offenders were subjected to certain and severe punishment. One of the controversies surrounding the Ray Rice incident is that after he was arrested for punching his fiancée into unconsciousness, he was offered pretrial intervention. When he completed the program in a year his arrest remained on his record but there would be no conviction. When the video of the Rice assault became public, there was a storm of protest that the intervention was too weak. In Florida, Marissa Alexander fired what she called a "warning shot" at her husband while the husband and his two children stood in the kitchen (see Chapter 5). Although Alexander claimed and documented that her husband beat her at least once, she was convicted and sentenced to 20 years in prison. Here the public response was that there was too much "control" in the response.

Compassion for the perpetrator is the typical response to child maltreatment. Criminal charges are rare—even if the case involves a significant injury to a child. The typical response is to remove the children from the home and provide the offenders with psychological and social services. Many argue that the compassionate approach to child maltreatment is warranted because most parents want to be good parents but may lack the psychological or social resources necessary to meet their children's needs. Others argue that it makes no sense that a husband who hits his wife gets arrested, but if he hits his child, he is assigned a social worker.

SUMMARY

These are but a few of the more significant controversies in the field of intimate violence and abuse. A number of other important issues and controversies will be examined in the following chapters.

What Is Violence and Abuse?

One of the earliest and most enduring problems in the field of intimate violence and abuse was the issue of developing useful, clear, and acceptable definitions of "violence" and "abuse." As noted earlier, estimates of the extent of intimate partner violence, child maltreatment, and sexual assault vary greatly, depending on the definition of the problem. Those who study child abuse have tried for years to develop an acceptable and accepted definition, and have found that after decades of conferences, workshops, and publications, there are perhaps as many definitions as there are scholars in the field (King & Chalk, 1998).

An example of an early definition of child abuse was the one used by C. Henry Kempe and his colleagues (1962) in their article "The Battered Child Syndrome." Kempe, a physician, defined child abuse as a *clinical condition* (i.e., with diagnosable medical and physical symptoms) having to do with those who have been deliberately injured by a physical assault. This definition restricts abuse to only those acts of physical violence that produce a diagnosable injury. The National Center on Child Abuse and Neglect, an agency of the federal government established in 1974,[4] expanded the definition of abuse to include non-physical acts as well. The agency's definition of abuse was the following:

> [T]he physical or mental injury, sexual abuse, negligent treatment, or maltreatment of a child under the age of eighteen by a person who is responsible for the child's welfare under circumstances which indicate that the child's health or welfare is harmed or threatened thereby. [Public Law 93-237]

This definition combines acts of omission and commission or acts of violence and nonviolence in the same category. On one hand, definitions like those used by the National Center on Child Abuse and Neglect include acts that go well beyond physical violence. On the other hand, this definition is restrictive in that *only* acts of violence that cause an injury are considered "abusive."

FORCE AND VIOLENCE

If a father takes a gun and shoots at his child and misses, there is no physical injury, and according to many definitions of abuse, this act would not be considered "abuse." There is, of course, harm in a father's shooting and missing, but the act itself does not qualify as abuse under the strict terms of the definition. Ideally, then, a definition of abuse should include harmful acts that, for some reason, do not produce an injury. At the other extreme, a father who spanks his child is not usually considered either abusive or violent—unless serious visible injuries occur. Most people believe that spanking a child is normal, necessary, and good. Many parents report that they spank their children, and some people believe that the true figure is a lot closer to 100% (Straus, Douglas, & Medeiros 2013). Consequently, some researchers believe that, in defining violence, it is a good idea to separate the so-called normal acts of "force" from the non-normal and harmful acts of "violence." While such a separation might seem desirable, distinguishing between acceptable and unacceptable acts proves more difficult than one might imagine. One major question is: Who decides which acts of violence are legitimate and illegitimate?" Is "force" hitting a child without physical evidence of an injury, while "violence" is hitting a child and causing a black and blue mark? Should the decision be left to the person who is being hit, to the person doing the hitting, or to agents of social control such as police, social workers, or judges? Should the decision be left to social scientists? An extensive study of the definitions of child abuse found that what is defined as "child abuse" varies by social category and profession. Police officers, social workers, physicians, and lawyers have differing views on what constitutes "child abuse." Similarly, the definition of abuse varies by social class, race, and ethnicity (Giovannoni & Becerra, 1979).

A DEFINITION OF VIOLENCE

The difficulty in defining what acts are violent and what acts are physical, but not violent, is due to varying cultural and subcultural views on whether certain behavior is or is not acceptable. It would be far too complex to have a definition that depended on the situation in which the behavior was used, the size of the offender, the size of the victim, and the reactions of those who observed or heard about the behavior. For that reason, this text uses the *definition of family violence* crafted by the National Academy of Sciences panel on "Assessing Family Violence Interventions":

> Family violence includes child and adult abuse that occurs between family members or adult intimate partners. For children, this includes acts by others that are physically or emotionally harmful, or that carry the potential to cause physical harm. Abuse of children may include sexual exploitation or molestation, threats to kill or abandon, or lack of emotional or physical support necessary for normal development.
>
> For adults, family or intimate violence may include acts that are physically and emotionally harmful or that carry the potential to cause physical harm. Abuse of adult partners may include sexual coercion or assaults, physical intimidation, threats to kill or harm, restraint of normal activities or freedom, and denial of access to resources. (National Research Council, 1998, p. 19)

TYPES OF VIOLENCE

Researchers sometimes identify subtypes of violent behaviors that may exist in intimate relationships. Johnson (1995) distinguishes three patterns of intimate partner violence: (1) situational violence, (2) intimate terrorism, and (3) violence resistance. He asserts that these classifications are based on patterns of control that are present throughout some relationships, and that they incorporate various types of violence. According to Johnson's model, violence that exists within the context of a specific argument or disagreement, in which one partner physically attacks the other, is described as Situational Violence. Intimate Terrorism, on the other hand, is defined as violence utilized as part of a general pattern of coercive control. Lastly, Violence Resistance is violence utilized in response to Intimate Terrorism. According to Johnson, the severest type of violence, Intimate Terrorism, is more likely to escalate over time, and less likely to be mutually violent. But situational violence is usually less severely violent, less likely to escalate, and can, at times, be bidirectional.

Physical violence, in all its forms, does not exhaust the range of harmful acts committed by family members against other household members. Students of child maltreatment identify neglect, emotional abuse, sexual abuse, educational neglect, medical neglect, and failure to thrive as forms of maltreatment. Researchers and practitioners often report that the impact and consequences of emotional and/or psychological abuse have a more profound and lasting effect on victims than the consequences of physical violence alone (Loseke & Kurz, 2005).

"Emotional and psychological abuse" covers a wide range of abusive behaviors. Emotional abuse includes attacks on an individual's self-esteem by the use of degrading and belittling remarks and/or acts. Name-calling, ridicule, blaming, swearing at, criticizing, and jealousy are only a few examples of tactics that can be used to gain power and control over another individual. Psychological abuse is any threat to do bodily harm to a partner, child, family member, friends, pets, or oneself (suicide threat). Victims of this form of abuse report that their partner has destroyed their prized possessions, thrown objects in their direction, punched walls, slammed doors, and threatened to harm the victim should she try to leave her abusive mate.

Summary

It is theoretically and practically important to differentiate acts of physical violence from other harmful but nonviolent coercive acts. Physical violence is qualitatively different from other means of harming and injuring people. Thus, although physical violence shares with other abusive acts the central characteristics of malevolence and harmful intent, the nature of the intended harm—physical pain and suffering—is unique. This text will examine the current research on the scope, nature, causes, consequences, and policy and practice interventions regarding the various forms of intimate partner violence and abuse.

Discussion Questions

1. Why is it useful to examine all forms of family violence instead of concentrating on just one single type, such as child abuse or intimate partner violence?

2. Why do the myths and controversies about family violence exist? What possible functions might these myths serve for practitioners who treat family violence? For society? What impact might these myths have on victims as well as abusers?

Notes

1. An exception that occurred simultaneously with the Rice and Pistorius cases was the indictment of Minnesota Vikings star running back Adrian Peterson for child abuse.

2. The AAU is organization of 62 leading public and private research universities in the United States and Canada. Founded in 1900 to advance the international standing of U.S. research universities, AAU today focuses on issues that are important to research-intensive universities, such as funding for research, research policy issues, and graduate and undergraduate education (see http://www.aau.edu/about/default.aspx?id=58), accessed October 19, 2015).

3. Source: https://www.washingtonpost.com/local/education/survey-more-than-1-in-5-female-undergrads-at-top-schools-suffer-sexual-attacks/2015/09/19/c6c80be2-5e29-11e5-b38e-06883aacba64_story.html. Downloaded October 19, 2015.

4. The agency is now named the Office of Child Abuse and Neglect (OCAN).

2 The Historical and Cultural Legacies of Family and Intimate Violence

VIOLENCE BETWEEN INTIMATES and toward children is not new. The Bible, while not a truly historical document, provides numerous examples of violence between family members. In *Genesis*, the Bible begins with sibling violence—Cain killing Abel. The book of *Genesis* also describes God's commandment that Abraham sacrifice his son, Isaac—which of course was not carried out. Later, in the New Testament, Jesus was presumably saved from Herod's "slaughter of the innocents."

If intimate violence and abuse is not a modern phenomenon, perhaps it is more common today than decades or centuries earlier. Many contemporary social commentators and some social scientists point to an "epidemic of family violence" as yet another sign of the disintegration of both the modern family and society in general. The question of whether we are more violent today than during previous times in history is difficult to answer. The selective inattention to the problem of intimate violence and child abuse and neglect means that few nations or societies kept official records of the occurrence of violence in homes. Anecdotal evidence exists in letters, diaries, and newspaper reports, but we have no way on knowing exactly the historical extent of intimate violence and child maltreatment. Similarly, until rather recently—the 1970s—researchers were reluctant to conduct surveys and ask questions about domestic violence or abuse. The first national surveys of partner violence and child maltreatment were carried out in the 1970s. Until follow-up surveys were carried out in the 1980s, we had no way of assessing the changing rates of violence towards children or between intimate partners.

The first section of this chapter examines the historical legacy of intimate violence and child abuse and neglect. Modern Americans are neither the first families to use violence on loved ones, nor are we the only society in the world to be violent towards intimates. The next section explores the social transformation of violence and traces the evolution of the issue of partner violence and child maltreatment from selective inattention, when nearly all that was written on violence in the home appeared on the front pages of tabloids such as the *National Enquirer*, to the present, when relationship violence is discussed and analyzed on social media, television and radio talk shows, television dramas, national magazines, among legislative bodies, and by government task forces.

We take it for granted that today's children have the right to live and to grow in order to develop fully. Women have struggled for centuries to achieve equal rights with men, and many take it for granted that they have a right to equality. The history of the subordination of women and children is closely connected to the history and causes of violence and abuse.

Infanticide and the Abuse of Women and Children

VIOLENCE TOWARD CHILDREN

The history of many of the world's societies is one in which children have been subjected to unspeakable cruelties. Historian Samuel Radbill (1987) reports that, in ancient times, infants had no protections until the right to live was ritually bestowed upon them by their fathers. If the right to live was withheld by fathers, infants were abandoned or left to die. Although we do not know how often children were killed or abandoned, we do know that infanticide was widely accepted among ancient and prehistoric cultures. Infants could be put to death because they cried too much, because they were sickly or deformed, or because they had some perceived imperfection. Girls, twins, and the children of unmarried women were the special targets of infanticide (Robin, 1982).

Many societies also subjected their offspring to rituals or survival tests. Some North American Indians threw their newborns into pools of water and rescued them only if they rose to the surface and cried. The Greeks exposed their children to the natural elements as a survival test.

Lloyd DeMause (1974) examined the history of childhood and graphically explains that, by A.D. 1526, the latrines of Rome were said to "resound with the cries of children who had been plunged into them." Infanticide continued through the eighteenth and nineteenth century. Even today, children born to unmarried women continue to run the greatest risk of infanticide. A few years ago, an old steamer trunk was opened in a mill town in southern New Hampshire. Inside the trunk were several small skeletons, alleged to have been children born out of wedlock and killed at birth. Contemporary news reports occasionally include mention of the bodies of newborns found in ladies' rooms or trash receptacles.

The killing of children was not the only form of abuse inflicted by generations of parents. From prehistoric times through colonial America, children were mutilated, beaten, and maltreated. Such treatment was not only condoned, it was often mandated as the most appropriate child-rearing method. Children were hit with rods, canes, and switches. Boys were castrated in order to produce eunuchs. Colonial American parents were implored to "beat the Devil" out of their children (Greven, 1990; Straus, 1994; Straus et al., 2014). "Stubborn child" laws were passed that permitted parents to put to death unruly children, although it is not clear whether children were actually ever killed.

FEMALE VICTIMS OF INTIMATE PARTNER VIOLENCE

The subordinate status of women worldwide is well documented. Since physical violence is the ultimate resource that can be utilized to hold subordinate groups in place, the history of women globally is one in which women are the victims of physical assaults.

Sociologists Rebecca and Russell Dobash (1979, 1998) explain that, in order to understand partner abuse within contemporary society, one must understand and recognize the centuries-old legacy of women as the victims of patriarchal cultures that dominate and control them. Roman husbands and fathers had control not only over their children, but over their wives as well. A Roman husband could chastise, divorce, or kill his wife. Not only that, but the behaviors for which these punishments were appropriate—adultery, public drunkenness, and attending public games—were the very same behaviors that Roman men engaged in daily (Dobash & Dobash, 1979).

As with children, women have been victimized and expected to be subservient to men as far back as the Bible. Eve is blamed for eating the forbidden fruit. For Eve's transgression, the Bible tells us that for all eternity women will be punished by having to bear children in sorrow and pain. The same passage in *Genesis* that multiplies women's sorrow and calls for them to bear children also approves of the husband's rule over women (Genesis 3:16). The expectation that "wives are to submit to and obey their husbands" is steeped in religious traditions (Ephesians 5:22–24).

One of the historical myths in the field of intimate partner violence is that Blackstone's codification of English common law in 1768 (*Commentaries on the Laws of England*) asserted that a husband had the right to "physically chastise" an errant wife, provided that the stick was no thicker than his thumb—and thus the "rule of thumb" was born. Christina Hoff Sommers (1994) points out however, that the "rule of thumb" passage cannot be found in Blackstone's writings (Sommers, 1994). In fact, since the time of the American Revolution, there have been laws prohibiting "wife beating" in the United States (Pleck, 1987). However, although laws existed, they were often indifferently enforced. Furthermore, although the laws outlawed assault and battery and prescribed fines and whippings as punishment, courts often allowed a certain amount of chastisement of "errant wives," within legal bounds. In 1824, a Mississippi court permitted corporal punishment of wives by their husbands. The right to chastise wives was finally overturned by courts in Alabama and Massachusetts in 1871.

A Global View of Intimate Violence and Abuse

Not only does conventional wisdom err when it argues that intimate violence and abuse are modern phenomena, it also errs when it asserts that violence is unique to American families, or if not unique, the problem is greater in the United States than in other societies. However, gathering information on partner violence and maltreatment of children in other societies is a difficult task. Only the United States, Canada, Botswana, and certain provinces in Australia have specific legislation that requires the reporting of child abuse and neglect; thus, there are no official report data on child abuse available in other nations. There is, however, an increasing number of local, regional, or national surveys conducted on intimate violence in other countries.

VIOLENCE AND THE ABUSE OF CHILDREN

Understanding the nature, scope, and consequences of child abuse and maltreatment proves a more difficult task than that of understanding violence between intimate partners. There are fewer national surveys of child abuse or child maltreatment. This is largely due to the difficulty that occurs when researchers attempt to develop a cross-cultural definition of *child maltreatment* (Gelles &

Cornell, 1983; Finkelhor & Korbin, 1988; Korbin, 1981). Korbin (1981) asserts that, since there is no universal standard for optimal child rearing, there can be no universal standard for what constitutes child abuse and neglect. Finkelhor and Korbin (1988) explain that a definition of child abuse that could be used internationally should accomplish at least two objectives: (1) It should distinguish child abuse clearly from other social, economic, and health problems of international concern; and, (2) it should be sufficiently flexible to apply to a range of situations in a variety of social and cultural contexts. They note that some of what is talked about as child abuse in Western societies has very little meaning in other societies.

Finkelhor and Korbin (1988) proposed the following definition of child abuse for cross-cultural research:

> Child abuse is the portion of harm to children that results from human action that is proscribed, proximate, and preventable. (p. 4)

The United Nations Children's Fund (UNICEF, 2003) estimates that, in the 27 richest and most industrially developed nations in the world, approximately 3,500 children under the age of 15 die from physical abuse and neglect every year (see Figure 2.1). The greatest risk appears to be among younger children. UNICEF reports that:

> Spain, Ireland and Norway appear to have an exceptionally low incidence of child maltreatment deaths; Belgium, the Czech Republic, New Zealand, Hungary and France have levels that are four to six times higher; and, the United States, Mexico and Portugal have rates that are between 10 and 15 times higher than those at the top of the league table. (UNICEF, 2003: p. 4)

Furthermore, the UNICEF study asserts, child maltreatment deaths appear to be declining in a majority of industrialized nations.

Israel is a country where it is believed there is little physical abuse of children. Hanita Zimrin (personal communication, 1992) noted that there was considerable attention paid to physical abuse in Israel after a child was beaten to death by a parent on a kibbutz. Zimrin explained, with some irony, that such a case challenged the notion of the "perfect society" and the "perfect childrearing setting"—the kibbutz.

Students of child maltreatment attempt to synthesize the various data that are available and come up with a general statement that explains why violence toward children is common in some societies and rare in others. Anthropologist

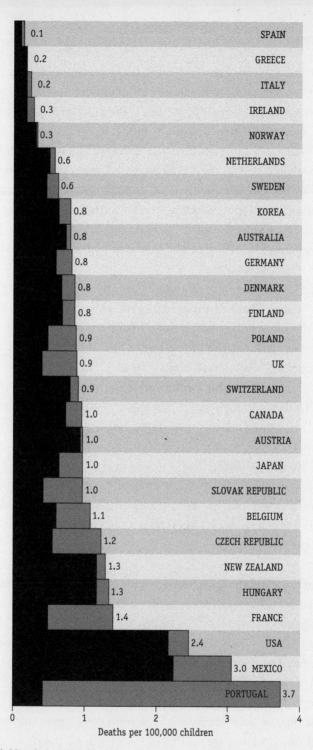

	Deaths per 100,000 children
0.1	SPAIN
0.2	GREECE
0.2	ITALY
0.3	IRELAND
0.3	NORWAY
0.6	NETHERLANDS
0.6	SWEDEN
0.8	KOREA
0.8	AUSTRALIA
0.8	GERMANY
0.8	DENMARK
0.8	FINLAND
0.9	POLAND
0.9	UK
0.9	SWITZERLAND
1.0	CANADA
1.0	AUSTRIA
1.0	JAPAN
1.0	SLOVAK REPUBLIC
1.1	BELGIUM
1.2	CZECH REPUBLIC
1.3	NEW ZEALAND
1.3	HUNGARY
1.4	FRANCE
2.4	USA
3.0	MEXICO
3.7	PORTUGAL

Deaths per 100,000 children

FIGURE 2.1 Child maltreatment deaths in rich nations. The table shows the annual number of deaths from maltreatment (dark part of bar) combined with those classified as "of undetermined intent" (pale part of bar). The data for children under the age of 15 years averaged over five years expressed per 100,000 chlidren in the age group.

Source: UNICEF, "A League Table of Child Maltreatment Deaths in Rich Nations," Innocenti Report Card No.5, September 2003. UNICEF Innocenti Research Centre, Florence: p. 4.

Jill Korbin (1981) concluded that, if children are valued for economic, spiritual, or psychological qualities, they are less likely to be maltreated. Certain children who are perceived to have undesirable qualities are at greatest risk of abuse. Thus, disabled children, orphans, stepchildren, females, or children born to unwed mothers are often at greatest risk of abuse.

The most recent examination of violence toward women and children is the United Nations' report *Hidden in Plain Sight* (2014). The report is a comprehensive examination of intimate partner violence, violence toward children, and violence between children. The report employs a broad definition of *intimate partner violence* and *violence toward children* that includes corporal punishment. In addition, the study examines the global extent of sexual violence, mental violence, and neglect and negligent treatment.[1]

The United Nations' report managed the issue of developing a uniform definition of violence toward children by gathering data through internationally comparable sources, including the UNICEF-supported Multiple Indicator Cluster Surveys (MICS), the U.S. Agency for International Development (USAID)–supported Demographic and Health Surveys (DHS), the Global School–based Student Health Surveys (GSHS), and the Health Behavior in School-aged Children Study (HbSC). The report did not examine certain forms of violence that, according to the authors, "take place within the context of shared community, cultural or social norms and values, such as female genital mutilation/ cutting (FGM/C)."

The examination of the global extent of violence toward children was comprehensive, using a variety of data sources, including surveys, and yielded an abundance of data regarding death (see Table 2.1), injury, and violence. Among the major findings are:

- Latin America and the Caribbean have the largest share of homicides among children and adolescents in the world (United Nations, 2014: p. 34).
- In almost all countries, parents and other caregivers are the most commonly cited perpetrators of physical violence against adolescent girls (United Nations, 2014: p. 51).
- In five countries (Uganda, Ukraine, Cameroon, Ghana, and Mozambique), at least one in four adolescent boys reports incidents of physical violence since age 15 (United Nations, 2014: p. 53).
- Forced sexual intercourse and other forms of sexual coercion are not uncommon in the lives of many girls (United Nations, 2014: p. 67).

TABLE 2.1

Latin America and the Caribbean have the largest share of homicides among children and adolescents in the world.

Number of homicide victims among children and adolescents aged 0–19 years and number of homicide victims among children and adolescents aged 0–19 years per 100,000 population in 2012, by region.

	Number of homicide victims	Homicide rate per 100,000
Latin America and the Caribbean	25,400	12
West and Central Africa	23,400	10
Eastern and Southern Africa	15,000	6
South Asia	15,000	2
Middle East and North Africa	3,700	2
Countries outside of these regions	3,800	2
Central and Eastern Europe and the Commonwealth of Independent States (CEE/CIS)	1,500	1
East Asia and the Pacific	7,100	1
World	94,900	4

Note: Figures in the table have been rounded.

Source: World Health Organization, Global Health Estimates (GHE) Summary Tables: Deaths by cause, age, sex and region, 2012. WHO, Geneva, 2014, recalculated according to UNICEF's regional classification.

Source: United Nations' Children's Fund, *Hidden in Plain Sight: A statistical analysis of violence against children*, UNICEF, New York, 2014: p. 133. Reproduced with permission. Produced in total from the UNICEF Publication without modification.

- Boys also report experiences of sexual violence, but to a lesser extent than girls (United Nations, 2014: p. 72).
- The use of violent discipline in the home is widespread, ranging from nearly 100% in Yemen to 45% in Panama (United Nations, 2014: p. 96).
- Over 40% of children experience severe physical punishment in Chad, Egypt, and Yemen (United Nations, 2014: p. 99).
- In most countries, boys and girls are at about equal risk of experiencing violent discipline (United Nations 2014: p. 102).

VIOLENCE TOWARD WOMEN

A World Health Organization's (WHO) international study of 24,000 women reveals that intimate partner violence is the most common form of violence experienced by women—more so than stranger or acquaintance assaults or rapes (Garcia-Moreno, Heise, Jansen, Ellsberg, & Watts, 2005). The United Nations Fourth World Congress on Women reported "epidemic proportions" of domestic violence in Third World countries. In Bangladesh, femicide (the murder of women by their partners) accounts for 50% of all homicides; it is estimated that in New Guinea, between 50% and 60% of women have been victims of partner violence (United Nations, 1995). UNICEF (2006) reports a steep rise in violence against women in Zimbabwe (no hard empirical evidence exist; data were collected through non-governmental agencies).

The United Nations' *Hidden in Plain Sight* (2014) examination of intimate partner violence experienced by adolescent girls found that (see Figure 2.2):

- Physical violence and emotional violence are the most commonly reported forms of partner violence perpetrated against adolescent girls. In 33 out of 43 countries, at least 1 in 10 adolescent girls (aged 15–19) who have ever been married or in union reported incidents of physical violence against them at the hands of their partners. The rates of physical violence among these girls vary considerably across countries— ranging from 2% in Ukraine to 71% in Equatorial Guinea (United Nations, 2014: p. 135).
- Comparable data from 43 low- and middle-income countries show that prevalence rates for partner violence against ever-married adolescent girls range from 2% in Ukraine to 73% in Equatorial Guinea (United Nations, 2014: p. 132).
- Partner violence is also pervasive in South Asia, where at least one in five girls who have ever been married or in union experienced partner violence in each of the four countries with available data (United Nations, 2014: p. 132).
- In East Asia and the Pacific, more than one in six ever-married or partnered girls experienced violence at the hands of their partners in all of the four countries with available data (United Nations, 2014: p. 132).
- Overall, the prevalence of partner violence is lowest in Central and Eastern Europe and the Commonwealth of Independent States (CEE/ CIS), ranging from 2% in Ukraine to 14% in Azerbaijan and 16% in Tajikistan (United Nations, 2014: p. 132).

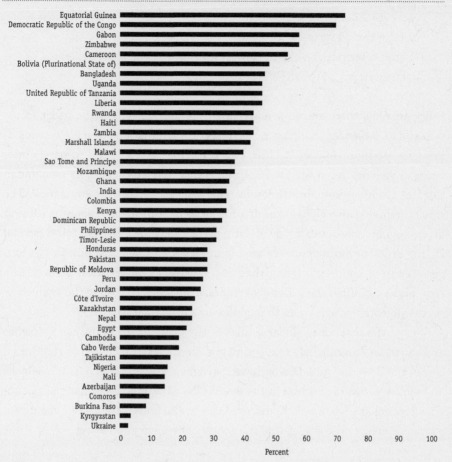

FIGURE 2.2 Percentage of ever-married girls aged 15 to 19 years who ever experienced any physical, sexual or emotional violence committed by their husbands or partners.
Source: United Nations, Children's Fund, *Hidden in Plain Sight: A Statistical Analysis of Violence Against Children*, UNICEF, New York, 2014: p. 133.

A World Health Organization report focused more specifically on intimate partner violence experienced by adult women (WHO, 2013). Here again, there is considerable evidence that women across the globe experience intimate partner violence. The report examined physical violence by intimate partners and sexual violence by someone other than a partner. Among the key findings are:

- Globally, the most violence women experience is at the hands of intimate partners (WHO, 2013: p. 2).
- As many as 30% of all female homicide victims are murdered by intimate partners (WHO, 2013: p. 2).
- The highest lifetime prevalence rates of intimate partner violence

occurred among women in Africa (38%), while the lowest was in the nations of the Western Pacific (24.6%) (WHO, 2013: p. 17).
- High-income nations had the lowest lifetime prevalence of intimate
partner violence (23.2%) (WHO, 2013: p. 17).

Unfortunately, there are no comprehensive global surveys of the other forms
of intimate violence. There are no systematic examinations of male victims of
intimate partner violence, sibling violence, elder abuse, child-to-parent violence, or violence among gay, lesbian, and transgendered couples. As we noted in
Chapter 1, female-to-male intimate partner violence is a controversial topic. The
most comprehensive global examination of female-to-male violence is Murray
Straus and his colleagues' study of dating violence (2004). Straus's International
Dating Study of dating violence among university students worldwide (31 universities in 16 countries) found that, at 21 of the 31 universities, more female
than males assaulted their dating partners. Even when confining the analysis to
severe violence, more females than males assaulted their partners.

Even in the absence of global studies of the other forms of intimate violence
and abuse, we can conclude that intimate violence is not confined to the United
States, nor does the United States have the highest prevalence of partner violence
and violence toward children in the world. The data on wealthy and poor countries foreshadow what we will discuss later in the book—that economic disadvantage increases the risk of almost all forms of violence and abuse.

The Social Transformation of Intimate Violence and Abuse

Although we find cases of intimate violence throughout recorded history, viewing intimate partner violence and child maltreatment as social issues and social
problems is a relatively new phenomenon. Violence between loved occurs behind
closed doors. During the 1960s and, more importantly, in the 1980s, intimate
violence and child abuse and neglect gradually became both a social issue—a condition that captures public attention and generates concern, controversy, and in
some cases collective action—and, finally, a social problem—a condition found
to be harmful to individual and/or societal well-being.

It is tempting to look for some dramatic change that took place 50 years ago
that propelled violence in the home out from secrecy into the public spotlight—
that, however, would be naïve. Rather, violence in the home came to public attention gradually. The fortress doors of the private family did not swing open, they
moved inch by inch over the decades.

DISCOVERING CHILDHOOD AND CHILDREN

Although abuse and neglect permeated the lives of children for centuries, the historical treatment of children was not entirely bleak. Children's rights were recognized, but slowly. Six thousand years ago, children in Mesopotamia had a patron goddess to look after them. The Greeks and Romans created orphan homes. Some historical accounts also mention the existence of foster care for children. Samuel Radbill (1987) reports that child protection laws were legislated as long ago as 450 B.C. At the same time, the father's complete control over his children was modified. Anthropologists note that nearly every society has laws and rules regarding sexual access to children.

Social historian Phillipe Aries, in his book *Centuries of Childhood* (1962), claims that the concept of childhood as a distinct stage emerged after the Middle Ages (from about A.D. 400–1000). Before then, childhood as a stage ended when an infant was weaned. Children were seen as miniature adults and were portrayed as such in the artwork of the Middle Ages. Paintings and sculptures of children pictured them with little heads and miniature adult bodies, dressed in adult clothing. Renaissance art was the first time children were portrayed as children.

Michael Robin (1982) traced the roots of child protection. He found that the Renaissance, a 300-year period spanning A.D. 1300–1600, was the beginning of a new morality regarding children. Children were seen as a dependent class in need of the protection of society. This was also a time when the family was looked to for teaching children the proper rules of behavior. At the same time, the power of the father increased dramatically.

While society paid more attention to children, this was not without some dire consequences. Colonial American leaders such as Cotton Mather instructed Puritan parents that the strict disciplining of children could not begin too early (Greven, 1990).

The Enlightenment of the eighteenth century brought children increased attention and services. The London Foundling Hospital was established during this period. The hospital not only provided pediatric care, but as Michael Robin (1982) recounts, it was also the center of the moral reform movement on behalf of children.

In the United States, the case of Mary Ellen Wilson is almost always singled out as the turning point in public concern for children's welfare. In 1874, the then–eight-year-old Mary Ellen lived in the home of Francis and Mary Connolly, but she was not the blood relative of either. Mary Ellen was the illegitimate daughter of Mary Connolly's first husband. A neighbor noticed the plight of Mary Ellen, who was beaten with a leather thong and allowed to go ill-clothed in bad weather.

The neighbor reported the case to Etta Wheeler—a "friendly visitor" who worked for the St. Luke's Methodist Mission in New York. In the mid-1800s, child welfare was church-based rather than government-based. Wheeler turned to the police and the New York City Department of Charities for help for Mary Ellen Wilson and was turned down—first by the police, who said there was no proof of a crime, and second by the charity agency, who said they did not have custody of Mary Ellen. A legend grew that claimed that Henry Berge, founder of the Society for the Prevention of Cruelty to Animals, intervened on behalf of Mary Ellen, and the courts accepted the case because Mary Ellen was a member of the animal kingdom. In reality, the court reviewed the case because the child needed protection. The case was argued, not by Henry Berge, but by his colleague, Elbridge Gerry.

Mary Ellen Wilson was removed from her foster home and initially placed in an orphanage. Her foster mother was imprisoned for a year, and the case received detailed press coverage for months. In December of 1874, the New York Society for the Prevention of Cruelty to Children was founded. Protective societies for children rose and fell during the next 80 years.

Two decades before the discovery of Mary Ellen Wilson and the formation of the Society for the Prevention of Cruelty to Children was formed, a phenomenon occurred that influenced the movement to protect children for harm. Charles Loring Brace, a young minister in New York City, became alarmed at the sight of thousands of immigrant children roaming the streets of New York. Some children formed gangs as a means of self-protection. Other children, many as young as five years of age, were arrested for being vagrants. Brace formed the Children's Aid Society with the purpose of protecting the street children. Brace's form of protection would be to raise money to fund trips for children to wholesome American families. Brace raised funds and sought legal permission to send children to families in Middle America. Brace believed that the synergy of the need for labor on farms and children's need for a wholesome upbringing would benefit both the farmers and the children. Between 1854 and 1929, Brace's efforts moved between 100,000 and 250,000 children on what became known as Orphan Trains (Scheuerman, 2007). Of course, the label was incorrect, since most of the children were not in fact orphans. Some children did in fact find warm and loving homes. Others were abused and mistreated. Orphans trains, like foster care in the twentieth and twenty-first century, were a decidedly mixed blessing for vulnerable children.

By the 1950s, public interest in abuse and neglect was practically nonexistent (Nelson, 1984). Technology helped pave the way for the rediscovery of child abuse. In 1946, radiologist John Caffey (1946) reported on a number of cases of children who had multiple long-bone fractures and subdural hematomas. Caffey used X-rays to identify the fractures, although he did not speculate about the causes. In 1953, P. V. Woolley and W. A. Evans (Wooley & Evans, 1953) speculated that the children's parents might inflict the injuries. Caffey (1957) looked again at his X-ray data and speculated that parents or caretakers could have inflicted such injuries. By 1962, physician C. Henry Kempe and his colleagues at the University of Colorado Medical Center (Kempe et al., 1962) were quite certain that many of the injuries they were seeing, as well as the healed fractures that appeared on X-rays, were intentionally inflicted by parents.

Kempe's article in the *Journal of the American Medical Association* became the benchmark of the public and professional rediscovery of child abuse. Kempe's article, and a strong editorial that accompanied the article, created considerable public and professional concern. The weekly news and feature magazines, *Time*, *Newsweek*, *The Saturday Evening Post*, and *Life*, followed up the Kempe article with news or feature stories. Barbara Nelson (1984) traced the record of professional and mass media articles on child abuse and neglect. Prior to 1962, it was unusual that a single mass media article on abuse would be published in a year. After Kempe's article, there was a tenfold increase in popular articles that discussed child abuse. Today, all forms of mass and social media routinely cover child maltreatment. Kempe founded his own professional journal, *Child Abuse and Neglect: The International Journal*, and thousands of professional articles are published annually in medical, sociology, psychology, social work, and other scholarly journals. There are now more than a dozen scientific journals devoted to family and intimate violence in general, or to some aspect of intimate violence such as sexual or emotional abuse.

That public, professional, and social media coverage of child abuse grew rapidly and in tandem was not a coincidence. Each professional journal article produced additional fodder for the mass media (many scholars and scholarly journals issue press releases to accompany the publication of a new article). Each popular article added legitimacy to the public concern about abuse and stimulated a new round of research and scholarly publication.

The symbiotic relationship between scholarly and popular media was not without some problems. The translation of scientific writing into popular presentation often leveled, sharpened, and distorted scientific findings and statements. For instance, the editorial that accompanied Kempe's article in the *Journal of the American Medical Association* (1962) stated, "It is likely that [the battered-child syndrome] will be found to be a more frequent cause of death than such well-recognized and thoroughly studied diseases as leukemia, cystic fibrosis, and muscular dystrophy, and might rank well above automobile accidents"(The battered-child syndrome. [Editorial]. (1962, July 7)). By the time the statement in the editorial had found its way to the public press, it had been slightly changed to state that child abuse *was one* of the five leading causes of the death of children, even though, at the time, there were no actual data to support such an assertion. Similarly, estimates of the incidence of child abuse and the possible causes were stated and restated so often that they took on lives of their own—apart from the initial speculative presentations in scholarly journals.

Legislative Action

Two other forces worked to move child abuse and neglect out from behind closed doors during the 1960s. The first was the passage of state child-abuse reporting laws; the second was the effort in the federal government to focus concern on the plight of abused children.

One of the concrete consequences of the rediscovery of child abuse after the publication of Kempe's 1962 article on the battered child syndrome was the passage of child-abuse reporting laws in each of the 50 states between 1963 and 1967. Reporting laws were the quickest and most concrete action states could take to demonstrate that they wanted to "do something" about the abuse of children. The underlying theme of many of the popular and professional publications on child abuse from the time of Mary Ellen Wilson was the fact that abused children were "missing persons" in social and criminal justice agencies. Many abused children came to public attention only at the point of death. Logic seemed to dictate that, if society were to help abused children, it would have to identify those in need of help. Not coincidentally, child-abuse reporting laws were often viewed as a no- or low-cost means for state legislators to "do something" about abuse. Few legislators who jumped on the reporting law bandwagon could foresee that reporting laws would lead to uncovering millions of children who required state-funded protective services. The prevailing myth that child maltreatment was rare had such a strong hold that most legislators assumed that the laws they passed would lead to uncovering only a handful of abused and neglected children in their state.

The Children's Bureau, first an agency in the Department of Labor, then an agency of the Department of Health, Education, and Welfare, and finally located within the Department of Health and Human Services, was the first federal focal point of discussion and concern for abused children. The Children's Bureau was active in the cause of abused children as far back as the 1950s. The Bureau was founded in 1912 by an act of Congress with the mandate of disseminating information on child development. The Bureau also acquired the budget and mandate to conduct research on issues concerning child development. The Children's

Bureau engaged in a variety of activities regarding child abuse and neglect. The agency participated in one of the earliest national meetings on child abuse, sponsored by the Children's Division of the American Humane Association. After the publication of Kempe's 1962 article, the Bureau convened a meeting to draft a model child-abuse reporting law. The model law was drafted in 1963. Finally, the Bureau funded a variety of research projects, including David Gil's first national survey of officially reported cases of child abuse. In 1974, Congress enacted the Child Abuse Prevention and Treatment Act (Public Law 93-247) and located the National Center on Child Abuse and Neglect in the Children's Bureau.

Prior to 1973, congressional interest in child abuse was limited to the passage of a reporting law for the District of Columbia and some attempts to pass national reporting laws. In 1973 the then–Senator (and later Vice President) Walter Mondale and Congressman John Brademas (later President of New York University) introduced the Child Abuse Prevention and Treatment Act (CAPTA). The Act, enacted in 1974, defined "child abuse and neglect," established the National Center on Child Abuse and Neglect, set forth a budget for research and demonstration projects, and called for a national survey of the incidence of child abuse and neglect.

Child abuse appeared to be a "safe" and non-controversial congressional issue. The general belief was that child abuse was rare and confined to the mentally ill. The problem was seen to be limited in scope and one that would not require substantial federal spending. Who could disagree, after seeing slides of horribly abused children, that they did not need care and protection? Mondale needed a "safe" issue. He had seen his Comprehensive Child Development Act vetoed by President Nixon. Even Nixon, Mondale would say, could not be in favor of child abuse (Hoffman, 1979).

Child abuse was not as "safe" an issue as it seemed, however. While one witness at Mondale's Senate hearings on CAPTA, "Jolly K.," a former child abuser and founder of Parents Anonymous, captured media and congressional attention with her testimony recounting her abuse of her child, another witness, social welfare expert David Gil, showed the "unsafe" side of the issue when he insisted on linking abuse to poverty. Moreover, Gil went beyond the narrow scope of the public stereotype of child abuse and introduced the issue of corporal punishment and spanking into his testimony. Finally, Gil concluded that the bill as written was too narrow to identify, treat, and prevent the real problem.

The Child Abuse Prevention and Treatment Act passed. It was never clear whether President Nixon could be for or against child abuse (although there is no evidence to support any claim that President Nixon would "support" child abuse)—he signed the bill in the midst of mounting public clamor over the

Watergate break-in scandal that eventually led to his resignation. The final amount of money made available for research and demonstration projects was relatively small, $85 million. Many child abuse experts who realized how extensive the problem was and how difficult it would be to treat, suggested that such a trifling amount was but a rounding error at the Pentagon. Yet, despite concern over the scope of the legislation and the narrowness of the mandate of the law, the passage of CAPTA succeeded in creating a federal presence and a federal agency that could serve as a focal point of public and professional awareness of child abuse and neglect.

UNCOVERING PARTNER VIOLENCE AND ABUSE

There was no historical "Mary Ellen" for battered women—no transport to safe haven—no technological breakthroughs such as pediatric radiology to uncover years of broken jaws and broken bones. No medical champion would capture public and professional attention in the way Henry Kempe had for battered children. There was no "Women's Bureau" in the federal government. And initially, there was no powerful senator who used a congressional committee chairmanship as a bully pulpit to bring attention to the plight of battered women.

The discovery of intimate violence was through a traditional grassroots effort. Attention to the problem of "wife-battering" came from women themselves. A women's center in the Chiswick section of London, founded by Erin Pizzey, became a refuge for victims of battering. Pizzey wrote the first book on wife abuse, *Scream Quietly or the Neighbors Will Hear* (1974) and produced a documentary movie of the same name. Both captured the attention of women in Europe and the United States. Women's groups began to organize safe houses, or battered wife shelters, as early as 1972 throughout the United States. In 1975, The National Organization for Women (NOW) created a task force to examine violence against women.

The results of research on violence against women began to be published in 1973. Those who believed that the abuse of women deserved the same place on the public agenda that child abuse had attained quickly seized the data on the extent, patterns, and factors associated with intimate violence. As with child abuse, the scholarly publications fed media articles, and the media articles fed public interest, which led to more research and professional attention.

Still, by the early 1980s, public and professional interest in violence against women had lagged far behind the public interest in child abuse. There were some congressional hearings on wife abuse and then–Congresswoman (now Senator) Barbara Milkulski introduced legislation for a National Domestic Violence

Prevention and Treatment Act. The Federal Office of Domestic Violence was established in 1979, only to be closed in 1981.

Some progress was made, however, in the mid-1980s. The National Domestic Violence Prevention and Treatment Act were passed into law, although spending from this legislation was almost insignificant. The United States Attorney General's Task Force on Family Violence held hearings across the country in 1984 and published the final report in September 1984.

The year 1994 was a watershed year for the issue of violence against women. Perhaps not coincidentally, this was the year that Nicole Brown Simpson and Ron Goldman were murdered and Brown Simpson's ex-husband, football Hall of Famer O. J. Simpson, was charged with the murders. At about the same time the murders took place, Congress was completing the 1994 crime bill, which included the Violence Against Women Act (VAWA—Public Law 103-322). The crime bill, with the VAWA, was passed by Congress in August 1994, and was signed into law by President Clinton on September 13, 1994. The VAWA appropriated $1.5 billion to fight violence against women, including $3 million over three years to reestablish a national hotline to assist victims of domestic violence. An additional $26 million was appropriated for state grants that would encourage states to take more creative, innovative, and effective approaches in law enforcement and prosecutor training, and develop and expand law enforcement and prosecution, such as special domestic violence units, improved data collection and communication strategies, improved victim service programs, and improved programs combating stalking. The VAWA also included various provisions to increase protection of battered women, including a civil rights title that declared, "All persons in the United States shall have the right to be free from crimes of violence motivated by gender." Lastly, an office on domestic violence was established within the U.S. Department of Justice (VAWA, Public Law 103-322, 1994).

At about the same time the VAWA was passed, the Family Violence Prevention Fund, along with the Advertising Council, began a national public awareness campaign entitled, "No Excuse for Domestic Violence." Public service announcements that were designed to educate the public about domestic violence and promote prevention and intervention appeared on television and in newspapers.

Legal reforms also occurred at the state level. States enacted legislation designed to establish domestic violence prosecution units, to criminalize female sexual assaults by their current or ex-partners, to improve protection for victims of stalking, and to develop more effective legal sanctions for domestic violence offenders.

The VAWA was reauthorized in 2000, again in 2005, and then again in 2013, adding components that provided services for immigrant, rural, disabled, and elderly women. The 2005 VAWA is of particular interest, as it contains language making it clear that all victims must be given equal standing, regardless of sex. In addition, Congress instructed the General Accounting Office (GAO) to conduct a study that examines the recipients of federal funding in order to investigate what types of services they provide and how many men versus women receive services. These are major steps. Male victims have not previously been recognized as "legitimate" victims of intimate partner violence with an equal right to treatment.

PUBLIC CONCERN FOR "PRIVATE" VIOLENCE

It is tempting to give credit for the discovery of a social problem to a single great person or a single tragic event. The field of child abuse and neglect certainly owes much to the late C. Henry Kempe. Walter Mondale was thought a hero by those concerned with child protection, while Senator (and Vice President) Joe Biden was instrumental in passing the Violence Against Women Act.

Another point of view is that no single person, journal article, or piece of legislation propels a problem from obscurity onto the public agenda. Rather, an issue slowly and gradually becomes a public issue. The "great man" and the "slow social movement explanations" of the social transformation of intimate violence and abuse are both inadequate. Rather, a variety of social movements and social concerns combined in the late 1960s to create a climate where people were ready and willing to listen to those concerned with the victimization of women and children.

The 1960s assassinations of John F. Kennedy, Robert Kennedy, and Martin Luther King focused public concern about violence. This focus led to the establishment of the President's Commission on the Causes and Prevention of Violence. The Commission's national survey on attitudes and experience with violence produced invaluable data for researchers in the field of family violence.

The 1960s were also a period of violent social protest and race riots, again focusing public concern on violence. The "baby boomers" of the 1950s were teenagers in the 1960s and, as is often the case for those 18–24 years of age, they engaged in innumerable acts of delinquency and violence, increasing the national homicide, assault, and rape rates. The general public believed that we were in the midst of an epidemic of violence. Fear of violent crime began to paralyze American society. The Figgie Report (Figgie, 1980),[2] found that four out of ten Americans were afraid of being assaulted, robbed, raped, or murdered in their homes or on the streets where they lived and worked.

Concern about violence would not have meant much had it not occurred at the same time as we were undergoing a resurgence of both the women's and the children's movements. These existing social movements provided the forum, the workers, and the energy to collect, organize, and present information on private victimization. Existing national groups, who lobbied on behalf of women and children, made it easier to lobby for national and regional attention to be paid to the problems of abuse and violence.

A final necessary and sufficient piece that helped shape public concern regarding violence into a portrait of a problem was the research being carried out by social and behavioral scientists. Until there could be scientific data that shattered the myths of abuse, it was impossible to convince the public and legislators that intimate violence was a social problem deserving a continued place on the national agenda.

Contemporary Attitudes and Beliefs

Violence between family members and intimate partners has a historical tradition that goes back centuries and cuts across continents. It should come as no surprise that contemporary social scientists have proposed that, in the United States and many other countries, "the marriage license is a hitting license" (Straus et al., 1980). Numerous surveys and situations emphasize the fact that some still believe that, under certain circumstances, it is perfectly appropriate for male partners to hit their female partners. Furthermore, parents who fail to physically discipline children are considered to be deviant, not the parents who hit.

At the end of the 1960s, the U.S. Commission on the Causes and Prevention of Violence conducted a study of violence in the United States. The primary purpose of the study was to attempt to understand the causes of the tragic rash of assassinations and riots that plagued the country between 1963 and 1968. Along with the questions on public violence, the commission asked a number of questions about private violence. Among the conclusions was that about one-quarter of all adult men, and one in six adult women, said they could think of circumstances in which it would be all right for a husband to hit his wife or for the wife to hit her husband. Overall, about one in five (21%) of those surveyed approved of a husband's slapping his wife (Stark & McEvoy, 1970). The same survey found that 86% of those surveyed agreed that young people needed "strong" discipline. Of the sample, 70% believed that it was important for a boy to have a few fistfights while he was growing up.

Fifteen years after the U.S. Commission on the Causes and Prevention of Violence conducted their research, Murray Straus, Suzanne Steinmetz, and I conducted the first national survey on family violence. Questions of people's attitudes toward violence in the home confirmed findings from earlier research.

Just under one in four wives and one in three husbands thought that a couple's slapping one another was at least somewhat necessary and normal (Straus et al., 1980). More than 70% of those questioned believed that slapping, for example, a 12-year-old child was a necessary means of discipline.

Anecdotal accounts further underscore the widespread cultural approval of private violence. In 1964, a young woman named Kitty Genovese was returning home to her apartment in the Queens borough of New York City. She was accosted and repeatedly stabbed by a man; and, while a number of her neighbors heard her screams for help and actually watched the assault from windows, no one called the police. The young woman's death led many people to conclude that American society was apathetic and anesthetized to violence, since bystanders seemed unwilling to get involved in a homicide. However, upon closer examination, it was suggested that the apathy of Kitty Genovese's neighbors was not the result of their lack of concern, or the fact that they were immune to violence after years of watching television. Rather, many of the witnesses believed that they were seeing a man beating his wife, and that, after all, is a "family matter."

Fairy tales, cartoons, television programs, video games, and popular music are full of violence against women and children. Hansel and Gretel, before they were lured into the witch's gingerbread house, had been abandoned by their parents to starve in the forest because money was scarce. Mother Goose's "Old Woman Who Lived in a Shoe" beat her children soundly and sent them to bed. "Humpty Dumpty" is a thinly disguised metaphor for the fragility of children, and "Rock-a-Bye Baby," with the cradle falling from the tree, is not even thinly disguised. Rap music hails the degradation of, and use of violence of against women. The television program "The Sopranos" underscores the subservient role of women, and the violent consequences for them when they "get out of line" or are deemed to be disloyal. The Lifetime television network made its reputation on portraying women as the inevitable, helpless victims of male violence and assorted other maladies. (Of late, Lifetime portrays stronger, much less helpless women.)

CHANGING ATTITUDES REGARDING DOMESTIC VIOLENCE

There is evidence from national surveys that attitudes regarding family violence are changing. Murray Straus and I repeated our National Family Violence Survey in 1985. Approval for a husband slapping his wife, and a wife slapping her husband, declined from the 1975 survey. In 1985, only 13% of those surveyed approved of a husband's slapping his wife in some situations. The level of approval of a husband's slapping his wife declined to 12% in 1992, and further declined to 10% in 1994. Approval for a wife's slapping her husband stayed relatively unchanged between

1968 and 1994, with about one in five respondents approving of a wife's slapping her husband in some situations (Gelles & Straus, 1988; Straus, Kantor & Moore, 1994).

More recent surveys also find decreasing public tolerance for violence against women. Surveys conducted for the Family Violence Prevention Fund (now named "Futures Without Violence") found that four out of five surveyed consider domestic violence an extremely important social issue, ranking it as more important than teenage alcoholism and pregnancy, and about as significant a problem as the environment. An increasing number of Americans believe outside interventions are needed if a man hits his female partner (87% agreed in 1995, compared to 80% in 1994). In the 1995 survey, 57% of men agreed that abusers should be arrested, compared to 49% agreement in 1994 (Family Violence Prevention Fund, 1995).

Bonnie Carlson and Alice Worden (2005) updated research on attitudes regarding domestic violence with a survey of 1,200 residents of six New York communities. Although not generalizable to any population other than the six communities, the survey found that respondents had considerable first- and secondhand experience with domestic violence. While respondents believed that acts of physical aggression should be labeled "domestic violence," there was uncertainty over whether such acts should be considered "criminal." When considering female-to-male violence, the respondents were less likely to view women's aggression as deviant or criminal compared to men's aggression.

As social norms change and adapt to contemporary cultures and societies, former attitudes regarding violence against women are increasingly considered unacceptable by many males worldwide, who reject the belief that violence and abuse against women, in any form, is acceptable. In fact, current studies suggest that many men seek mutual agreement within their interpersonal relationships and are uncomfortable with attitudes, beliefs, and behaviors that objectify and demean women (Berkowitz, 2004).

For an examination of cross-cultural attitudes regarding violence toward women, see Global Perspectives Box 2.1.

ATTITUDES REGARDING CHILD ABUSE AND VIOLENCE TOWARD CHILDREN

Assessing public opinion about child abuse and neglect and violence toward children turns out to be considerably more complex than examining attitudes toward intimate partner violence. If, for example, we were to carry out a public opinion poll and ask whether respondents thought child abuse, child neglect, or sexual abuse were deviant and/or criminal, there would be little variation from 100% agreement. However, were we to change the questions and ask whether specific forms of behavior constituted abuse or neglect, beyond homicide and

GLOBAL PERSPECTIVES BOX 2.1
ATTITUDES TOWARD INTIMATE PARTNER VIOLENCE

The most recent examination of attitudes toward intimate partner violence is Rachael Pierotti's analysis of data collected from hundreds of thousands of people in 26 countries[3] (2013). The data were collected as part of demographic and health surveys funded by the United States Agency on International Development (USAID). Male attitudes were assessed in 15 of the 26 countries. Men were more likely than women to reject domestic violence in Benin, Ethiopia, Ghana, Indonesia, Madagascar, Malawi, Nigeria, Rwanda, Tanzania, Uganda, and Zambia. Over time, both men and women in Madagascar and Indonesia actually declined in their rejection of domestic violence.[4]

There, surveys included questions about whether use of violence in certain circumstances (such as going out without telling the man, neglecting the children, or arguing) was justified. Overall, both men and women were most likely to believe domestic violence was justified when the wife neglected the children. Violence was least justified when the wife burned the food.

Domestic violence was most likely to be rejected by people who lived in urban areas and had more education, compared to those living in rural areas who had less education. Finally, people with access to mass media (newspapers, television, and radio) were most likely to reject domestic violence.

Source: Pierotti, R. S. (2013). Increasing rejection of intimate partner violence: Evidence of global cultural diffusion. *American Sociological Review, 78,* 240–265.

obvious cruelty, there would be considerable variation in responses. While there have been studies of what professionals define as "child abuse and neglect" (see Giovannoni & Becerra, 1979), there were very few polls or surveys that asked the public whether certain behaviors are abusive or neglectful.

The National Committee to Prevent Child Abuse (now called Prevent Child Abuse America) conducted one of the few annual surveys of public attitudes and child abuse and neglect. There were annual public opinion polls from 1987–1995 that measured the extent to which the public perceives child abuse to be a serious social problem, as well as the extent to which the public is committed to preventing the abuse of children. Each survey found that the majority of the public viewed physical punishment and repeated yelling and swearing as harmful to children's well-being. In 1995, only 22% of the public felt that physical punishment *never* leads to injury, and only 6% believed repeated yelling and swearing *never* leads to long-term emotional harm (Daro, 1995; Daro & Gelles, 1992).

Paradoxically, although the general public appears to be more willing to view physical punishment, yelling, and swearing as harmful to children, the general public, still, overall endorses spanking. From data gathered through a nationally representative sample of 991 U.S. families, Straus and Stewart (1999) concluded that a little over one-third of infants (children under one year of age) were hit by their parents, and that by ages four to five, 94% of parents surveyed stated that they had used corporal punishment (that is, the use of physical force with the intention of causing pain, but not injury, to a child) for the purpose of correction or control of the child's behavior (Straus, 1994). Furthermore, 40% of parents admitted to having used corporal punishment as a disciplinary tactic with their children until the age of 13.

Child Trends (2013) published a summary of national surveys of attitudes toward spanking. Data from 1986–2000 came from Child Trends' "Charting Parenthood: A Statistical Review of Fathers and Mothers in America" (2002). Data from 2002–2012 were gathered by the National Opinion Research Center at the University of Chicago. One of the key questions in the surveys asked respondents whether they agreed or disagreed that it is sometimes necessary to discipline a child with a "good hard spanking." Over 30 years, men were more likely than women to agree or strongly agree that a good hard spanking is sometimes appropriate. Over time, there has been a gradual decline in support for the good hard spanking from a high of 84% for men and 82% for women in 1985, to 77% for men and 65% for women in 2012. Looking at racial and ethnic differences in 2012, the greatest support for the occasional good hard spanking comes from African-American respondents, while the least support comes from Asian and Pacific Islander respondents (see Figure 2.3).

Summary

The remaining chapters of this book:

(1) Document the extent of intimate violence and abuse in the United States today;
(2) Consider the factors that are associated with acts of intimate violence;
(3) Examine the various theories that have been brought to bear to explain violence in the home; and, finally,
(4) Consider methods of treating and preventing family violence.

The tragic nature of violence among family members and intimates and the emotions that arise in reaction to specific instances of child, partner, sibling, or elder abuse frequently focus our attention on the immediate situation or on a specific

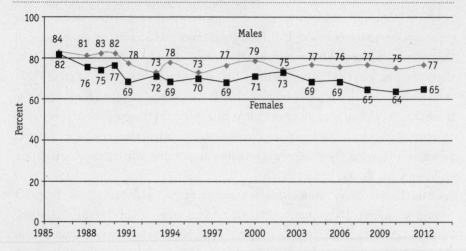

FIGURE 2.3 Percentage of males and females ages 18–65 who agree or strongly agree that it is sometimes necessary to discipline a child with a "good, hard spanking," selected years 1986–2012.

Source: Child Trends. (2013). Attitudes towards spanking. Retrieved May 15, 2015. Reproduced with permission, Child Trends.

case. It is important to keep in mind that what we are experiencing is neither new nor particularly unique to our own society. While we look for causes and solutions in individuals, within families, or even in communities, we should remember that cultural attitudes about women, men, children, and the elderly, and cultural attitudes about violence as a means of self-expression and solving problems, are at the root of private violence.

We will demonstrate that socioeconomic factors, gender, race, ethnicity, and other social-psychological factors are related to acts and patterns of intimate violence, but one needs to consider that people have choices as to how they will respond to intra- and interpersonal factors and social and cultural norms. A historical and sociocultural legacy of violence in the home is a powerful means of influencing what choices people consider appropriate. Current research demonstrates that someone's exposure to and/or experience of violence as a child significantly increase the risk for engaging in later adult parent violence, as well as in acts of child maltreatment and abuse (Holmes & Sammel, 2005).

Discussion Questions

1. Why have women historically been the primary victims of intimate violence?
2. Identify the problems that hamper our ability to understand and

compare the extent of intimate violence in other cultures and societies to the context and extent of family intimate violence in the United States.

3. What are the possible harmful effects on children who have experienced corporal punishment as children? In your view, why is corporal punishment a common method of discipline?

4. Identify and discuss any perceptions and/or beliefs that you may have had about intimate violence and child maltreatment that have been challenged by what you have read in this chapter.

Suggested Assignments

1. Read the Old and New Testaments of the Bible and identify examples of intimate violence (implicit or explicit).

2. Examine some nursery rhymes, children's stories, or children videos and identify themes or messages that seem to condone violence and abuse of children.

3. View prime-time television programs, videos, or films and note how many threats of violence and/or abuse against women and men are included per ten-minute segment.

Notes

1. The definitions were adapted from: United Nations Committee on the Rights of the Child, General Comment No. 13 (2011): The right of the child to freedom from all forms of violence, UN document CRC/C/GC/13, Office of the High Commissioner for Human Rights, Geneva, April 18, 2011.

2. This report presents the results of a survey investigating the pervasiveness of fear of crime among the general public in the United States, the ways that people cope with fear of crime, and public views on the police and the criminal justice system. The study was commissioned by businessman Harry E. Figgie in 1980: https://www.ncjrs.gov/App/publications/abstract.aspx?ID=74041. Retrieved August 26, 2015.

3. The countries were: Armenia, Benin, Bolivia, Cambodia, Dominican Republic, Egypt, Ethiopia, Ghana, Haiti, India, Indonesia, Jordan, Kenya, Madagascar, Malawi, Mali, Nepal, Nigeria, Philippines, Rwanda, Senegal, Tanzania, Turkey, Uganda, Zambia, and Zimbabwe.

4. Data were collected using nationally representative, repeated cross-sectional surveys.

3 The Youngest Victims

VIOLENCE TOWARD AND THE MALTREATMENT OF CHILDREN AND ADOLESCENTS

KAYA MCKEAN WAS six years old when her stepfather beat her to death. After he beat the child to death, Richard Adams buried her in a shallow grave in the Ocala National Forest. There were numerous warning signs that Kayla was in danger. Kayla was reported to the Florida Department of Children and Families at least three times. Each time the report of suspected abuse was investigated, and each time the caseworkers accepted Adams's claims that Kayla was hurt in some kind of accident.

Carlette Talbot was 23 years old and a single mother when she suffocated her six-week-old daughter. The baby's body lay in the bedroom for eight hours until Ms. Talbot's boyfriend returned home for dinner. The couple ate dinner, went out until 2:30 a.m., and then came home and went to sleep. The next morning, Carlette told her boyfriend about what she did, and then they both disposed on the baby's body in a nearby dumpster.

Danieal Kelley was 14 years old when she was found dead in her home in Philadelphia. Danielle had cerebral palsy and weighed 42 pounds at the time of her death. Her body was found in a hot room, with no fan, no curtains, and no light. She was covered with bedsores and lay in a urine-soaked bed. Danielle's mother, who was sentenced to 20–40 years in jail for the death of her daughter, had refused to feed Danielle or provide water, and never sought medical care for Danielle, nor enrolled her in school.

In Rhode Island, his foster mother and her boyfriend beat three-year-old T. J. Wright to death. Both were convicted, and both received life sentences for second-degree murder.

Each of the above cases made headlines in the local newspapers. Although the names and locations change, the stories are numbingly familiar—a child, usually an infant or toddler, is killed or horribly injured by his or her caregivers. The death or injury is tragic enough, but it is often compounded by the fact that the child or his or her caregivers were known to be at risk by the local child welfare agency. Occasionally, a death is so horrific that it captures national attention.

When the most lurid and horrifying cases of child maltreatment receive media attention, there is little doubt that the children have been maltreated; however, the clear and obvious cases of abuse and maltreatment are relatively rare. The severest cases of child maltreatment and sexual abuse are but the tip of an iceberg. At the lower regions of the iceberg are hundreds of thousands of cases of neglect, sexual abuse, and physical punishment that do not get headlines.

In most cases of suspected child maltreatment, hospital child-abuse diagnostic teams, a Child Protective Service investigator, a teacher or counselor, or a police officer will not have clear evidence about how an injury to a child, or a condition of a child, occurred. Typically, in cases of suspected abuse and neglect, a child is observed at school or in a hospital emergency room with a cut, a bruise, or some other injury. Physical examinations, interviews with the child and the parent(s), and an examination of the child's medical history (if available) can sometimes help unravel the case and separate true accidents from inflicted injuries. When a child experiences violence that does not produce a black and blue mark, cut, or injury, determining whether the child has been harmed is even more complex, since variable community standards and definitions of abuse have to be applied to an act that has produced no gross visible harm. The problem of detecting abuse is even more difficult when the victim is an adolescent. Observers of suspected physical abuse of adolescents tend to write off the injuries as "typical" of teenagers unless the adolescent victim comes forward to report suspected abuse. Even when an adolescent reports maltreatment, some responders wonder what the teenager did to provoke the incident or maltreatment.

Diagnosing neglect, emotional abuse, psychological abuse, and sexual abuse are even more difficult, since these forms of maltreatment rarely leave overt physical signs of injury. Child neglect, the most common form of reported and confirmed child maltreatment, is difficult to diagnose since child abuse and neglect laws stipulate that child neglect cannot be a condition produced as a direct result of poverty.

Determining the extent of child abuse and violence toward children in the United States and in other countries or societies is a difficult task because not all cases of abuse and violence are as obvious as those of Kayla McKean, Danielle Kelly, or T. J. Wright. Estimates of the extent of maltreatment vary, as do definitions and community standards. Moreover, the majority of cases of suspected child maltreatment are not even reported to child welfare authorities—despite the existence of mandatory reporting laws in all states (Zellman, 1990).

This chapter begins by first discussing the definition of child abuse and neglect. We then review various sources of information on the extent and nature of violence, abuse, and the maltreatment of children. Before considering who abuses children, we examine the process by which child abuse is recognized and reported in the United States. Official reports of child abuse tend to over-represent specific populations—poor and minority families—and under-represent other families—middle class and professionals—in part because minority and poor families are more likely to be identified and reported for maltreatment. As a result, relying on official reports as a basis for estimating the extent and patterns of child maltreatment leads to the perpetuation of the myth that only poor people abuse their children. Finally, the chapter reviews the evidence on the consequences of child abuse.

Defining Child Abuse and Neglect

There is no uniform, national definition of child abuse and neglect. The current federal Child Abuse Prevention and Treatment Act (CAPTA) (42 U.S.C.A. § 5101 note), as amended by the CAPTA Reauthorization Act of 2010, defines *child abuse* and *neglect* as, at minimum:

- "Any recent act or failure to act on the part of a parent or caretaker which results in death, serious physical or emotional harm, sexual abuse or exploitation"; or
- "An act or failure to act which presents an imminent risk of serious harm."

This definition of child abuse and neglect refers specifically to parents and other caregivers. A "child" under this definition generally means a person who is younger than age 18 or who is not an emancipated minor.

The Child Abuse Prevention and Treatment Act also provides definitions for sexual abuse and the special cases of neglect related to withholding or failing to provide medically indicated treatment. The law does not provide specific definitions for other types of maltreatment such as physical abuse, neglect, or emotional abuse. The federal definition is *a minimum standard* each state must meet if it is to receive funding authorized under CAPTA. States are free to develop their own definitions of what constitutes child maltreatment beyond the federal minimum standards. In short, there are actually 51 definitions of child abuse and neglect in the United States (50 states plus the District of Columbia).[1] And it is true that this produces some confusion. For example, take the case of sexual abuse committed by former Pennsylvania State University football coach Jerry Sandusky. Sandusky was found guilty of 45 counts of criminal sexual acts against numerous boys. Yet Sandusky's behavior did not fall under the definition of "child sexual abuse" in the Commonwealth of Pennsylvania. The state statute at the time defined a sexual abuse perpetrator as someone who was related to the victim or had a supervisory relationship with the victim.[2] Sandusky had neither type of relationship with his victims. Thus, although he committed criminal acts, the acts themselves did not fall under the legal definition of sexual abuse in Pennsylvania, were not subject to the state's mandatory reporting law, and would not show up in the state's annual reporting on cases of child abuse and neglect. Had Sandusky's acts of sexual molestation occurred in New Jersey, the behavior would be considered sexual abuse since New Jersey law defines a perpetrator of sexual abuse as "any adult."[3] Thus, there is no standard legal or policy definition of child abuse and neglect that we could use to assess the extent, risk factors, and consequences of child maltreatment, since what is child abuse in one state may be recorded as only a crime in a second state.

The federal government faced the definitional dilemma when responding to a congressional mandate, included in the original Child Abuse Prevention and Treatment Act, that there be a "full and complete study and investigation of the national incidence of child abuse and neglect" [Public Law 03-247; §2(b)(6)]. For the purposes of carrying out the study and investigation, the study defined six major types of child abuse and neglect (see National Center on Child Abuse, 1988; Sedlak et al., 2010):

1. *Physical abuse*: Acts of commission that result in physical harm, including death, to a child.
2. *Sexual abuse*: Acts of commission including intrusion or penetration, molestation with genital contact, or other forms of sexual acts in which children are used to provide sexual gratification for a perpetrator.

3. *Emotional abuse*: Acts of commission that include confinement, verbal or emotional abuse, or other types of abuse such as withholding sleep, food, or shelter.

4. *Physical neglect*: Acts of omission that involve refusal to provide health care, delay in providing health care, abandonment, expulsion of a child from a home, inadequate supervision, failure to meet food and clothing needs, and conspicuous failure to protect a child from hazards or danger.

5. *Educational neglect*: Acts of omission and commission that include permitting chronic truancy, failure to enroll a child in school, and inattention to specific education needs.

6. *Emotional neglect*: Acts of omission that involve failing to meet the nurturing and affection needs of a child, exposing a child to chronic or severe spouse abuse, allowing or permitting a child to use alcohol or controlled substances, encouraging the child to engage in maladaptive behavior, refusal to provide psychological care, delays in providing psychological care, and other inattention to the child's developmental needs.

PHYSICAL PUNISHMENT OF CHILDREN

Of note, neither the study nor the definition took up the issue of physical punishment of children by parents or others. Spanking children is the most common form of family violence in the United States (Straus, et al., 2013), and because it is considered acceptable and appropriate, many people object to calling it violence or child abuse. In fact, the Adoption and Safe Families Act of 1997 (PL 105-89) included a provision that stated:

SEC. 401. PRESERVATION OF REASONABLE PARENTING.

Nothing in this Act is intended to disrupt the family unnecessarily or to intrude inappropriately into family life, to prohibit the use of reasonable methods of parental discipline, or to prescribe a particular method of parenting.

On the other hand, the main objective of a spanking or slapping of a child is to teach the child a lesson, to get the child to stop a certain behavior (running into the street, touching a hot stove, etc.), or to relieve a parent's own pent-up frustration. Thus, the punishment must inflict enough pain to be adverse to the person hit and painful enough to hopefully deter the undesirable behavior. While physical punishment might be legal, it is still a form of violence. As we saw in

Chapter 2, many parents feel that children "*need*" to be hit. Justifications from a number of parents illustrate this attitude:

> "I spank her once a week—when she deserves it—usually when she is eating. I believe that a child should eat so much and that is it."

> "Once in a great while I use a strap. I don't believe in hitting in the head or in the face—although, Rhoda, I slapped her in her face a couple of times because she was sassing. That she needed."

> "But right now she doesn't understand that much. I mean you can't stand and explain really something in detail that she'll understand. So I slap sometimes. She understands when she gets a slap when she's done something wrong."

> Gelles, 1974, pp. 62–63

The justifications for physical punishment are not limited to striking young children. Parents also justify the physical punishment of teenagers on the basis of the teen's "mouthiness," obnoxious behavior, or the "need" to control an uncontrollable adolescent.

Social surveys conducted over the past 50 years consistently indicate that physical punishment of children is used by 80–97% of all parents at some time in their children's lives (Blumberg, 1964; Bronfenbrenner, 1958; Erlanger, 1974; Harris Poll, 2013; Stark & McEvoy, 1970; Straus, 1994; Straus et al., 2013; Straus & Gelles, 1990; Finkelhor, Ormrod, Turner, & Hamby, 2005). The most current estimate of the extent of the use of corporal punishment is that the rate of self-reported physical punishment of children is 67% (Harris, 2013). The current estimate indicates that spanking has declined in the past 50 years but is still widespread.

Despite parents' descriptions of how and why they use violence, and the claim that physical punishment is used because parents cannot reason with very young children, physical punishment of children does not cease when the children are old enough to walk, talk, or reason with (Straus, et al., 2013; Wauchope & Straus, 1990). Studies of college and university students found that half were hit when they were seniors in high school (Straus, 1971; Steinmetz, 1971; Mulligan, 1977; Wolfner, 1996). One of these studies (Mulligan, 1977) reported that 8% of the students questioned reported that they had been "physically injured" by their parents during the last year they lived at home before entering college.[1] Sociologist David Finkelhor and his colleagues (Finkelhor, Ormrod, Turner, & Hamby, 2005) surveyed a nationally representative sample of 2,030 children aged 2–17 years of age. Among their findings was that the rate of reported physical abuse was highest for

teenagers aged 13–17. Teens also reported the highest rates of sexual assault and psychological and emotional abuse. Teen rates were lowest, and those of children 2–5 years of age were highest, in reports of experiencing neglect.

The Extent of Child Abuse and Neglect

ESTIMATES FROM OFFICIAL REPORTS

The major and official government effort to assess the extent of child maltreatment in the United States is the National Child Abuse and Neglect Data System (NCANDS). NCANDS is a national data collection and analysis project carried out by the U.S. Department of Health and Human Services (DHHS), Office of Child Abuse and Neglect.

In 2014, according to the National Child Abuse and Neglect Data System, there were 3.6 million referrals for suspected child maltreatment involving 6.6 million children (U.S. DHHS, 2016). As a result of the investigations, an estimated 702,208 children were considered victims of maltreatment at the hands of parents or caregivers (see Figure 3.1). Of 702,208 victims of maltreatment for whom there are data on type of maltreatment, 119,517 (17%) experienced physical abuse; 526,744 (75%) experienced neglect; 58,266 (8.3%) experienced sexual abuse; 42,290 (7%) experienced psychological maltreatment; and the remainder experienced medical neglect or other forms of maltreatment (U.S. DHHS, 2016).

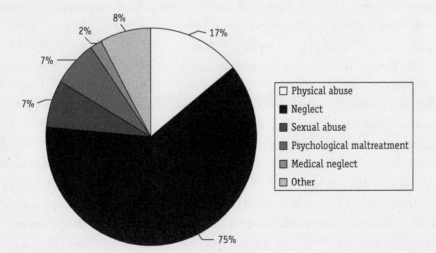

FIGURE 3.1 Maltreatment, type of victims, 2014.[4]

Source: U.S. Department of Health and Human Services, Administration for Children and Families, Administration on Children, Youth and Families, Children's Bureau. (2016).*Child Maltreatment 2014.* At http://www. acf.hhs.gov/programs/cb/research-data-technology/statistics-research/child-maltreatment.

There are limitations to the estimates of the extent of child maltreatment that are based on official reports. First, as noted earlier in this chapter, definitions of maltreatment and reporting practices vary from state to state and from agency to agency. Pennsylvania, for example, reported only 110 substantiated reports of child neglect in 2014. This is because Pennsylvania only considers acts of physical and sexual abuse as reportable acts of child maltreatment. Physical and sexual abuse reports in Pennsylvania are received through the Child Protective Service (CPS) system. Acts of neglect are received and responded to as General Protective Services (GPS) cases. Pennsylvania GPS cases are not reported as part of the NCANDS process. NCANDS also does not capture occurrences of abuse and neglect among Native American children, as there is no mechanism for tribes to report data to the system (Petersen, Joseph, & Feit, 2014).

In addition, each profession has a somewhat different definition of child abuse. Individual, agency, and state participation in the surveys is variable. Finally, some states provide complete data to the National Center on Child Abuse and Neglect, while other states do not provide complete data. For an example of how another county, Israel, implements mandatory reporting, see Global Perspectives Box 3.1.

THE NATIONAL INCIDENCE SURVEYS

GLOBAL PERSPECTIVES BOX 3.1
CHILD MALTREATMENT IN ISRAEL

In 1989, Israel joined the handful of nations that enacted legislation requiring the reporting of suspected child abuse and neglect. The criminal code was amended, making it mandatory to report any reasonable suspicion of instances of children at risk of physical, sexual, or emotional abuse as well as children whose physical needs were neglected. Reports would be made to the police or to a social services "child protection officer."

Asher Ben-Arieh and Muhammad Haj-Yahia (2006) collected data on reported child maltreatment. The researchers contacted the directors of all 276 localities in Israel that receive reports of suspected maltreatment. The researchers followed up initial requests for data multiple times, and 184 of the localities provided data.

The agencies received 31,168 reports of suspected maltreatment in the year 2000. Projecting to the total population, Ben-Arieh and Haj-Yahia estimated that 37,500 children were subjects of child abuse and neglect reports in the country.

The rate of reported child maltreatment was surprisingly high. The rate of reported maltreatment in Israel in 2000 was 17.8 children per 1,000. This compares to a rate of 11.8 per 1,000 in the United States and 2.6 per 1,000 in the United Kingdom. The largest category of reports was neglect (34.6%), followed by physical abuse (30.5%).

The distribution of suspected maltreatment was also something of a surprise. Geographic areas that were primarily Jewish reported rates of 20.1 per 1,000. The lowest rate of reported maltreatment was in primarily Arab localities, where the rate was 9.2 per 1,000. Equally surprising was that the rate of reported maltreatment was highest in affluent neighborhoods (18.9 per 1,000), compared to disadvantaged neighborhoods (13.1). Finally, although the number of maltreatment reports is low (*n* = 34), the rate of kibbutzim was the highest for type of localities (29.6 per 1,000).

Keeping in mind that the data are about suspected and reported maltreatment and not the actual occurrence of child abuse or neglect, the data from Israel suggest that reporting is influenced by the availability of service organizations, the willingness of individuals to make reports, and the amount of surveillance available.

Source: Ben-Arieh, A., & Haj-Yahia, M. M. (2006). The "geography" of child maltreatment in Israel: Findings from a national data set of cases reported to the social services. *Child Abuse and Neglect, 30*, 991–1003.

The federal Office of Child Abuse and Neglect has a second means of assessing the extent of child maltreatment in the United States. There have now been four National Incidence Surveys of Child Abuse and Neglect that survey a nationally representative sample of professionals—physicians, nurses, social workers, teachers, and others—and ask respondents to report on recognized and reported cases of child maltreatment (Burgdorf, 1980; National Center on Child Abuse and Neglect [NCCAN], 1988, 1996; Sedlak, Mettenburg, Basena, Petta, McPherson, Greene, & Li, 2010). A total of 1.25 million maltreated children were known by the agencies surveyed in 2005–2006.[5] (See Table 3.1.)

SELF-REPORT SURVEYS

Another means of determining the extent of child maltreatment are self-report surveys—either interviews or questionnaires. The National Family Violence Surveys (NFVS), conducted by Murray Straus and his colleagues—interviewed two nationally representative samples of families: 2,146 family members in 1976 (Straus, Gelles, & Steinmetz, 1980) and 6,002 family members in 1985 (Gelles & Straus, 1988). The surveys measured violence and abuse by asking respondents to report their behaviors towards their children during the previous 12 months. "Mild" forms of violence—such as those thought of as "physical punishment" by most people—were the type reported most commonly. More than 80% of the parents/caregivers of children three to nine years of age reported hitting their

TABLE 3.1

Severity of Outcomes from Harm Standard Maltreatment in the NIS-4 (2005–2006), and Comparison with the NIS-3 (1993) and the NIS-2 (1986) Harm Standard Findings

			Comparisons with Earlier Studies						
Severity of Injury or Harm	NIS-4 Estimates 2005–2006		NIS-3 Estimates, 1993			NIS-2 Estimates, 1986			
	Estimated Total	Rate per 1,000 Children	Estimated Total	Rate per 1,000 Children		Estimated Total	Rate per 1,000 Children		
Fatal	2,400	0.03	1,500	0.02	ns	1,100	0.02	M
Serious	487,900	6.6	565,000	8.4	ns	141,700	2.3	*
Moderate	694,700	9.4	822,000	12.2	ns	682,700	10.8	Ns
Inferred	71,500	1.0	165,300	2.5	*	105,500	1.7	*
TOTAL	1,256,600	17.1	1,553,800	23.1	m	931,000	14.8	Ns

* The difference between this and the NIS-4 incidence rate is significant at $p < .05$.

m The difference between this and the NIS-4 incidence rate is statistically marginal (i.e., $.10 > p > .05$).

ns The difference between this and the NIS-4 incidence rate is neither significant nor marginal ($p > .10$).

Note: Estimated totals are rounded to the nearest 100.

Sedlak, A.J., Mettenburg, J., Basena, M., Petta, L., McPherson, K., Greene, A., & Li, S. (2010). Fourth National Incidence Study of Child Abuse and Neglect (NIS-4): Report to Congress (pp. 3–11). Washington, DC: U.S. DHHS, Administration for Children and Families.

children at least once during the previous year. Among older children, the reported rates were lower: 67% of the parents/caregivers of preteens and young adolescents reported hitting their youngsters during the previous year, and slightly more than 33% of caregivers/parents of teenagers 15–17 years of age reported hitting their adolescents during the prior year.

Even with the severest forms of violence, the reported rates were surprisingly high. Slightly more than 20 parents in 1,000 admitted to engaging in an act of "abusive violence" during the year prior to the 1985 survey. "Abusive violence" was defined as an act that had a high probability of injuring the child, including kicking, biting, punching, beating, hitting or trying to hit a child with an object, burning or scalding, and threatening to use or using a gun or a knife. Seven children in 1,000 were hurt as the result of an act of violence directed at them by a parent or caregiver during the previous year. Based on these findings, it is projected that 1.5 million children in the United States under the age of 18 who live with one or both parents are the victims of acts of abusive physical violence each year, and 450,000 children are injured annually as a result of parental violence.

David Finkelhor and his colleagues conducted a national survey of child victimization in 2002–2003 (Finkelhor, Ormrod, Turner, & Hamby, 2005). The survey collected data on children 2–17 years old. Interviews were conducted with parents and youth. Slightly more than one in seven children (138 per 1,000) experienced child maltreatment. Emotional abuse was the most frequent type of reported maltreatment. The rate of "physical abuse" (meaning that children experienced physical harm) was 15 per 1,000, while the rate of neglect was 11 per 1,000. The overall projected extent of maltreatment was 8,755,000 child victims (Finkelhor, Ormrod, Turner, & Hamby, 2005).

One of the important limitations of all self-report surveys is that the studies measure only self-reports of violence toward, or victimization of, children. Thus, the results indicate the rates of violence and/or maltreatment *admitted to* by respondents or victims, not the true level of violence and victimization. Nevertheless, national surveys do yield valuable information regarding the maltreatment of children and a projection of a rate of child abuse that is considerably higher than most other estimates of reported physical abuse.

UNDER-REPORTING AND DISPROPORTIONALITY

No matter what method is used to measure the extent of child maltreatment, the general consensus is that not all cases of abuse and neglect come to the attention of authorities or professionals. Even though self-report surveys yield higher rates of admitted child maltreatment, it is clear that neither offenders nor victims report every case of abuse or neglect (Finkelhor & Dziuba-Leatherman, 1994; MacMillan et al., 2013; Petersen, Joseph, & Feit, 2014).

There is also the matter of the fact that what is officially recognized by authorities, medical professionals, school professionals, and social service professionals over-represents certain groups and under-represents others. Even a cursory review of NCANDS data indicates that African American and Native American children are reported and substantiated at higher rates than their proportion of the population. Conversely, Asian and Latino children are reported at lower rates. Disproportionality travels through the child welfare system, from reporting, to substantiation, to placement in foster care, and finally to termination of parental rights (Roberts, 2002; Miller, Cahn, & Orellana, 2012).

While there are abundant and consistent data that demonstrate disproportionality in child abuse and neglect reporting, there is rigorous debate over the reason for disproportionality. Dorothy Roberts (2002) argues that disproportionality is a form of racism in which disadvantaged minority families are more likely to have their children reported and substantiated for child maltreatment than white children with similar injuries or circumstances. Elizabeth Bartholet (2009) counters that what she calls the "Racial Disproportionality Movement" has not proven that disproportionality is a result of racial discrimination. Bartholet argues that, taken together, the data indicate that African American children are in fact more likely to be victimized, and that the cause of racial equity would be better served by insuring the protection of children from victimization.

One important study that addresses the disproportionality debate is Emily Putnam-Hornstein's (2011) examination of a birth cohort of children and assessing the rates at which children became child maltreatment fatalities. Putnam-Horntstein reports that African American and American Indian children were disproportionally likely to be victims of intentional and unintentional fatal injuries, while Asian and Latino children's fatality rates were lower than their percentage of the general population. Assuming there is no bias or discrimination in determining child fatalities, the rates of child deaths in Putnam-Hornstein's study mirror the NCANDS data in terms of referrals for suspected child abuse.

CHILD FATALITIES

The NCANDS estimated that parents or caregivers killed 1,239 children in 2014 (U.S. DHHS, 2016).[6] Expressed in rates, 2.13 children per 100,000 children under 18 years of age are victims of fatal child abuse and neglect. This rate is higher than the rate of 1.84 in 2000, and lower than the 2009 rate of 2.3, which was the highest in the previous six years.

Young children are the most vulnerable to fatal child maltreatment. More than 44 (44.2%) percent of child maltreatment fatalities were under the age of one year old. Overall, 70.7% of all child maltreatment fatality victims are three years of age or younger. Boys are slightly more likely than girls to be killed by parents or caregivers (2.48 per 100,000 for boys; 1.82 per 100,000 for girls).

We noted earlier that there is a controversy in the field of child maltreatment about whether minorities are more likely to maltreat their children or are more likely to be labeled child abusers. The data on homicide, again as we noted earlier, are not as prone to biases or selective reporting or substantiation. The child fatality data from NCANDS do find certain racial and ethnic groups either over- or under-represented. African Americans had the highest rates of child fatalities (4.36). The rate for white and Pacific Islands children was 1.79. The NCANDS data do not include case-level information on socioeconomic status, so the data cannot answer the question of whether economic disadvantage plays a substantial role in over- and under-representation of racial and ethnic groups.

While the stereotypical portrait of a child maltreatment fatality may be one of a child being cruelly beaten to death, the actual reality is often closer to the case of Danieal Kelly that introduced this chapter (although Danieal was actually much older than the typical child-fatality victim). Neglect makes up nearly seven in ten (72.3%) cases of child fatalities. An additional 8.9% of the fatalities result from medical neglect. Typically, medical neglect occurs when a parent or caregiver fails to seek medical treatment for an ill child. Physical abuse leads to 41.3% of child fatalities.

Child-abuse fatality perpetrators are mostly parents' acts of omission or commission—79.2%. Of the parent offenders, 28% were mothers acting alone, 15% were fathers acting alone, and 21.8% were both parents. Perpetrators who were not biological parents of the children committed 15.7% of fatalities. A male relative was the most common non-parental perpetrator.

IS CHILD MALTREATMENT INCREASING?

Since the early 1960s, there has been a widespread belief that the rates of child abuse and violence toward children have been increasing. This belief has been partially supported by the fact that the number of cases of child abuse that are reported to social service agencies rose steadily between 1976 and 1992—see Figure 3.2 (American Association for Protecting Children, 1989; U.S. DHHS, 1995). The rate of reported child maltreatment actually stayed even for the first time between 1992 and 1993.

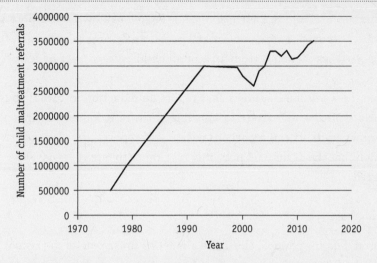

FIGURE 3.2 Estimated number of child-maltreatment reports, 1976–2013.

Source: Data derived from: U.S. Department of Health and Human Services, National Center on Child Abuse and Neglect. (1995). *Child maltreatment 1993: Reports from the states to the National Center on Child Abuse and Neglect.* Washington, DC: U.S. Government Printing Office; U.S. Department of Health and Human Services, Administration for Children and Families, Administration on Children, Youth, and Families. (2016). *Child maltreatment 2014.* Washington, DC: US Department of Health and Human Services; National Child Abuse and Neglect Reporting System and the American Association for Protecting Children. American Association For Protecting Children. (1989).Highlights of Official Child Neglect and Abuse Reporting, 1987. Denver: American Humane Association.

As it turns out, answering the question about whether child maltreatment is increasing, decreasing, or staying the same is as complicated as answering the question about how much child maltreatment occurs—and for the same reason. Each source of data has limitations and problems; thus, assessing the trends is complicated by the strengths and weaknesses of each data source.

Child Sexual Abuse

The most consistent trend data are for child sexual abuse. Using NCANDS data, David Finkelhor and Lisa Jones (2012) point out that child sexual abuse is down 62% since 1992. The most substantial decline occurred in the late 1990s. The National Incidence Survey (NIS) also reports a decline in child sexual abuse. The Fourth National Incidence Survey (NIS-4) reported a 47% decline in reported and recognized sexual abuse between the mid-1990s and 2005 (Finkelhor & Jones, 2012). The National Academy of Sciences (Petersen, Joseph, & Feit, 2014) report on child maltreatment states that the decline in sexual abuse is mirrored in the National Crime Victimization Survey (NCVS) conducted by the U.S. Department of Justice. The NCVS data on unreported sexual assault (i.e., a sexual assault the victim experienced but did not report to the police) declined 68% between

1993 and 2010 (White & Lauritsen, 2012). Finkelhor's own self-report survey of children exposed to violence (Finkelhor & Jones, 2012) reported a decline of self-reported sexual abuse from 3.3% of all children aged 2–17 in 2003 to 2.0% in 2008.

While there are some surveys that report no reduction in sexual abuse victimization, the overall pattern is a decline in the rate. Moreover, since the decline shows up in official reports as well as self-reports, the plausible rival explanation that the decline reflects only reluctance to report sexual abuse is not supported.

Physical Abuse

The trend data for physical abuse are almost as consistent as the sexual abuse data. NCANDS data show a decline of 56% in physical abuse from 1992–2010 (Finkelhor et al., 2010), and that trend continued through 2012. NIS-4 also echoed the NCANDS finding and reports a 29% drop in what is referred to as "endangerment physical abuse." But self-report survey data are somewhat more dramatic. The NCVS surveys report a decline of 69% in physical assault from 1993 through 2008 (Finkelhor & Jones, 2009). The NCVS data cover a broader spectrum of violence than parent-to-child violence. Many of the physical assaults are peer-to-peer or sibling violence. Other survey data that measure parent-to-child violence do confirm a decline across decades (Zolotor et al., 2011; Gelles & Straus, 1987).

There are some data that demonstrate contrary results. Most specifically, data on hospital admissions due to head trauma injury demonstrated a small but worrisome increase from 1997–2009 (Leventhal & Gaither, 2012). While hospital admissions for head trauma constitute a rather small percentage of the overall number of cases of child maltreatment that the spike occurring during the time of economic recession is notable.

Child Neglect

Child neglect, the largest portion of child maltreatment, shows a decidedly more mixed trend picture. Overall NCANDS data show a 10% decline in neglect between 1990 and 2010 (Finkelhor & Jones, 2012). But unlike sexual and physical abuse, the within-state trends are much more variable. During the period from 1990–2010, neglect declined 90% in Vermont but increased 189% in Michigan. Although the National Incidence Surveys trend data were consistent with NCANDS for physical and sexual abuse, the NIS-4 data showed no change in the rate of reported and/or recognized child neglect (Sedlak et al., 2010). Of note, there are no child-neglect self-report surveys that can be used to estimate trends (Petersen, Joseph, & Feit, 2014).

Fatalities

Data on child fatalities may be the most reliable and valid measure of child maltreatment. Yet here the trend data are remarkably inconsistent with data for non-fatal child maltreatment. According to NCANDS data, abuse and neglect fatalities rose 46% between 1993 and 2007. (As noted in the previous section, the rate peaked in 2009 before declining in 2010.) Official data on child homicides, on the other hand, fell 43% overall and 26% for children aged newborn to five years old between 1980 and 2008 (Finkelhor & Jones, 2012). Since the majority of young children are killed by their parents (Cooper & Smith, 2011), it is unclear why such an inconsistency exists for data that should be consistent across agencies that collect official data.

RISK AND PROTECTIVE FACTORS

Before we examine the risk and protective factors associated with child abuse and neglect, we need to highlight two important caveats. Although the literature uses the terms "child maltreatment" and "child abuse and neglect" interchangeably, these are broad terms that refer to distinct kinds of behavior. While some individuals may physically neglect their children, or abuse their children, each form of maltreatment has different generative causes and consequences. Simply said, there is not a profile of risk and protective factors for child maltreatment— instead, there are risk and protective factors for abuse, sexual abuse, and the different forms of neglect. As we will discuss below, although income disadvantage is a risk factor for physical abuse and neglect, it is not a risk factor for sexual abuse.

A second important caveat is that what we believe we know about risk and protective factors very much depends on the source of data we use to assess the factors. We begin this section by briefly reviewing the three sources or data and the strengths and weaknesses of each source.

Clinical Studies

Most of the early research on child maltreatment was based on data collected from clinical populations. Clinical studies depend on information collected by clinicians such as social workers, psychiatrists, physicians, psychologists, and marriage counselors. Clinicians can collect a considerable range of data with considerable detail because the clinicians see their patients over a period of time. However, clinical data typically are based on only a few cases (clinicians can only see a certain number of patients per week), and these cases are not randomly or representatively selected. Consequently, although data from clinical studies may be rich in descriptive information, one cannot generalize from these small numbers of cases to any larger population. Another limitation is that clinicians typically do not compare the information they obtain from cases of abuse to other families where abuse does not occur. Thus they cannot be sure that the factors they find in the abusive families are unique to, or are even associated with, the acts of abuse.

Official Reports

As we discussed in the section on assessing the extent of child maltreatment, each state has its own official reporting system and records, and the federal government collects data using the NCANDS system. Official reports provide information about a large number and wide range of cases of abuse. However, the data speak as much to the factors that lead someone to get reported or identified for abuse and neglect as to what factors are actually associated with the child abuse. Earlier in the chapter we discussed over-representation of certain groups as child abusers to be the possible result of lower income and lower social-status individuals (e.g., ethnic minorities, in particular blacks or some Spanish-speaking ethnic groups) being over-represented in official reports. Child-abuse researchers find considerable bias in the process of officially labeling and reporting child abuse (Hampton & Newberger, 1985). Physician Eli Newberger and his associates (1977) reported that lower-class and minority children seen with injuries in a private hospital are more likely than middle- and upper-class children to be labeled "abused." Patrick Turbett and Richard O'Toole (1980), using an experimental design, found that physicians are more likely to label minority children and lower-class children as "abused" (a mock case was presented to the physicians, with the injury remaining constant and the race or class of the child varying).

Self-Report Survey Data

Self-report data collected from representative, and often non-representative, samples of a given population also have limitations. First, and most obviously, respondents may be unwilling to report engaging in behavior that is thought to be deviant. Second, respondents may fail to remember engaging in or being victimized in violent or abusive behavior or may not remember being hit, maltreated, or sexually abused (Williams, 1994).

Our discussion of factors associated with child abuse draws from all three of these sources of information. Where the three sources agree, we find the most powerful explanations of what child factors and parent factors are related to the abuse and neglect of children.

PSYCHOLOGICAL AND INTRA-INDIVIDUAL FACTORS

The first research articles on physical child abuse and neglect characterized offenders as suffering from various forms of psychopathology (see, e.g., Bennie & Sclare, 1969; Galdston, 1965; Steele & Pollock, 1974). Thus, the initial approach to explaining, understanding, and treating maltreatment was to identify the personality or character disorders that were thought to be associated with abuse and neglect. Marc Parent, for example, described his experiences as a Child Protective Service investigator (1998). One of the calls he responded to involved a women who was clearly psychotic. She told Parent she heard voices and saw blood pouring from her walls. She was completely unable to care for her children while in such a delusional state, and Parent had no choice but to substantiate the claim of neglect and seek a court order to remove the children from her care. In other cases, the presenting problem of the suspected maltreators may be substance abuse, alcoholism, or clinical depression.

The presentation of the individual who abuses or neglects a child may strongly suggest a psychological disorder, and the very nature of the maltreatment may convince an observer that the perpetrator must have a psychological problem, but these observations are insufficient evidence on which to base a claim that psychological disorders are risk factors of maltreatment.

One of the consistent risk factors for physical abuse and child neglect is a family history of child abuse or neglect, or what researchers label "the intergenerational transmission of child maltreatment." The "intergenerational transmission" hypothesis often is presented as overly deterministic; resulting in the myth that all maltreated children will grow up to be child abusers or neglectors. Early testing of the "intergenerational transmission" hypothesis concluded that the proportion of maltreated children who grow up to become abusers or neglectors is between 25% and 30% (Kaufman & Zigler, 1987). Twenty-five to thirty percent is quite a bit greater than the overall rate of child maltreatment, but nowhere near even a majority of those who have a history of child maltreatment. The risk is greater for those who experienced physical abuse, and statistically significant for such abuse, but not strong for child neglect (Stith et al., 2009; Thornberry et al., 2012).

There are cautions in interpreting the data on the intergenerational transmission hypothesis. Cathy Spatz Widom and her colleagues (Widom, Czaja, & DuMont, 2015) carried out a 30-year follow-up study of individuals who had documented histories of childhood abuse and neglect. The study examined maltreatment using data from state Child Protective Service (CPS) records (official report data), as well as self-reports by parents, nonparents, and offspring of the parents who had documented histories of child abuse and neglect. The strength of the intergenerational link depended on the source of the data. Individuals with a history of child maltreatment had higher rates of being reported to CPS agencies compared to those with no maltreatment history. But, those with histories of child maltreatment did not self-report more physical or sexual abuse than the matched comparisons with no history of maltreatment. To complicate the picture, children of parents with histories of child maltreatment reported more sexual abuse and neglect than the comparison group whose parents had no history of child maltreatment. Thus, the most recent and comprehensive test of the intergenerational hypothesis suggests a complex picture that depends on both the type of maltreatment examined and the source of the data on maltreatment. Those who have experienced maltreatment tend to be under more surveillance by CPS agencies, thus producing a stronger relationship between experiencing maltreatment and becoming a perpetrator.

Early Parenthood

There is a shorthand phrase for the risk factor of early childbearing—many clinicians refer to the risk factor as "babies having babies." Official report data as well as self-report studies concur that the children of younger mothers are at greater risk of physical abuse and neglect than are the children of older mothers (Parrish et al., 2011; Putnam-Hornstein & Needell, 2011). Of course, economic disadvantage is a confounding factor when we look at early childbearing. Very young mothers are more likely to be poor or be on welfare than older mothers are (Klerman, 1993). The NCANDS data, however, do not support the idea that early childbearing is a risk factor (Petersen, Joseph, & Feit, 2014); however, the general finding from studies *other* than NCANDS is that early childbearing *is* a risk factor.

Psychopathology, Depression, and Antisocial Personality Disorders

As noted earlier and in Chapter 1, conventional wisdom and clinical experience point to parental psychopathology as a major risk factor for all forms of child maltreatment (Gelles, 1993). Research, on the other hand, fails to find that a significant number of perpetrators exhibit diagnosable psychopathology separate from the abusive or neglectful behavior (Wolf, 1999). There are a few high-quality studies that do find some important psychological characteristics as risk factors. The most important psychological risk factor is depression. Numerous studies report high rates of depression among parents who physically abuse and/or neglect their children (Brown et al., 1999; Bishop & Leadbetter, 1999; Kotch et al., 1999). Some of the research on the link between depression and abuse and neglect is limited because the studies are retrospective—carried out after the maltreatment occurred. Thus, as Belsky (1993) warns, the depression might be a consequence of maltreating one's child. Prospective studies, such as Kotch et al. (1999), do find that the depression precedes the abusive or neglectful behavior.

One risk factor that cuts across all forms of child maltreatment is antisocial personality disorder (ASPD). Various studies, including a prospective longitudinal study (Brown et al., 1999), find child maltreators to be more likely to have an ASPD than non-maltreators (Belsky & Vondra, 1989; Capaldi & Stoolmiller, 1999).

Drugs and Alcohol

Chapter 1 went to some length to debunk the notion that alcohol and drugs disinhibit people and that that leads to physical abuse, neglect, and sexual abuse. While alcohol and drugs might not disinhibit people, there is a strong correlation between substance abuse and many forms of child maltreatment (Chaffin et al., 1996; Dubowitz et al., 2011; Yampolskaya & Banks, 2006). While alcohol and drugs themselves might not cause abuse or neglect, in some instances, alcohol and drugs are used as an excuse for deviant behavior, and the research is consistent that drug and alcohol abuse are consistent risk factors for physical abuse and neglect.

CHILD CHARACTERISTICS

Another type of individual-level risk factor is the question of whether certain children are at greater risk of child maltreatment. Compared to research on offenders, there has been somewhat less research on victims of child abuse and neglect that focuses on factors that increase or reduce the risk of victimization.

The very youngest children are at the greatest risk of being physically abused, especially by lethal forms of violence (U.S. DHHS, 2013; Wulcszn, Barth, Yuan, Harden, & Landsverk, 2005). However, older children are at the greatest risk of non-lethal physical abuse, and the youngest children (age one to three years) have the highest rate of being reported for child neglect (U.S. DHHS, 2013).

Early research suggested that there were many factors that raised the risk of a child's being abused. Low birthweight babies (Parke & Collmer, 1975), premature children (Elmer, 1967; Newberger et al., 1977; Parke & Collmer, 1975; Steele & Pollack, 1974), and handicapped, retarded, or developmentally disabled children (Friedrich & Boriskin, 1976; Gil, 1970; Steinmetz, 1978a) were all described as being at greater risk of being abused by their parents or caretakers. According to the most recent NCANDS data, children who were reported with any of the following risk factors were considered as having a disability: mental retardation, emotional disturbance, visual or hearing impairment, learning disability, physical disability, behavioral problems, or another medical problem (U.S. DHHS, 2016.) On the other hand, a review of studies that examines the child's role in abuse has questioned many of these findings (Starr, 1988). One major problem is that few investigators used matched comparison groups. Secondly, other studies find the evidence is weak that children with disabilities are more likely to be maltreated (Govindshenoy & Spencer, 2007).

Factors Associated with Sexual Abuse of Children

There has been a great deal of research on the characteristics of sexual abusers; however, current research has failed to isolate characteristics, especially demographic, social, or psychological factors, that discriminate between sexual abusers and non-abusers (Black, Heyman, & Slep, 2001; Quinsey, 1984). One of the key questions raised in discussions about sexual abuse is whether all children are at risk for sexual abuse, or whether some children, because of some specific characteristic (e.g., age, sex, or poverty status), are at greater risk than others. Current research is unclear as to definitive factors that can predict future sexual abuse. Finkelhor, Moore, Hamby, and Straus (1997) found that a child's sex does not necessarily predict later victimization. However, Sedlak (1997) asserts that female children are at an increased risk for sexual abuse, and the relationship between a child's sexual victimization and age is also associated with family structure and race.

SOCIAL FACTORS

Although conventional wisdom points to intra-individual factors such as psychopathology as major causes of child abuse and neglect, only a minority of abusing parents—no more than 10 percent—have a primary psychiatric disorder related to abuse or neglect (Wolfe, 1999). The percentage may be higher for fatal abuse and sexual abuse and even lower for child neglect. Even when psychological risk factors are present they are often accompanied and sometimes exacerbated by social factors (Gelles, 1993; Gelles, 2004).

Poverty, unemployment, and low socioeconomic status are all risk factors for physical abuse and neglect—but not sexual abuse (Petersen, Joseph, & Feit, 2014). While not all, nor even most, low-income parents maltreat their children, the rate of abuse and neglect in households with low income is considerably higher than the rate in higher income families. The risk is not just a risk of being labeled a child abuser, but is genuine real risk factor that is found across studies using different methodologies and data sources.

Official and clinical data show a disproportionate amount of abuse in households with single parents or among parents who have children with multiple partners (Gelles & Harrop, 1991; Sedlak et al., 2010). The risk in single parent families is closely connected to the fact that single parent households are more likely to be below the poverty line than dual parent homes, and poverty, not family structure per se, is the risk factor (Gelles & Harrop, 1991).

The notion of the wicked stepparent portrayed in numerous fairly tales, such as Hansel and Gretel and Cinderella is echoed in research on child maltreatment that finds children who live with married parents have the lowest rates of child maltreatment while children living with a single parent and cohabitating partner have the highest rates of abuse and neglect (Sedlak et al., 2010).

Clinical and anecdotal evidence points to social isolation as a possible risk factor. Parents, particularly parents with limited social and economic resources, appear to be limited in their ability to cope with social stressors and difficult children. Another plausible explanation is that caregivers deliberately isolate their families so that how they treat their children will be shielded from family, neighbors, teachers, and others. The actual research on social isolation as a risk factor for child maltreatment is a mixed bag with widely varying findings (Petersen, Joseph, & Feit, 2014). It does appear that abusing and neglectful families do lack social connections and what social scientists refer to as "social capital" (Connelly & Straus, 2010; Coulton, 2007; DePanfilis, 1996; Dubowitz, 1999). Even studies of families from countries other than the United States, such as Spain and Columbia, find the risk of maltreatment higher in families with limited social connections and community integration (Gracia & Musitu, 2003).

Consistent with our discussion on Chapter 1, research finds a connection between intimate partner violence and child maltreatment. While the rate of the overall association is variable—ranging from 18 to 67 percent (Edleson, 1999; Jouriles et al., 2007) there is clear evidence that households with domestic violence are more prone to child maltreatment compared to non-violent households. Not only do perpetrators direct their violence at partners and children, but victims are more likely to mistreat their children compared to non-victims (Coohey & Braun, 1997; Zolotor et al., 2007).

Neighbor factors are also related to higher risk of child maltreatment—even allowing for greater risk of being identified and reported for suspected abuse or neglect. A community self-report survey carried out by Claudia Coulton and her colleagues (2007) found the rates of maltreatment highest in high poverty neighborhoods with high child care burdens. Other research also points to high rates of poverty as well as high concentration of alcohol outlets as neighborhood risk factors (Freisthler et al., 2007).

PROTECTIVE FACTORS

There is very little research that specifically focuses on factors that protect children from victimization. This is partially because the professional focus of children protective service work is to identify risk factors that place children in harm's way (Gelles & Bingham, 2011). A second explanation for the lack of specific work on protective factors is the obvious conclusion that protective factors are the opposite of risk factors. This, households that have sufficient economic and social resources will have lower rates of child maltreatment.

One important study on protective factors is Byron Egeland and his colleague's (1988) longitudinal examination of mothers thought to be at high risk of maltreating their children. Following high-risk mothers Egeland found that mothers who themselves had been abused would not maltreat their own children if they, the mothers, received emotional support from a non-abusive adult during childhood. Additional factors that reduced the likelihood that abused mothers would abuse their own children were participating in therapy and having a stable relationship with their current partner.

SUMMARY

As tempting as it might be to attribute all forms of child maltreatment to some intra-individual character or personality flaw, the knowledge base consistently supports a more multi-variable, multi-level complex of risk factors. And, to reinforce the introduction to this section, some risk factors are more salient for particular forms of maltreatment and may not be relevant for other forms. Finally, a risk factor does not mean a causal factor. Chapter 7, which presents theories of intimate violence and abuse, takes up the issue of causal factors and causal models.

Consequences of Child Abuse

The consequences of child abuse and neglect can be devastating. Researchers and clinicians have documented physical, psychological, cognitive, and behavioral consequences of physical abuse, psychological abuse, sexual abuse, and neglect. Physical damage can range from death, brain damage, and permanent disabilities, to minor bruises and scrapes. The psychological consequences can range from a lowered sense of self-worth to severe psychiatric disorders, including dissociative states. Cognitive problems range from severe organic brain disorders to reduced attention and minor learning disorders. Maltreated children's behavioral problems can include severe violent and criminal behavior and suicide as well as an inability to relate to peers (National Research Council, 1993).

Not only are there consequences for the victims of abuse and neglect, but there are also consequences for their families, communities, and society in general. In terms of actual economic costs, My colleague Stacy Perlman and I calculated that the annual direct and indirect costs of child maltreatment for the nearly 1,000,000 cases of maltreatment each year is $80 billion, or $220 million each day. These costs include the direct costs of medical care, child protective service costs, foster care, and educational costs. Indirect costs include juvenile delinquency and adult criminality as well as lost worker productivity and long-term mental health costs (Gelles & Perlman, 2012).

As severe and significant as the consequences of child abuse and neglect are, it is also important to point out that the majority of children who are abused and neglected do not show signs of extreme disturbance. Despite having been physically abused, psychologically abused, or sexually abused, many children have social support and effective coping abilities, and thus are able to deal with their problems better than other maltreated children. There are several protective factors that insulate children from the effects of maltreatment. These include: high intelligence and good scholastic attainment; temperament; cognitive appraisal of events—how the child views the maltreatment; having a relationship with a significant person; and the types of interventions, including placement outside of the home (National Research Council, 1993).

It is also important to note that, even when there are major negative consequences of maltreatment, there may be other factors that lead to the poor outcomes. The same factors that are related to child maltreatment—poverty, family structure, occurrence of domestic violence in the home, alcohol or drug problems of the parents—may also contribute to the psychological, cognitive, and behavioral outcomes for maltreated children. In additional, the child's age and developmental status at the time of the maltreatment may influence the outcomes of the maltreatment experience.

The consequences of child abuse and neglect differ by the age of the child. During childhood, some of the major consequences of maltreatment include problematic school performance and lowered attention to social cues. Researchers have found that children whose parents were "psychologically unavailable" functioned poorly across a wide range of psychological, cognitive, and developmental areas (Egeland & Sroufe, 1981). Physical aggression, antisocial behavior, and juvenile delinquency are among the most consistently documented consequences of abuse in adolescence and adulthood (Aber et al., 1990; Dodge et al., 1990; Widom, 1989a, 1989b, 1991). Evidence is more suggestive that maltreatment increases the risk of alcohol and drug problems (National Research Council, 1993).

Research on the consequences of sexual abuse finds that inappropriate sexual behavior, such as frequent and overt sexual stimulation and inappropriate sexual overtures to other children, is commonly found among victims of sexual abuse (Kendall-Tackett et al., 1993). Cathy Spatz Widom (1995) has found that people who were sexually abused during childhood are at higher risk of arrest for committing crimes as adults, including sex crimes, than are people who did not suffer sexual abuse. However, this risk is no greater than the risk of arrest for victims of other childhood maltreatment, with one exception: Victims of sexual abuse are more likely to be arrested for prostitution than are other victims of maltreatment.

In summary, the legacy of child abuse is more than the physical scars that children carry with them. Research indicates that there are emotional and developmental scars as well. Family violence can also spill out onto the street. Moreover, there is the issue of quality of life—the day-to-day impact of violence and its threat on children and the entire family.

Discussion Questions

1. What techniques have been used to measure the extent of child abuse in the United States? Discuss the advantages and disadvantages of each technique.
2. Are poor people more likely to abuse their children, to be correctly or incorrectly labeled "child abusers," or both?
3. What are the implications for clinicians, who must diagnose and treat child abuse, of the conclusion that there are multiple factors associated with the abuse of children?

Suggested Assignments

1. Observe how parents discipline children in a public place. Develop a "coding" form by which you can keep track of how frequently parents use physical punishment to discipline their children. Try to observe in different locations and see whether the setting, situation, and social class of the parents influence their public behavior.
2. Contact your local child welfare agency (state, city, or local). Ask for the official tally of child abuse reports for the last ten or even twenty years. See whether you can see any trends in the changes.

Notes

1. American Samoa, the Commonwealth of Puerto Rico, the Commonwealth of North Mariana Islands, Guam, and the Virgin Islands have mandatory reporting laws for child abuse and neglect.

2. P.A. C.S.A. § 3490.4 Definitions.

3. Pursuant to *N.J.S.A.* 9:6-1(e): Abuse of a Child includes the performance of any indecent, immoral or unlawful act or deed in the presence of a child that is likely to debauch or endanger the morals of the child. Pursuant to *N.J.S.A.* 2C:24-4, Endangering the Welfare of a Child includes any person who engages in "prohibited sexual acts" with a child under the age of 16 which is a crime of the third degree. Pursuant to *N.J.S.A.* 2C:24-4(b) (1) (a) "prohibited sexual act" includes sexual intercourse or penetration. See, *In the Matter of Registrant R.B.*, 376 *N.J. Super.* 451, 466 (App. Div. 2005) *cert. den.* 185 *N.J.* 29 (2005) (the debauching, endangering or degrading of the morals of the child includes prohibited sexual conduct).

4. A "victim" is defined as a child whose case was either "substantiated" or "indicated" after an investigation by a Child Protective Service agency. "Substantiated" is defined as

a type of investigation disposition that is used when the allegation of maltreatment was supported or founded by state law or state policy. This is considered the highest level of finding by a state agency. "Indicated" is defined as a type of investigation that concludes that maltreatment could not be substantiated under state law or policy but there is reason to suspect that the child may have been maltreated or was at risk of maltreatment (U.S. DHHS, 1995).

5. The estimate is based on what the study refers to as the stringent "Harm Standard," which requires that an act or omission result in demonstrable harm to a child.

6. The estimate is based on reports from 49 states. The 49 states reported 1,593 fatalities. Case level data are from 44 states.

4 Violence Against Women in Heterosexual Relationships

ON WEDNESDAY, MARCH 9, 1977, Francine Hughes, a mother of four children in Michigan, woke at 5:00 a.m., drank a cup of coffee, and reviewed her term paper once more before setting off for school. When she returned home from classes at 1:40 p.m., she was confronted by her husband, Mickey. Mickey, who previously was physically and emotionally violent toward Francine, was drunk and in a rage because Francine was ten minutes later than her usual time to be home. Mickey began screaming and swearing at Francine, and his rage continued off and on for the rest of the afternoon until Francine began to prepare dinner. Mickey's rage intensified when he threw the bag of groceries Francine and the children purchased for dinner. Things quieted for a while; then suddenly Mickey jolted from the living room, grabbed Francine by the arm, forced her to sit on the living room couch, and screamed: "Listen to me you bitch, I've made up my mind. You're quitting school right now" (McNulty, 1980, p. 167). Mickey's next move, after finishing another beer, was to grab Francine's book bag, dump the books on the floor, grab her wallet and car keys, and throw them on the floor as well. When Francine protested, Mickey slapped her across her face. Mickey then screamed, "Pick up that stuff on the floor! Clean it up right now, or I'll break your fucking neck!" (McNulty, 1980, p. 169). Mickey grabbed her by the neck and squeezed. When Mickey released her, she picked up the debris, put it in the trash barrel, and burned the contents of her wallet and all her schoolwork and books.

According to Francine's account, the emotional and physical violence she experienced on March 9th was typical of her volatile relationship with Mickey. She had even asked Mickey to leave after a previous violent episode, but had taken him back after he was injured in an automobile accident.

The evening of March 9th lurched forward, with Francine trying to feed her children and enraged husband. At one point Mickey threw a beer at Francine. When she jumped up, he threw her down and began punching her, all the while calling her, in Francine's words, "every filthy name in the book." He threatened to kill her, a threat that was not exactly new. Finally Francine called for her daughter to call the police. The police arrived in 20 minutes and stayed 20 minutes. One of the deputies asked Francine if she wanted to leave, but she declined.

Mickey had another violent outburst after dinner. Finally, Mickey topped off the day by calling Francine to the bedroom and demanding sex, to which she reluctantly agreed—if only to avoid yet another battle.

When Mickey was finally asleep, Francine gathered her thoughts, rounded up her four children, and hustled out of the house. Then Francine turned and went back into the house. She picked up a can of gasoline, unscrewed the top, and poured the contents onto the sleeping Mickey. She did not remember lighting a match, but in an instant there was flame and she ran from the house to her screaming children. Francine drove to the local police station and admitted what she had just done.

Francine Hughes was charged with first-degree murder. Michigan law would not allow her to plead self-defense because she was not in imminent danger when she set the bed and her husband on fire. Her lawyer sought acquittal based on a plea on temporary insanity, and the jury found Francine not guilty on that basis.

Francine Hughes's story would have been one of thousands of stories of women in the 1970s who defended their lives by killing their abusive husbands. In the later 1970s, as we noted in Chapter 2, violence against women, or wife abuse, was still pretty much a personal trouble and only a fledgling social issue. But in Francine's case, something different occurred. A well-respected author of children's books, Faith McNulty, was commissioned to write the story of Francine. The book, *The Burning Bed: The True Story of Francine Hughes—A Beaten Wife Who Rebelled,* had respectable reviews and sales. The book was optioned as a "made-for-television" movie, and the movie cast actress Farrah Fawcett to play Francine. At the time, Farrah Fawcett was something of a "sex symbol" with television credits including the original *Charlie's Angels* series, and there was a famous best-selling poster of her in a red swimsuit.

The movie, *The Burning Bed*, aired on the NBC network in October 1984. NBC invited researchers,[1] advocates, and social workers and counselors to watch the show at Rockefeller Center in New York City. At that time, the three major broadcast networks dominated the airways. The rating services stated that one-third of all television sets and more than half of all viewers in the United States tuned in to *The Burning Bed*.[2]

Most researchers and advocates agree that the television movie *The Burning Bed* was a major inflection point that increased public awareness of wife abuse. A little less than ten years after *The Burning Bed*, a second and vastly different television event rekindled public awareness of violence toward women.

One the night of June 17, 1994, an estimated 94 million viewers[3] watched Los Angeles police slowly chase a white Ford Bronco on Interstate 405 in California. Inside the now legendary white Bronco was former football star, movie actor, and celebrated TV pitchman[4] O. J. Simpson. Simpson was wanted for questioning in the murder of his former wife, Nicole Brown Simpson, and a waiter from a local restaurant, Ronald Goldman. Brown Simpson and Goldman had been brutally stabbed to death, and Simpson was a prime suspect. The chase ended, Simpson was taken into custody, and after a widely televised trial, he was found not guilty by the jury. Nonetheless, the Bronco chase and trial provided another platform on which the issue of wife abuse was presented and identified as a major social problem.

Jump ahead another 20 years and we have the case of football player Ray Rice punching his wife in an Atlantic City casino elevator. When the video first became available, it was shown almost every hour on cable news and sports channels. As of the current writing, the YouTube video had been watched more than 10 million times since September 8, 2014. As with *The Burning Bed* and the O. J. Simpson case, the Ray Rice case ignited more public awareness of the problem of violence toward women. Almost immediately after the Ray Rice video became public, the National Football League began to run "NO MORE,"[5] a series of public service announcements about domestic violence.

Each of the three episodes of violence against women that received national exposure was instrumental in moving intimate partner violence from a shielded private trouble to a significant social problem. The O. J. Simpson case was probably instrumental in the enactment of the federal Violence Against Women Act of 1994 (Public Law 103-322).

The three episodes also had another consequence—they established the prototypical narrative that the problem of intimate partner violence is mainly violence against women in heterosexual relationships. Francine Hughes's act of fatal violence was considered justifiable self-defense. Commentators ignored the portions of the video showing Ray Rice's fiancée striking him.

There is no question that violence against women in general, and violence against women in heterosexual relationships, are significant social problems. But these are not the only forms of intimate partner violence. Relationship violence includes mutual violence; some women are violent towards non-offending partners; and both women and men experience violence in same-sex intimate relationships.

This chapter examines the prototypical narrative—violence toward women in heterosexual relationships. Chapter 5 examines the other forms of intimate partner violence.

The Nature of the Problem

We provided a definition of intimate violence in the opening chapter. It is worth repeating here:

> For adults, family or intimate violence may include acts that are physically and emotionally harmful or that carry the potential to cause physical harm. Abuse of adult partners may include sexual coercion or assaults, physical intimidation, threats to kill or harm, restraint of normal activities or freedom, and denial of access to resources. (King & Chalk, 1998, p. 19)

Dating Violence

When the first researchers to study intimate partner violence uncovered significantly higher rates of domestic violence compared to the rate of violence individuals experience outside of the home, they proposed that the "marriage license is a hitting license" (Straus, Gelles, & Steinmetz, 1980). But later, other researchers found that high rates of violence occurred in intimate relations outside of marriage (see, e.g., Sugarman & Hotaling, 1989). Scholars who examined nonmarital violence used the now "quaint" term "courtship violence" to describe violence and abuse that occurred outside of marriage. We do not hear the term "courtship" much anymore, and the violence that does occur is not tied to just the process of selecting a mate. Even the term we use now, "dating violence," may be out of fashion and is too narrow. What we are concerned about is violence between individuals who are in intimate relationships prior to marriage. For now, "dating violence" is the best shorthand for this type of intimate violence and abuse.

A variety of small studies of secondary school and college students yields estimates of dating violence between 10% and 60% (Sugarman & Hotaling, 1989). The most recent and comprehensive examination of dating violence defined the behavior as "physical, sexual or psychological violence within a dating relationship" (Centers for Disease Control and Prevention [CDC], 2006). The CDC conducts the Youth Risk Behavior Survey (YRBS). The YRBS focuses on high school–aged youth. For the year 2003, the survey revealed that fewer than 9% of females (8.8%) had reported violent victimization at the hands of a dating partner in the previous 12 months.[6] The 9% prevalence is probably a lower boundary number since the subjects were not asked whether or not they actually dated in the prior year. Thus, some of the "no" responses were due to not being in a dating relationship. Foreshadowing what we will see in the next section, the rate of dating violence was highest among black students (14% for females) and lower for whites (7.5% for females).

The rate of dating violence among college students is higher than for high school students. Within the United States, estimates of dating violence among college students range from 10–50% (Kaukinen, 2014). Murray Straus (2004) analyzed data gathered on 31 college campuses in 16 countries and reported that 29% of students had assaulted a dating partner in the previous 12 months.[7] The prevalence ranged from 17–45%. The highest prevalence was at a university in Louisiana, while the lowest was at a university in Amsterdam, the Netherlands. In terms of severe violence—violence that has a high probably of causing an injury—the rates were also high. The median prevalence of severe violence was 9%, with a range from a low of 4% to as high as 20%. In terms of violence that inflicted an injury, the rates were also high, with a range from 1.5–20%. No university had a rate of injury-producing violence that was zero, and the median was 2%.

SEXUAL VIOLENCE

As noted in the definition of "dating violence," violence between young intimates is not limited to physical violence. Sexual assault is also a significant risk in intimate relationships. The stereotype that strangers pose the greatest risk of sexual assault is pervasive. College campuses generally offer escorts to students traversing the campus in the evening or late at night. On the other hand, colleges offer no escorts for students when they go out on dates—and yet more sexual assaults occur during social interactions, parties, and other social events, than on dark nights on campuses.

According to data collected as part of the National Crime Victimization Survey (NCVS), 6.1 per 1,000 college females (ages 18–24) reported they had experienced

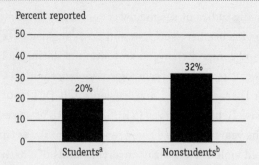

FIGURE 4.1 Rape or sexual assault victimizations against females ages 18–24 reported to police, by post-secondary enrollment status, 1995–2013.

Notes: [a] Includes victims ages 18–24 enrolled part time or full time in post-secondary institution (i.e. college or university, trade school, or vocational school).
[b] Includes female victims ages 18 to 24 not enrolled in post-secondary institution.

Source: Sinozich, S., & Langton, L. (2014, Dec.). Rape and Sexual Victimization Among College-Age Females, 1995–2013. Special Report. Washington, DC: U.S. Department of Justice, Office of Justice Programs, Bureau of Justice Studies.

a rape or sexual assault between 1995 and 2013. Eighty percent of the victims stated that they knew the offender (Sinozich & Langdon, 2014). The rate for women 18–24 who were not attending college was slightly higher—7.6 per 1,000. Only one out of ten assailants used a weapon (see Figure 4.1).

Sexual assault on campus is no longer hidden and is much discussed of late— because of victims are now pressing colleges and universities to develop and enforce polices punishing sexual assaults. Still, 80% of college students and two-thirds of non-college students did not report their victimization to the police.

RISK FACTORS FOR DATING VIOLENCE

High school students with lower grades, who engage in delinquent acts, who are sexually active, and who come from risky social settings and communities are more likely to engage in dating violence (CDC, 2006; Oudekerk, Balchman-Demner, & Mulford, 2014). Kaukinen's (2014) review of the research on dating violence among college students points to a number of important risk factors, including exposure to and experience with violence in one's family of origin; negative emotional states such as anger, anxiety, and depression; drug and alcohol use and abuse; and sexual risk-taking.

Adult Intimate Partner Violence

When the study of violence toward women began, various terms like "conjugal violence," "domestic violence," and "marital violence" were used to describe the phenomenon. According to the U.S Bureau of the Census, in 1960, nearly three-quarters of those over 18 years old were married (U.S. Bureau of the Census, 2014). Today that figure is down to 50.3%—a 93-year-low. While the decline of marriage has important implications for society, it also requires some adjustment in the terminology used by those who study intimate violence. For at least the last two decades, the prevailing term and acronym are *intimate partner violence,* IPV.

In terms of available data to determine the extent of IPV, with the exception of the Federal Bureau of Investigation's (FBI) Uniform Crime Reporting data, there are no official data collected. Early in the emergence of violence against women as a social issue, advocates resisted enacting laws requiring mandatory reporting of violence and abuse of women. The core argument against mandatory reporting was that it would reduce the victim's self-efficacy and subject her to the control of the criminal justice system. Thus, unlike child maltreatment, nearly all of the data we have on the extent of IPV come from self-report surveys.

SELF-REPORT DATA

The National Crime Victimization Survey, which we mentioned earlier when discussing dating violence, is an annual survey conducted by the United States Justice Department's Bureau of Justice Statistics. The NCVS surveys a nationally representative sample of about 90,000 households comprising 160,000 individuals. In order to be interviewed, the subject must be 12 years of age or older, Each household is interviewed two times each year and asked a series of questions about crime victimization. The Bureau of Justice Statistics began carrying out the NCVS in 1972, but it was not until 1993 that the survey began asking specific questions about IPV.

The most recent data on IPV are for 2011 (Catalano, 2013). Among the major findings are:

- The rate of serious intimate violence victimization (rape, sexual assault, robbery, and aggravated assault) for women was 5.9 victims per 1,000 females age 12 and older.
- The rate of simple assault against women by intimate partners was 10.3 per 1,000 females aged 12 and older.
- Of the violence against female victims, 8% involved some form of sexual violence, and 4% reported that they were shot at, stabbed, or hit with a weapon.
- Half of the female victims reported suffering an injury in the previous year as a result of intimate partner violence.

There are two noteworthy comments about estimates of IPV. First, the rates of victimization are lower than the rates reported by other self-report surveys (see next section). Second, the rate of female victimization is considerably greater than the rate of reported male victimization (see Chapter 5). Many other studies find similar rates of female and male intimate partner victimization. One plausible and likely explanation for the anomalies in the NCVS data is that the NCVS introduces the study as a "crime victimization" study. Many respondents may not view IPV as a criminal act and thus, may choose not to report violence by an intimate partner.

A second self-report survey of intimate violence is the National Intimate Partner and Sexual Assault Survey carried out by the CDC (Black et al., 2011). The initial survey collected data in 2010 and reports the annual and lifetime extent of intimate violence and sexual assault. A nationally representative sample of adults 18 years of age or older (9,086 women and 7,421 men) was interviewed by telephone.

The study's major findings are:

- About 1 in 3 women (35.6%) experienced rape, physical violence, or stalking by an intimate partner in their lifetime.
- About 1 in 4 women (24.3%) have experienced severe violence by an intimate partner at some point in their lifetime.
- An estimated 1 in 17 women (5.9%) experienced rape, physical violence, and/or stalking in the 12 months prior to responding to the survey.
- Approximately 1 in 20 women (5.6%) experienced sexual violence victimization in the 12 months prior to the interview. About the same percentage experienced a physical assault in the year prior to the survey (6.3%).
- About 4% of women were stalked in the 12 months prior to the survey.
- Nearly 1 in 5 women (18.3%) report being raped in their lifetime. Most of the female victims of rape (51.1%) were sexually assaulted by an intimate partner.

Of course, the CDC survey and the NCVS surveys are not directly comparable. As noted above, the NCVS survey focuses on crime, while the CDC survey does not present the questions in the context of being a crime victim.

There is some criticism of the CDC data on sexual assault. The criticism echoes concerns about advocacy statistics raised in Chapter 1. Christina Hoff Sommers (2014) believes the CDC study inflates the rates of rape by using a broader definition of "rape" than would be used in the criminal justice system. One of the

CDC survey questions used to assess rape was "When you were drunk, high, drugged, or passed out and unable to consent, how many people had vaginal sex with you?"[8] Sommers points out that more than half of the subjects (61.5%) who reported being sexually victimized experienced some form of alcohol- or drug-facilitated penetration. "Sexual violence" also included affirmative answers to questions such as "being pressured to have sex by someone telling you lies, making promises about the future that they knew were untrue." Of note, this is not the first time such criticisms were raised in rape research. As noted earlier, Mary Koss and her colleagues (1985) employed the same questions in their study of campus assault.

HOMICIDE

The only official data on IPV are reports of homicide provided to the FBI as part of the annual Uniform Crime Reports. The Supplemental Homicide Reports provide a breakdown of homicide by relationship between the offender and the victim. In 2012, 2,844 adult women were victims of homicide. Of that number, 26.4%, or 752, were victims of a current or former spouse, boyfriend, or girlfriend (Catalano, 2013). For trend data on IPV homicide, see Figure 4.2.

For a discussion of a unique form of marital homicide, see Global Perspectives Box 4.1 for an examination of dowry homicide in India,

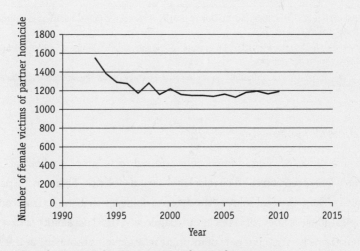

FIGURE 4.2 Female victims of intimate partner homicide, 1993–2011.
Source: Catalano, S. M. (2013). Intimate Partner Violence: Attributes of Victimization, 1993–2011. Washington, DC: US Bureau of Justice Statistics (NCJ243300).

GLOBAL PERSPECTIVES BOX 4.1
DOWRY MURDER IN INDIA

In 2006, more than 8,000 women (8,093) in India were murdered in "dowry-related" incidents. An additional 3,148 women committed suicide as a result of dowry incidents. The number of dowry homicides increased 74% between 1995 and 2007, while dowry-related suicides increased 31% (Babu & Babu, 2011).

Dowry is the practice of the bride's family providing clothing, jewelry, and household items to the groom (Shenk, 2007). In recent years, dowry in India has been more likely to be cash or large consumer items, such as motor scooters. Historically, the bride's family in upper- and middle-caste families provided dowry. The practice of dowry varies across India, with cash and consumer items becoming more common dowry offerings in North India (Shenk, 2007).

As the practice of dowry spread during the twentieth century, reports emerged about suicide, abuse, and the murder of wives by grooms dissatisfied with the content and size of the dowry (Shenk, 2007). So, in the early 1960s, the Indian Parliament began to enact laws to combat what was becoming the "social evil" of dowry. Parliament continued to enact legislation, including the Dowry Prohibition Amendment Act of 1984. Demanding and advertising for dowry became illegal. "Dowry death" was ruled a crime in 1986. Nonetheless, dowry continues to be practiced in various parts of India. Gift exchanges are still allowed, thus offering a loophole to the law, and brides who are harassed, abused, and threatened are still reluctant to report the groom/husband's abuse (Shenk, 2007).

Jane Rudd (2001) points out that dowry-murder is an archetypal example of how the dominance of men in a patriarchal society is the root cause of violence toward women.

Source: Babu, G. R., & Babu, B. V. (2011). Dowry deaths: A neglected public health issue in India. *International Health*, 3(1), 35–43.

Rudd, J. (2001, Oct.). Dowry-murder: An example of violence against women. In *Women's Studies International Forum*, 24, 513–522.

Shenk, M. K. (2007). Dowry and public policy in contemporary India. *Human Nature*, 18, 242–263.

PSYCHOLOGICAL ABUSE

Psychological abuse, or what is sometimes referred to as "emotional abuse," receives considerably less attention than physical and sexual violence. This may be partly due to the lower risk of physical injury. Another possibility is that the harm produced by psychological abuse is not visible or easy to diagnose. A third possibility is that psychological abuse is such a frequent part of intimate relationships that neither the offender nor the victim think of psychological mistreatment as a social issue or problem. An example of this possibility was a divorce case trial in which a woman was alleging that her husband's psychological abuse created considerable emotional harm. I appeared as an expert witness on behalf of the woman. I interviewed the woman and administered the "Psychological Aggression" scale from the Conflict Tactics Scales (Straus, 1979). The woman, based on her responses to the questions, experienced frequent and significant psychological aggression, including being yelled at, insulted or sworn at, had something done to spite her, and had an object thrown at her. The husband's attorney asked me to define, beyond the items in the Conflict Tactics Scales, what was meant by "psychological abuse." Drawing from one of my publications (Vissing, Straus, Gelles, & Harrop, 1991), I stated that the definition we used, and was used by others, was:

> A communication intended to cause psychological pain to another person, or a communication perceived as having that intent. The communicative act may be active or passive, and verbal or nonverbal. Examples include name calling or nasty remarks (active, verbal), slamming a door or smashing something (active, nonverbal), and stony silence or sulking (passive, nonverbal). (Vissing, Straus, Gelles, & Harrop, 1991, p. 224)

The judge pondered the answer, and before the husband's attorney could pose a follow-up question, the judged addressed me and said, "Given that definition, I have done some of those things." I wisely did not respond.

There is tendency in the area of IPV and abuse to think that violence and abuse are things someone else does. That belief is challenged by both the definition of psychological abuse and the research that demonstrates the harmful effects of psychological abuse (O'Leary, 1999).

Murray Straus and his colleagues employed the Psychological Aggression scale from the Conflict Tactics Scales in two national surveys of family violence (Straus, Gelles, & Steinmetz, 1980; Gelles & Straus, 1988; Straus & Sweet, 1992). The Second National Family Violence Survey found that 74% of men used at least one form of psychological aggression toward an intimate partner in the year prior to the survey (Straus & Sweet, 1992).

The more recent National Intimate Partner and Sexual Violence Survey (Black et al., 2011) reported somewhat lower rates of psychological aggression, with about half of all men and women reporting they had ever experienced some form of psychological aggression in their lifetimes (48.4% of males and 48.8% of females).

Is Intimate Partner Violence Decreasing?

Across the board, all data point to a dramatic decrease in IPV over the past two decades. Data from the National Crime Victimization Survey reveal a 72% decrease in serious female IPV victimization between 1994 and 2011 (see Figure 4.3).

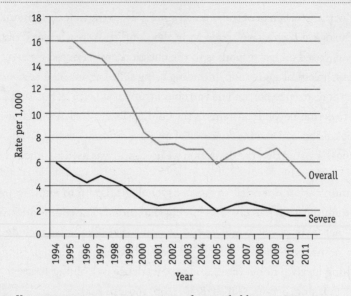

FIGURE 4.3 Year rate per 1,000 women 12 years of age and older, 1993–2011.
Source: Catalano, S. M. (2013). Intimate Partner Violence: Attributes of Victimization, 1993–2011. Washington, DC: US Bureau of Justice Statistics (NCJ243300).

In terms of absolute numbers, there were about 1.1 million fewer female victims of intimate violence in 2011 compared to 1994.

The rate of simple IPV against women decreased by 70% over the same time period. Overall, the total number of victims of IPV declined by 1.2 million in little less than two decades.

Of course, given that the data from the NCVS come from self-reports, one could doubt that the decline is real and could possibly be the result of changes in willingness to report victimization. That plausible explanation seems unlikely, given the fact that the interviews afford respondents the privacy of being interviewed by telephone. Second, given the increase of public attention to and concern about IPV, it seems unlikely that victims would be *less willing* to report intimate violence and abuse.

The question of whether the NCVS data could be the result of reporting and not actual behavior change can partly be resolved by turning to the data on intimate partner homicide. Obviously, data on homicide are not based on self-reports, so there is a much lower chance that reporting bias will affect the data. The data on intimate partner homicide reveal the same pattern as the NCVS data—a substantial decline in the occurrence of intimate partner homicides. In 1994, intimate partners killed 1,386 women. As noted above, this number declined to 752 adult women in 2012—a decline of 45.7% (see Figure 4.2).

Thirty years ago, the first reports of a decline in IPV were met with considerable skepticism (Straus & Gelles, 1986). Either the method of interviewing subjects was faulty, or people simply were unwilling to truthfully and accurately report their offenses and/or victimization. But, beginning in 1994, all forms of criminal violence (see, e.g., Conklin & Jacobson, 2003), including IPV and homicide and most forms of child maltreatment, have declined. So while there may be debates about *why* there is such a dramatic decrease in overall and intimate violence crime, the reality is that the decline is quite real.

Risk Factors and Perpetrators

There is an abundance of research on risk factors for IPV. But there are three cautions that go along with the research. Almost every time there is a highly publicized case of IPV—from Francine Hughes and *The Burning Bed* through O. J. Simpson, and most recently, football player Ray Rice, there is a barrage of emails and some phone calls to experts on intimate violence—researchers and advocates. The question is always the same—How would a woman be able to identify or predict whether a man will be an abuser? Although we have quite a bit of consistent research on risk factors, the question is impossible to answer at the individual level. No matter what rate of IPV we employ, the majority of men are not going to be violent in a given year or over the course of a relationship. When trying to predict what scientists call a "low base rate" phenomenon—whether it is IPV or an earthquake, there is a substantial risk of "false positives." In other words, even when adding up all we know about risk factors, when applying the data to individual cases, there will be a high rate of falsely predicting someone will be an abuser—even when the individual has all of the risk factors present. And of course, there are always false negatives—O. J. Simpson and Ray Rice had very few risk factors for severe physical violence.[9] The bottom line is that no one should apply the risk factors we discuss below to try to predict IPV in individual cases.

A second caution is not to place too much emphasis on individual risk factors apart from social factors. The earliest publications on the subject of wife abuse took a distinctively psychiatric view of both offender and victim. Abused women were believed to suffer from psychological disorders, as were the men who abused them. Research conducted since the 1970s finds this view of wife battery inaccurate and too simplistic. There are many individual, demographic, relational, and situational factors related to violence toward women. These factors are interrelated. For example, certain relationship patterns are probably more common in certain social classes than in others.

INDIVIDUAL FACTORS

Men who strike or batter their partners have lower self-esteem and are more likely to have vulnerable self-concepts than do non-violent men (CDC, 2014; Stith et al., 2004). A remark, insult, or comment that might not affect someone else, may be interpreted as a slight, insult, or challenge to many violent men. As we discussed in Chapter 1, alcohol and most illicit drugs do not produce disinhibition or directly lead to violent behavior. Nonetheless, illicit drug use and alcohol misuse are highly correlated with IPV and abuse (Capaldi et al., 2012; Stith et al., 2004).

As with child abuse and neglect, there are almost as many personality disorders linked to IPV as there are publications on risk factors. There is not a great deal of consistency in the findings, however. Two important systematic reviews of risk factors for IPV focused on perpetrator depression as a moderate risk factor (Capaldi et al., 2012; Stith et al., 2004). Of all the various personality and mental health variables examined, conduct problems and antisocial behavior emerge as the strongest risk factors for partner violence (Capaldi et al., 2012; Hotaling & Sugarman, 1986).

FAMILY OF ORIGIN

Given what we know about risk factors for child maltreatment, it would be a surprise if experience with, and exposure to, violence as a child would not be a risk factor for IPV. And, indeed, there are no surprises in the literature. Although there are no surprises, it is important to understand that experience of and exposure to violence are only moderately associated with adult IPV (Capaldi et al., 2012; Stith et al., 2004). The majority of individuals who experience violence as children and/or witness IPV do not go on to become perpetrators. There are numerous intervening events and factors to moderate or amplify one's childhood experience with violence.

SOCIAL AND DEMOGRAPHIC FACTORS

One of the most important risk factors for IPV, or for that matter, all forms of interpersonal violence, is age. Data from the National Crime Victimization Survey (Catalano, 2012) reveal that women 18–34 years of age have the highest rates of intimate partner victimization. Among women 50 years of age and older, the rate of victimization is consistently low across the last two decades.

The fact that age is such a strong correlate of IPV addresses one of the myths we raised in Chapter 1. That myth was that violence "always gets worse over time." In reality, intimate violence is most likely to occur among younger couples. After age 34, the likelihood of any form of violent behavior, including violence toward a partner, declines. Does the violence decline because the perpetrator desists or because the relationship ends? That, we do not know. What we do know is that, by middle age, the likelihood of intimate violence occurring is much lower than in early adolescence or young adulthood.

As with child maltreatment, one needs to examine race and ethnicity as a risk factor with some caution. While there are differences in the rates of IPV in terms of race and ethnicity, the differences are relatively small and are moderated by economic factors. The National Crime Victimization Survey reveals that, in 2010, blacks had the highest rates of reporting IPV, with whites slightly lower, and Hispanics the lowest of the three major groups (Catalano, 2012). Interestingly, the rates declined significantly for all three groups from 1994–2010. The small differences become even smaller when controlling for family income.

SOCIAL ISOLATION AND SOCIAL SUPPORT

Abusers often isolate their partners (Dutton & Goodman, 2005). In one instance, for example, a man became jealous of his wife when she was pregnant. As soon as he learned his wife was pregnant, the man decided to move from their apartment in the city to a hillside cottage miles from the nearest neighbor. After the family moved, the husband sold his pickup truck and purchased a motorcycle. His wife was cut off from her family and former friends and had no means of transportation. The husband's psychological aggression eventually escalated to physical violence. The wife had no social support, and the violence took place far away from the eyes and ears of any witnesses.

On the other side of the social isolation coin is social support. There is a small body of research that indicates that the greater social support a woman has, the less likely it is that her partner will engage in IPV (Capaldi et al., 2012).

LIFE STRESS

Economic stressors such as poverty and unemployment are risk factors for IPV and abuse (Capaldi et al., 2012; Stith et al., 2004). The strength of the association of economic stressors and IPV is small to moderate. In addition to financial stress being a risk factor, other individual and family stressors increase the likelihood of partner violence and abuse. Parenting stress is an important factor than can lead to partner aggression (Probst et al., 2008).

RELATIONSHIP FACTORS

As we mentioned earlier, more than three decades ago, Murray Straus and his colleagues opined that a marriage license is a hitting license (Straus, Gelles, & Steinmetz, 1980). Since then, considerable research finds higher rates of IPV among dating couples than among married individuals. The data collected for the National Crime Victimization Survey support claims by advocates that the most dangerous time for women is when they leave a marital relationship. The victimization rate for women separated from their partners is 60 per 1,000 women, compared to 2 per 1,000 for married women. The rates for never-married women (8.5 per 1,000) and divorced or widowed women (6.5 per 1,000) also exceed the rate for married women (Catalano, 2012). Various other studies point out that the rate of IPV among cohabiting couples exceeds the rate for married couples (Catalano, 2012).

Types of Offenders

Beginning in the mid-1990s, the field of IPV went in a different direction than the research by those who study and treat child abuse and neglect. Up until the mid-1990s, the study of offenders assumed that the greater the risk factors and the fewer the protective factors, the more an offender would be violent and abusive. Said another way, the assumption was that offenders would differ only by degree and not in kind. Following from this assumption, if one could decrease risk factors or increase protective factors, the escalation of violence could be deterred or even stopped.

Michael Johnson (1995), however, pointed out that most IPV was relatively minor—pushes and slaps—and the majority of violent men never escalated to more severe or even lethal forms of violence. Johnson labeled the minor violence "Common Couple Violence" and referred to the severe violence (choking, beating, using a weapon) as "Intimate Terrorism."

At the same time as Johnson published his theoretical argument, Neil Jacobson and John Gottman (Gottman et al., 1995) published the results of their laboratory experiments. Gottman and his colleagues recruited couples in which the male reported engaging in an act of physical violence toward his partner. The couples were subjected to a stressful event in the laboratory, and the researchers monitored the heart rate activity as the experiment moved from an "eyes closed" baseline to a conflictual interaction. The majority of men's heart rates increased with the increase in conflict. However, a second and smaller group of men's heart rates decreased. The men whose heart rates decreased were labeled "Type I" and were also called "Vagal Reactors." The Type I men reported higher levels of severe and emotional violence compared to the "Type II" men, whose heart rates increased during the conflict. Gottman and Jacobson not only differentiated types of violent men, they also linked the type to differences in brain and neurological traits.

Numerous other researchers followed the path of Johnson, Jacobson, and Gottman. Edward Gondolf (1988) had previously developed typologies from interviews with 6,000 women who experienced violence over an 18-month period. Gondolf labeled his types: Type I, the sociopathic batterer, distinguished by high levels of physical and emotional abuse; Type II, the antisocial batter, who is less violent and less likely to be arrested; and Type III, the typical batterer, who uses the least severe physical and emotional abuse. Other scholars who developed typology approaches included Holtzworth-Munroe and Stuart (1994) and Hamberger and his colleagues (1996). Mary Cavanaugh and I (2005) synthesized the research on violent typologies and developed a three-typology model of violent offenders (see Chapter 1, Table 1.1).

The "Low-Risk Batterer" engages in fewer acts of violence and less severe violence, presents with little or no psychopathology, and has no criminal history. "Moderate-Risk Offenders" are, as the name suggests, moderate in frequency and severity. Moderate-risk offenders have moderate to high psychopathology, with a tendency toward presenting with borderline personality disorders. Finally, the "High-Risk" abuser is high in both severity and frequency of abuse, presents with high levels of psychopathology, and has a criminal history. The high-risk offender does not confine his violence to intimate partners.

The typology approach to IPV has obvious implications for policy and practice. First, if offenders differ by type and not degree, a one-size-fits-all intervention is not likely to be effective across the range of offenders. What might deter a "low-risk" offender might be totally ineffective with the other two types of offenders. Second, interventions designed to create a "firewall" to prevent violent escalation may be the wrong approach. An intervention that first determines what type of offender someone is will be more appropriate than assuming all offenders are likely to escalate to severe or even fatal abuse.

Lastly, the idea that there are different types of offenders may influence how the social problem of intimate violence is framed. The typical framing that every man is capable of being an offender and every man is capable of escalating his violence and abuse directs us to intervening even when the violence is minor and infrequent. As toxic as any form of violence may be to the victim and family, it might be better to reserve our resources for the most dangerous offenders. Evan Stark, who began his career with the "every man can be violent" frame, revised his approach in light of the research on typologies and now argues that our best policy and use of resources is to target the truly dangerous offenders and vulnerable victims (Stark, 2007).

Of course, nearly all of the research and conceptualizations on types of violent offenders are based on data gathered on male-to-female violence in heterosexual relationships. We do not know whether the typologies are applicable to other forms of IPV.

The Consequences of Intimate Partner Violence

For female victims of domestic assault, the consequences extend beyond physical injury. Researchers consistently find a high incidence of depression and anxiety as well as increased risk of suicide attempts among victims of intimate abuse (Christopoulos et al., 1987; Gelles & Harrop, 1989; Hilberman, 1980; Burgess & Crowell, 1996; Schechter, 1982; Schumacher, Feldbau-Kohn, Slep, & Heyman, 2001; Walker, 1984).

Ann Coker and her colleagues (Coker et al., 2002) analyzed data from the National Violence Against Women Survey (NVAWS) and reported that both male and female victims of IPV reported increased risk of poor health, depressive symptoms, substance abuse, developing chronic diseases and chronic mental illness, and injuries compared to men and women who did not experience intimate violence. Michele Black's (2011) review of the research on the health consequences of intimate partner victimization concurs that for both female and male victims, physical, emotional, and sexual victimization are associated with higher risk of adverse health outcomes. Jacqueline Campbell (2002) examined the health care outcomes for female victims of IPV in both the United States and Canada. Her analysis was based on reviews of population-based (not clinical) samples. Here again, victims presented in healthcare settings with a variety of healthcare issues ranging from physical injury to mental health problems, including post-traumatic stress disorder (PTSD), as well as gastrointestinal disorders.

The CDC (National Center for Injury Prevention and Control, 2003) calculated that the costs of IPV in 2003 dollars were $8.3 billion per year. The costs of IPV persist for as many as 15 years after the cessation of violence (Rivara et al., 2007). For society as a whole, the costs of IPV include the time lost from work by victims, the medical care that victims require, and the investment of resources from social and criminal justice agencies. According to the CDC (National Center for Injury Prevention and Control, 2003), female victims of IPV lose nearly a million days of paid work annually as a consequence of being victims of physical, emotional, and sexual violence.

Why Do They Stay?

Even before the book and movie *The Burning Bed* raised the question, one consistent response to accounts of domestic abuse has been "Why do they stay?" The prevailing narrative was that perhaps battered women "liked" being abused. To an outsider, especially an outsider who never experienced a battering and who has access to social and economic resources, it seemed baffling that Francine Hughes would allow her abuser and ex-husband to live with her and continue to physically and emotionally abuse her.

The question of "Why do they stay?" actually inhibited the development of appropriate safe havens for battered women. Some observers opined that the solution to intimate violence was not to fund shelters, but for the victims—the women—to just leave.

Lenore Walker (1979) offered an early argument for why victims stay with offenders. Walker, drawing on the research of psychologists Steven Maier and Martin Seligman (1976), proposed that battered women become helpless after repeated victimizations. Walker applied the concept of "learned helplessness" as an expert witness in cases where women used deadly force (much like Francine Hughes) to kill their abusers. Walker noted that women who experience repeated physical assaults at the hands of their husbands have much lower self-concepts than women whose marriages were free from violence. Walker postulated that the repeated beatings and lower self-concepts leave women with the feeling that they cannot control what would happen to them. They feel they are unable to protect themselves from further assaults and feel incapable of controlling the events that go on around them. Thus, like laboratory animals that experience repeated shocks from which there is no apparent escape, battered women eventually learn that they are helpless to prevent violent attacks.

"Learned helplessness" implies a rather passive nature of battered women, and it is important not to confuse the situation of women who are battered with the situation of the laboratory animals from which the theory of "learned helplessness" was derived. Walker (1993) later revised her initial conceptualization of "learned helplessness" and proposed that women in battering relationships experience a constellation of effects that make up the "battered woman syndrome" (BWS). The "battered woman syndrome" is a pattern of psychological symptoms called "post-traumatic stress disorder" (PTSD). Criteria of PTSD include:

1. Experiencing a stressor (such as battering) that can cause a traumatic response;
2. Psychological symptoms lasting more than a month;
3. Measurable cognitive and memory changes;
4. At least three measurable avoidance symptoms; and,
5. At least two measurable arousal symptoms, such as hypervigilance or an exaggerated startle response.

Walker argues that the psychological trauma caused by repeated battering explains some women's reluctance to flee a battering relationship or other women's decisions to kill abusive husbands.

Over time, the "learned helplessness" theory did not hold up. Researchers found that, rather than being helpless, victims of domestic violence employed many strategies in attempts to deter the offender or flee the abusive household (Bowker, 1983, 1993; Gelles & Straus, 1988). Lee Bowker (1993) explained that women's reactions to experiencing domestic violence and their decisions about whether to stay or leave a violent relationship are not the products of the personalities of battered women, but rather are the result of the many social, psychological, economic, and physical factors that hold women in abusive relationships. Although many battered women do not leave their abusers, and many who leave return again, battered women do resist their husbands and utilize a variety of strategies to protect themselves and their children.

In my own research (Gelles, 1976), I compared battered women who stayed with their violent husbands to women who called the police, sought a divorce, or went to a mental health agency for help. I found that certain factors distinguished women who stayed in the violent relationship from women who sought help or left a violent husband. First, the women who leave seem to experience the most severe and frequent violence. Second, women who experienced more violence as children were more likely to remain in violent relationships. In addition, women with limited educational attainment and occupational skills were more likely to stay with battering husbands. The fewer resources a woman had, the less power she had, the more she was entrapped in a marriage, and the more she suffered at the hands of her husband. Sociologists Michael Strube and Linda Barbour (1983) talked with 98 battered wives and also confirmed that economically dependent women were more likely to remain with an abusive husband. They also found that wives who stayed with violent men reported they were more "committed" to the marital relationship.

Ola Barnett and Alyce LaViolette (1993) came closest to capturing why victims of intimate partner remain with, or return to, offenders. They placed the issue of staying or leaving in a larger cultural context. They explained that the socialization of girls to women both within the family and in the larger culture involves the learning of a belief system that devalues women, especially unmarried women, and creates a sense of female responsibility for the maintenance of an emotionally stable family. Thus the failure of a relationship or marriage, even as a result of severe violence and abuse, is assumed to be the woman's fault. Victims of IPV learn to endure abuse and remain in unhealthy relationships. Barnett and LaViolette refer to this learning process as *learned hopefulness*. Learned hopefulness is a battered woman's ongoing belief that her partner will change his abusive behavior or that he will change his personality.

Discussion Questions

1. Compare the nature of dating violence to the nature of violence within marriage. Is the marriage license a "hitting license," or are there other factors that increase the risk that intimates will be violent toward one another?
2. Discuss the various ways economic factors influence the chances that IPV will occur.
3. Why is it unfair to "blame" victims of IPV for remaining with their battering spouses? What resources or facilities in the community could help women who wanted to leave their violent partners?

Suggested Assignments

1. Identify the services that exist for IPV in your community (e.g., shelters or safe houses, hotlines, counseling groups, and so on).
2. Talk to someone who works in a shelter or a safe house. Is the address of the shelter public or a secret? How many women and children can the shelter hold? Does the shelter ever turn away women? Why? What is the philosophy of the shelter—how do they approach the problem of violence toward women?
3. Create a resource book for victims of IPV in your community—include the names, addresses, and telephone numbers of all resources that could be used by victims of IPV.
4. Find out what services (if any) are available for victims of dating violence and sexual assault at your college or university.

Notes

1. Myself included.

2. Available at http://www.nytimes.com/1984/10/18/arts/nbc-wins-decisively-in-nielsen-tv-ratings.html.

3. Availableathttp://www.nbcnews.com/storyline/o-j-20-years-later/o-j-simpsons-bronco-chase-theater-absurd-n129071.

4. For Hertz rental cars.

5. Available at http://nomore.org/nflplayerspsa/.

6. The question used to measure dating violence was: "During the last 12 months, did your boyfriend or girlfriend ever hit, slap, or physically hurt you on purpose?"

7. "Dating" was defined as a dyadic relationship involving meeting for a social interaction and joint activities with the explicit or implicit intention to continue the relationship until one of the parties terminates or until some other, more committed relationship is established.

8. Of course, the wording of that question excludes men reporting rape.

9. Simpson was acquitted for homicide in the death of his ex-wife and Ronald Goldman. He was found liable for the deaths in a civil trial.

5 Mutual Violence; Violence Toward Men; Violence in Gay, Lesbian, and Transgender Relationships

THE CASE OF Marissa Alexander and Rico Gray illustrates the complexity of the issue of intimate partner violence (IPV).[1] In 2010, nine days after she gave birth to her daughter, her husband and the father of the baby confronted Marissa Alexander. Rico Gray, Marissa's husband, found out that Marissa had texted photos of the newborn to her ex-husband. Marissa fled to the bathroom as Rico swore and screamed at her. Gray had previously struck Marissa hard enough to send her to the emergency room and had also choked her and left red marks on her neck. During his testimony and depositions, Rico Gray admitted, but then recanted, that he had physically struck his other "baby mamas" (mothers of his other children). The "baby mamas" also testified that they had been struck and then also recanted the same testimony. There was no evidence in the trial testimony or depositions that Marissa knew Rico was violent toward other women, but she had certainly experienced his violence firsthand on two occasions.

During a lull in the screaming, Rico rounded up his two children with the intent to leave the home. At the same time, Marissa went into the garage and retrieved her licensed revolver. She took time to load the weapon and returned to the kitchen, where she confronted Rico and his two children. Marissa fired a single shot that struck the wall above Rico's head—clearly a warning shot. The two children did not see Marissa fire the weapon, as they were standing in a room off the kitchen.

After the shot, Rico left the home with his children and called 911. The police arrived and arrested Marissa. Marissa was charged with three counts of assault with a dangerous weapon.

The case received considerable publicity. One factor leading to the national publicity was that the case occurred in Jacksonville, Florida, and the district attorney was the same one who had prosecuted George Zimmerman for the murder of Trayvon Martin. Zimmerman was acquitted based on a "stand your ground" defense. Marissa attempted to use the same defense, but the defense was dismissed because there was no evidence she was, or believed she was, in imminent danger when she fired the shot. Marissa could not use a self-defense argument because she was not in imminent danger.[2]

The jury convicted Marissa in 12 minutes, and she was sentenced to 20 years in jail. The case then took three more turns. First, the conviction was overturned on appeal because the judge had provided inaccurate instructions to the jury. Part of the appeals court ruling was that the 20-year sentence for each count could not be served concurrently, but must be served consecutively. In other words, if convicted in a second trial, Marissa would be sentenced to 60 years in jail. Finally, after she was released, Marissa had had a confrontation with Rico and assaulted him to the point of injuring him.

The media and advocates' portrayal of Marissa was that of a victim of a serial abuser who was defending herself from another attack. Gray had abused Marissa twice, but he was not in any way attacking her on the night she fired her gun. Did Gray abuse the other women in his life? No one knows for sure, and Marissa certainly did not know for sure. Did Marissa act in self-defense? Not according to Florida law. Irrespective of the law, was she acting in self-defense? Based on the available evidence and testimony, that would be a difficult conclusion to reach. In the end, there would be no second trial. Marissa agreed to a plea agreement in which she served 60 days and would serve two years of house arrest with a bracelet monitor.

So how would we characterize the case of Marissa Alexander and Rico Gray? Even advocates would agree that Marissa Alexander is not the "perfect" victim of IPV. She herself had used violence on at least two occasions. Rico Gray was also violent toward Marissa and possibly toward other women.

In the end, this was a couple that engaged in bidirectional, or what is often referred to as "mutual," violence. Bidirectional violence is hardly uncommon. In their national surveys of family violence, Straus and his colleagues found that about one-third of violent couples engaged in mutual violence (Straus, Gelles, & Steinmetz, 1980; Gelles & Straus, 1988). Male-only violent households made up another third, and female-only violent households made up the final third.

Mutual Violence

Mutual violence may be the most common form of IPV, but it is the least studied. Violence against women is clearly the most researched form of IPV. Many surveys, including all of the national studies of IPV, ask both men and women whether an intimate partner has victimized them and whether they have used violence toward an intimate partner. However, few studies actually report data on bidirectional or mutual violence in relationships.

Jennifer Langhinrichsen-Rohling and her colleagues (2012) provide the most comprehensive examination of the extent of bidirectional IPV compared to unidirectional IPV. Langhinrichsen-Rohling and her colleagues examined journal articles and book chapters[3] that report the results of 48 empirical studies and one meta-analysis[4] that reported rates of unidirectional and bidirectional IPV.

Bidirectional violence was as common as unidirectional violence across all the studies. In fact, bidirectional violence was the most common form of violence in most of the studies examined. Irrespective of the samples examined (e.g., population studies and criminal justice samples), criminal justice and military samples yielded higher ratios of male-to-female violence than of bidirectional violence. Lastly, rates of bidirectional violence varied by race and ethnicity, with blacks having higher rates of bidirectional violence.

The fact that many couples are mutually violent does not mean that the violence is the same. One partner may slap or push, while the other may punch or hit with an object. Michael Johnson and Kathleen Ferraro (2000) examined types of violent offenders and described couples who engage in mutual violence. In many couples, the husband or male partner engaged in what Johnson (1995—see also Chapter 4) calls "intimate terrorism," while the wife or female partner engaged in "violence resistance." But that pattern is but one of a variety of patterns of bidirectional violence. Jennifer Langhinrichsen-Rohling (2010) points out, based on a review of the IPV literature, that there are at least three sub-types of mutually violent couples:

1. Both partners use violence to control the other;
2. Mutual violence occurs because both partners have difficulty regulating their emotions and behaviors; and
3. Violence is dyadic/reciprocal, in which both partners engage in common couple, situational violence (see Chapter 4).

Raul Caetano and his colleagues (Caetano et al., 2005, 2008), whose study was included in the Langhinrichsen-Rohling review, found that mutual violence was least common among older individuals. Bidirectional violence was also more common among blacks and Hispanics than among white couples.

Lynette Renner and Stephen Whitney (2012) used a different approach to examine bidirectional violence. They analyzed data from Wave 3 of the National Longitudinal Study of Adolescent Health. The study consisted of a nationally representative sample of 10,187 young adults who stated they were in a romantic relationship at the time of the study. As with other studies of "dating violence," the occurrence of violence was quite common—47% of the sample reported experiencing some form of IPV. In terms of bidirectional violence, a history of sexual abuse and a childhood history of neglect were associated with perpetration by males. For female perpetrators in mutually violent relationships, childhood neglect and physical abuse were risk factors. For both males and females, a history of suicide attempts was associated with bidirectional violence.

GLOBAL PERSPECTIVES BOX 5.1
GENDER SYMMETRY IN PARTNER VIOLENCE AMONG UNIVERSITY STUDENTS

As a multi-decade participant in the controversy over whether women perpetrate the same amount of intimate partner violence as men, Murray Straus (2008) collected data from 4,239 students enrolled at 68 institutions of higher education in 32 nations. Straus's research team distributed questionnaires in college classes—mainly courses on sociology, psychology, criminology, and family studies, and collected data. The participation rates—the percentage of students who deposited a completed questionnaire at the conclusion of class—ranged from 42–100%, with most classes falling between 85% and 100%.

The analysis focused on respondents who self-reported being in a relationship of a month or more. Intimate partner violence was measured using the revised Conflict Tactics Scales—CTS2 (Straus et al., 1996).

Based on his review of the literature on IPV, Straus's hypothesis was that bidirectional violence would be the most common form of physical assault reported by college-student subjects. The second hypothesis proposed that "dominance" by one partner, regardless of gender, is associated with an increased risk of partner violence.

As predicted, and consistent with studies carried out in North America, bidirectional violence was the most prevalent pattern of IPV reported by college students around the globe. The second most common form of partner violence was female-to-male, followed by male-to-female. The findings applied to severe as well as minor violence.

Straus's second finding was that dominance by either partner increased the risk of IPV. That result applied to both minor and severe violence. From the college student sample, it appears that the generative source of partner violence does not differ by gender, but arises out the desire to dominate the other person.

Straus's study adds fuel to the controversy over gender symmetry and IPV. Yet these results are remarkably consistent with other general population surveys. The prevalence of bidirectional violence creates a challenge for prevention and treatment programs that tend to follow the stereotyped narrative of male perpetrator and female victim.

Sources: Straus, M. A. (2008). Dominance and symmetry in partner violence by male and female university students in 32 nations. *Children and Youth Services Review, 30*, 252–275.

Straus, M. A., Hamby, S. L., Boney-MscCoy, S., & Sugarman, D. B. (1996). The revised Conflict Tactics Scales (CTS2) development and preliminary psychometric data. *Journal of Family Issues, 17*, 283–316.

Although it is less commonly studied than violence toward women, it is clear that mutual or bidirectional IPV is common. Not surprisingly, many of the same correlates and risk factors for violence toward women, including alcohol use, are risk factors for mutual partner violence. Although there is a growing body of research on bidirectional violence, this form of IPV has barely moved from being a private trouble to a social issue. There is virtually no public or policy conversation about the violence that occurs when both partners strike each other. The stereotype that female violence is reactive and resistant to male violence remains the dominant narrative for bidirectional violence. For a review of an international study of bidirectional violence among university students, see Global Perspectives Box 5.1.

Violence by Women

I am 32 years old and live in the southeast part of the United States. I am a victim of domestic family violence. I know that it seems like most cases are the man abusing the woman, but in my case it's the other way around. The violence has been going on for 2 1/2 years, till I finally called the police on my wife. I didn't know what else to do; she was getting worse and worse. Many times my wife would use harsh words, and profanity towards me with our child standing right next to me. She would often tell me to get out of the house, and go f___ myself. She would get angry and throw fits, and 30 to 45 minutes later she would say that she was sorry, and that she loved me. She told me that it will not happen again, but this continued to be a daily thing for her. It got so bad that she started hitting me, and even at times when I was holding our 2 yr. old son. Men are often mistreated by women like in my case, but everyone always points to the man to blame. That is not always the case. Many women like my wife who knows that I will not hit or harm her, take advantage of the situation.

Emails and letters like the one above show up on a fairly regular basis in the mailboxes of researchers who study IPV and include examinations of female-to-male violence in their books and articles. While bidirectional or mutual violence remains below the radar screen in the field of IPV, unidirectional IPV by women remains an extremely controversial topic. In Chapter 2 I briefly discussed how contentious the issue of female-to-male violence is as a topic. Both Suzanne Steinmetz and Murray Straus actually received death threats in the 1970s and 1980s as a result of their public presentations and professional publications on the topic of female-to-male violence. The fervor has not died down. At the time of this writing, a blast email went out soliciting papers for a special issue of *The Journal of Family Violence*. The title of the special issue is *"Current Controversies Over Gender Differences in Perpetration of Physical Partner Violence."* That such a special issue is planned is not a great surprise, but the response to the call for papers revealed that the issue of violence by women and mutual violence remains a controversial topic. Among the online responses to the call for papers was the following:

> ... Funny for two reasons, he doesn't name the guest editor(s) which, I bet, means its one of the FR [Father's rights] nuts I met at the SD [San Diego] Conference.... I wouldn't go near this with a pole (unless they asked me for something and guaranteed publication). Also, for me, this issue is resolved and I see no reason to continue to hash it out in public.

It is not clear what the writer meant by "this issue is resolved." As we noted earlier, the reaction to the first papers and presentations on violence toward men was that no such behavior existed. A second response was a methodological critique of the method Straus and his colleagues (Straus, 1979; Straus, Gelles & Steinmetz, 1980) used to measure IPV. The main measure was an instrument titled the "Conflict Tactics Scales" (CTS) (Straus, 1979). The critics pointed out that the initial version of the CTS did not measure outcome—what was the consequence of the violent act—and also failed to measure who initiated the violence (Loseke & Kurz, 2005; Kurz, 1993). Failing to measure consequences meant that those who used the CTS could not know whether female-to-male violence was as injurious as male-to-female violence was. The assumption of the critics was that men did far more damage when they used violence than did women. Failing to assess who initiated the violence, the critics pointed out, meant that using the CTS to measure IPV obscured women's predominant use of violence as a self-defense mechanism.

In later applications of the CTS, Straus and his colleagues (Straus, 1993, 2005; Gelles & Straus, 1988) added questions to the interview schedule on outcome and sequence of events in the course of a violent incident. Straus (2005, 2011) rebutted criticism of the CTS and demonstrated that, in terms of injury, men do cause more injuries than women do. In terms of initiating violence, men and women initiate violence at about the same rates.

Given the quick and sardonic reaction to a simple call for papers, it is clear the controversy and issue are not at all resolved.

THE EXTENT OF FEMALE-TO-MALE VIOLENCE

We need to point out an important caveat when presenting data on both the extent of female-to-male violence as well as the risk factors. There are three types of IPV: (1) Male-to-female only; (2) Female-to-male only; and (3) Bidirectional.

Very few of the articles that examine the rate of IPV break the data down into rates by each of the three forms of IPV. Most analyses of male-to-female violence presented in Chapter 4 combine male-to-female violence only with bidirectional violence. Similarly, in the discussion that follows, data on female perpetrators and the rate of perpetration include unidirectional and bidirectional violence. When the analysis differentiates between unidirectional and bidirectional violence, we will specifically make note of that.

Dating Violence

The Centers for Disease Control and Prevention's Youth Risk Behavior Survey (2006) focused on the behavior of high school students. For the year 2003, a little less than 9% of males (8.9%) and females (8.8%) reported violent victimization at the hands of a dating partner in the previous 12 months.[5] The rate of dating violence was highest among black students (13.7% for males; 14% for females) and lower for whites (7.5% for females; 6.6% for males).

As with studies of dating violence in high school, the data from colleges show that females are as, or more, likely than males to use violence toward a dating partner. Across the universities, the rates of severe assault by females were higher compared to males (Kaukinsen, 2014; Straus, 2014). Males in nonmarital relationships generally exceeded females only in terms of inflicting injury, but the difference was quite small.[6]

Sexual Violence

It is fair to say that males are generally overlooked in studies of sexual violence. And yet, across numerous self-report surveys, males do report being victims of rape or sexual assault. Data from the National Violence Against Women Survey (Tjaden & Thoennes, 2000) included responses from 8,000 representatively sampled men. Two men in 100 stated they were victims of a completed rape, while

9 men in 1,000 reported they were victims of an attempted rape. A more recent national survey reports that 1 in 59 U.S. adults (2.7 million women and 978,000 men) experienced unwanted sexual activity in the 12 months preceding the survey, and that 1 in 15 U.S. adults (11.7 million women and 2.1 million men) had been forced to have sex during their lifetime (Basile et al., 2007). Sixty percent (60.4%) of females and 69.2% of males were 17 years old or younger at the time the first forced sex occurred. Some of the sexual victimization reported in that survey was sexual abuse of a minor and non–intimate partner sexual abuse. Most recently, the National Intimate Partner and Sexual Abuse Survey (Black et al., 2011) found that 1 in 17 men (1.4%) reported being raped at some point in their lives. That number probably includes sexual assault by individuals other than intimate partners. In terms of sexual assaults, more than half of the men reported a sexual assault by an acquaintance. Of the men who reported they were forced to penetrate another partner, nearly half (44.8%) reported they penetrated an intimate partner. A considerable amount of the sexual assault experienced by men (27.8%) first occurred when the men were ten years of age or younger.

Adult Intimate Partner Violence

The most recent data on female-to-male intimate partner violence from the National Crime Victimization Survey (NCVS; Catalano, 2013) indicate that:

- The rate of serious intimate violence against males was .04 per 1,000 for males aged 12 and older.
- The rate of simple assault of males by intimate partners was 1.1 per 1,000 males aged 12 and older.
- Eight percent of male victims reported being shot, stabbed, or hit with a weapon.
- Forty-four percent of male victims of intimate partner violence reported suffering an injury in the previous year.

The National Intimate Partner and Sexual Assault Survey (NIPSAS- Black et al., 2011) collected self-reports from men on IPV victimization. A nationally representative sample of adults 18 years of age or older (9,086 women and 7,421 men) were interviewed by telephone. In terms of female-to-violence, the major findings are:

- About 1 in 4 men (28.5%) experienced rape, physical violence, or stalking by an intimate partner in their lifetime.

- About 1 in 7 (13.8%) men have experienced severe violence by an intimate partner at some point in their lifetime.
- An estimated 1 in 20 men (5.0%) experienced rape, physical violence, and/or stalking in the 12 months prior to responding to the survey.

Of course, the NIPSAS survey and the NCVS surveys are not directly comparable. As noted in Chapter 4, the NCVS survey focuses on crime, while the NIPSAS survey does not present the questions in the context of being a crime victim.

If the matter of female-to-male violence is settled, as claimed by the email poster referring to a special issue of an academic journal on gender and violence, then, according to the best data available, it is fair to conclude that women are violent towards men across the age span and ranging from dating violence to domestic homicide. If the question is, are men and women equal in terms of perpetrating IPV, the answer needs to be more nuanced. Men commit more intimate partner homicides. Male sexual assault is greater than female intimate partner sexual assault. There is greater symmetry for the less serious, more common forms of violence, and less symmetry for fatal and injurious violence.

While many women use violence in self-defense, many other women use violence for the same reason men do—for the purposes of power and control. And it is also the case that many couples are violent with no specific person responsible for always initiating the violence. Males perpetrate the more injurious and lethal forms of violence.

Forty years after violence against women emerged as a social issue and social problem, the issue of female-to-male violence is still very much a personal trouble, with rare sparks of being a social issue. Research on female-to-male violence is limited, with very few sources of federal and foundation grant support. Advocates no longer dismiss female-to-male violence as nonexistent, but there is also no attempt to embrace the issue as a significant component of the problem of IPV.

CHANGING RATES

The rate of violence toward women, as collected by the National Crime Victimization Survey (Catalano, 2012), has declined by 63% between 1993 and 2010 (see Chapter 4). Similarly, the rate of female-to-male violence also declined from 3.0 victimizations per 1,000 men to 2.1 per 1,000—a decline of 64% (see Figure 5.1).

Looking at intimate partner homicides, the changing rates show a different picture. FBI data indicate that the number of female victims of intimate partner

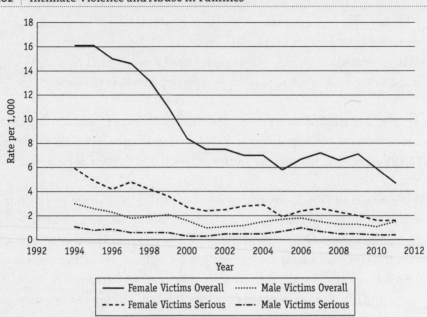

FIGURE 5.1 Rates of Male to Female and Female to Male Violence 1993–2011.

Source: Catalano, S. M. (2013). Intimate partner violence: Attributes of victimization, 1993–2011. Washington, DC: US Bureau of Justice Statistics (NCJ243300).

homicide declined from a peak of 2,000 victims in 1993 to around 1,500 in 2010 (Fox, 2012). The decline for male victims was even more dramatic. About 1,500 men were killed by intimate partners in 1993. The number declined to about 500 in 2010 (Fox, 2012).

RISK FACTORS

By and large, with the few studies we have that separate unidirectional violence from bidirectional violence, the risk factors for female-to-male unidirectional violence appear to be similar to the risk factors for the other forms of IPV in heterosexual relationships. Langhinrichsen-Rohling and her colleague's (2012) review of research comparing unidirectional to bidirectional IPV concludes that, across the studies that provided data on directionality and race/ethnicity, there were either very small differences in the rates of female-to-male unidirectional violence, or the rates were highest among white females.

Denise Hines and Emily Douglas (2009) also extracted data from existing research and examined factors related to female-to-male unidirectional violence. They report IPV by women against men may be associated with mental health problems in men, such as depression, stress, and other psychological issues.

CONSEQUENCES FOR MALE VICTIMS

As with the entire scope of research on female-to-male IPV, there is a paucity of research—beyond anecdotes—that discusses the consequences of male victimization. Hines and Douglas's (2009) review of research on women who perpetrate IPV is one of the few resources available. Hines and Douglas point out that, although criminal justice data and advocacy claims conclude that while women may strike men often, women suffer the most frequent and grievous injuries. Nonetheless, men are injured, and intimate partners kill some 500 men each year. The ratio of injury rates between men and women often depends on the sample from whom data are collected. Men do report experiencing anger, emotional hurt, shame, and fear as a result of victimization. As with women, men who experience IPV report high rates of depression, stress, and physical and psychological distress.

As noted in Chapter 4, Ann Coker and her colleagues (Coker et al., 2002) reported that male victims of IPV who responded to the National Violence Against Women Survey reported increased risk of poor health, depression, substance abuse, and chronic illnesses. Data from the most recent national intimate violence survey (Black et al., 2011) echo the earlier results about poor outcomes for male victims of IPV.

The limited research that is available suggests that male victims experience many of the same physical, social, and psychological sequelae as female victims.

Gays, Lesbians, Bisexuals, and Transgendered Violence and Abuse

Until this decade, violence in gay, lesbian, bisexual, and transgendered (LGBT) relationships constituted the most overlooked form of intimate violence. In the 1970s and 1980s, the use of the term "family violence" resulted in a focus on violence that occurred within traditional heterosexual marriages. The term "intimate violence" allowed for the expanding the focus on violence to nonmarital relationships. The feminist theoretical perspective (see Chapter 7) conceptualized intimate violence as something men do mostly to women. Traditional services for treating intimate violence were shelters for women who were victimized by men, arrest for male batterers, and treatment groups for violent men. Primary prevention efforts aimed at confronting and changing cultural values that supported male domination of women. Cultural attitudes about gays and lesbians, including homophobic attitudes and behavior, constrained victims of gay and lesbian violence from speaking out about their victimization. With the exception of surveys on sexual behavior, few researchers routinely asked subjects to self-report their gender identity or sexual preferences. All of the above-listed factors contributed to a myth that only heterosexual women were battered. The perceptual blackout of male victims extended to gay men.

The first definitive data on the extent of intimate violence in same-sex couples came from the National Violence Against Women Survey—NVAW (Tjaden & Thoenne, 2000). The NVAW survey did not actually ask respondents to self-report gender identify or sexual orientation. The survey did include a question about whether the respondent lived as a couple with a same-sex partner. One percent of the women and .8% of the men reported they had a history of living as a couple with a same-sex partner. For women and men who had ever lived with a same-sex partner, the lifetime victimization rates were:

- Eleven percent (11.4) of women reported ever being raped.
- Thirty-five percent of women (35.4) reported physical assault.
- Thirty-nine percent (39.2) of women reported lifetime victimization.
- No men reported being raped.
- Twenty-one percent (21.5) of men reported physical assault.
- Twenty-three percent (23.1) of men reported lifetime victimization.

In every instance, the rate of victimization of women and men who ever lived with a same-sex partner was significantly greater than the rate of respondents who only lived as a couple with an opposite sex partner. As it turns out, reporting that you ever lived with a same-sex partner does not mean you were abused or struck by a same-sex partner. Of the women victims who reported they ever lived with a same-sex partner, a male victimized 30.4%, and a female victimized only 11.4%. Similarly, for the men who reported ever living in a same-sex relationship, the rate of victimization at the hands of a male offender was 14.4%, compared to a rate of 10.8 from female offenders.

A second source of data on the extent of violence in same-sex relationships is the National Epidemiological Survey on Alcohol and Related Conditions (Roberts et al., 2010). The survey collected data from a nationally representative sample of 34,552 adults 18 years of age or older living in the United States. A single item assessed IPV. Heterosexual women reported the highest rate of intimate partner victimization—23.8%. Four in every hundred heterosexual men reported intimate partner victimization. Of the women responding that they were bisexual, 20.2% reported victimization, compared to 16.1% for lesbians, 11.5% for gay men, and zero percent for bisexual men.

The most recent survey of IPV is the Centers for Disease Control and Prevention's National Intimate Partner and Sexual Assault Survey—NIPSAS (Black et al., 2011). A supplemental report of the survey results examined intimate violence and sexual assault in terms of victimization and sexual orientation (Walters, Chen, & Brieding, 2013). The NIPSAS asked subjects the following question to measure their sexual orientation: "Do you consider yourself to be heterosexual or straight, gay or lesbian, or bisexual?" Bisexual respondents were not asked about the sexual orientation of their partner/offender. Given the low base rate of self-reported annual victimization and the low base rate of self-reported gay, lesbian, or bisexual sexual orientations, the study results present only lifetime prevalence rates.

The study sample consisted of 9,086 females and 7,421 men. The sexual orientation of the sample included 96.5% females identified as heterosexual, 2.2% bisexual, and 1.3% lesbian. For males, 96.8% identified as heterosexual, 1.2% bisexual, and 2.0% gay. Looking at all forms of victimization, the results were:

- Bisexual women had significantly higher lifetime prevalence of rape, physical violence, and/or stalking by *an intimate partner* when compared to both lesbian and heterosexual women.
- Lesbian women and gay men reported levels of intimate partner violence and sexual violence equal to or higher than those of heterosexuals.

Looking only at physical violence, the comparative rates of IPV by sexual orientation of the victim are:

For *women*:
Lesbian—29.4%
Bisexual—49.3%
Heterosexual—23.6%

For *men*:
Gay—16.4%
Bisexual—numbers too small
Heterosexual—13.9%

Lastly, the study examined the sex of the perpetrator. Again, we have no way of knowing the sexual orientation of the perpetrator. Most bisexual and heterosexual women (89.5% and 98.7%, respectively) reported having only male perpetrators of IPV. Two-thirds of lesbian women (67.4%) reported having only female perpetrators of IPV. The majority of bisexual men (78.5%) and almost all heterosexual men (99.5%) reported having only female perpetrators of IPV. Most gay men (90.7%) reported having only male perpetrators of IPV.

Unquestionably, we know that IPV is not restricted to heterosexual couples. Moreover, the rate of violence and abuse experienced by bisexual men and women exceeds the rate of intimate violence in reported by heterosexual men and women.

The data from the two national surveys of intimate violence and sexual orientation firmly establish the extent of intimate violence experienced by lesbians, gays, and especially bisexual women. However, the low rates of victimization and non-heterosexual sexual orientations preclude a more extensive analysis of individual and social risk factors associated with intimate victimization of those who reported lesbian, gay, and bisexual sexual orientations. And, of course, neither study provides any data on the violent and sexual victimization of transsexuals.

PATTERNS OF GAY AND LESBIAN VIOLENCE

The vast majority of the scholarly literature on gays, lesbians, and bisexual's experience with IPV focused on establishing an estimate of the extent of the violence. Studies were either clinical or small regional samples. The two national data sets rendered much of the literature prior to 2011 out of date.

The extensive focus on exploding the myth of exclusively heterosexual IPV limited researchers from carrying out other examinations of IPV in the LGBT community. Research efforts are also constrained, as noted earlier, by the low base rates of victimization and non-heterosexual gender identification. We do, however, have some evidence about the nature and patterns of intimate violence in LGBT relationships.

In the 1980s and 1990s, if violence in gay and lesbian relationships was recognized at all, there was the assumption that the nature of the violence conformed to stereotypical roles that gays and lesbians were believed to play in relationships. Thus the offender in the lesbian couple was believed to be the masculine or "butch" partner, while the victim was the "femme" or feminine partner. Claire Renzetti (1995) reported, however, that the available data on gay and lesbian violence demonstrated that stereotypical sex roles or physical size are not related to offender and victim roles. Researchers also believe that, although the partners are the same sex, there is no pattern of prevalent mutual violence in gay and lesbian relations (Letellier, 1994; Renzetti, 1992). Neither of the national surveys reports on the occurrence of bidirectional or mutual violence in these couples.

Those who have examined psychological and physical abuse explain that, as with violence in heterosexual couples, power and power imbalances are key triggers to the occurrence of gay and lesbian violence (Lockhart et al., 1994). It is presumed that egalitarian lesbian and gay relationships have lower levels of violence than do couples with greater resource and power imbalances.

Going forward, it is reasonable to assume that there will a considerable increase if not an explosion of research on IPV in the LGBT community. The Supreme Court removed the legal barriers to same-sex marriage in 2015. As other barriers and taboos fall, researchers will be more willing to ask questions about sexual orientation, and members of the LGBT community may be more willing to self-identify their gender orientation and sexual preference. The LGBT community is enormously successful in advocating for their rights and equitable treatment in society. It is reasonable to expect the LGBT community will be equally successful in addressing social problems such as violence and sexual assault.

Summary

It is quite clear that the rates of the "hidden" forms of intimate violence are as high as or higher than the better-recognized types of violence. It is also evident that the harm caused by violence and abuse is comparable to that experienced by women in heterosexual relationships. The big difference is that, with the exception of intimate violence experienced by gays, lesbians, and bisexuals, there are very few effective social movements that are pushing to move the other forms of intimate partner victimization into the public and policy spotlights. Men's rights groups and conservative women public intellectuals have attempted to level the playing field for male victims of intimate violence. Nonetheless, the vast majority of attention, funding, and policy is focused on female victims. Male victims find little in the way of local services or protections, and there is virtually no research that examines how to intervene with female offenders.

Discussion Questions

1. Why would there be such resistance to data demonstrating that females hit males in intimate relationships?
2. What do you think accounts for the substantial decline in male victims of intimate partner homicide between 1993 and 2010?
3. Does dominance and control play the same role in IPV between gays, lesbians, bisexuals, and transgendered couples as it appears to play in IPV among heterosexuals?

Suggested Assignments

1. Check out the ongoing debate about gender symmetry and bidirectional violence by doing a web search of the following terms: "gender symmetry" and "bidirectional IPV."
2. Interview staff at a shelter for battered women and ask them about whether they encounter instances of lesbian violence and what services they provide for victims of violence in lesbian relationships. Ask if they have policies for dealing with the situation when both victim and offender seek services from the shelter.

Notes

1. The information presented is based on my serving as an expert witness in the case and reading all of the depositions and documents associated with the arrest and trial of Marissa Alexander.

2. Florida does not have an "imperfect self-defense" statute, therefore, in order to plead self-defense, a perpetrator must be in imminent danger.

3. The studies reviewed articles published after 1990.

4. A meta-analysis is a statistical technique that combines findings from independent studies.

5. The question used to measure dating violence was: "During the last 12 months, did your boyfriend or girlfriend ever hit, slap, or physically hurt you on purpose?"

6. Among universities where an injury was reported, the rate of injury-producing violence was highest for men, at 78% of the universities.

6 Hidden Victims

CHILDREN AND WOMEN receive nearly all of the advocacy, media, and policy attention with regard to intimate victimization. Yet, children and women are not the most vulnerable victims of intimate violence, nor are they the most commonly victimized family members—siblings are.

This chapter examines violent intimate relationships that have largely been overlooked by the public, researchers, and members of the social service and public policy communities. Each form of violence is hidden for a slightly different reason. Violence between siblings is so common that people rarely think of these events as "family violence." We briefly mentioned adolescent victims of child maltreatment in Chapter 3. Discussions of child abuse rarely extend beyond the youngest victims. Older victims of parental violence tend to be blamed for their own victimization. Teenagers are thought of as causing their own victimization, and, as we blame the victim, we tend to overlook this particular form of violent family relationship. Parent abuse is almost considered humorous by those who first hear of it. Many parent victims are so shamed by their victimization that they are reluctant to discuss anything but the severest incidents; and, when they do report, they, like adolescent victims, are often blamed for being hit.

The elderly are also victims of intimate violence at the hands of their partners, children, and caregivers. Elders may be the most hidden victims, since one of the aspects of aging in our society is the departure of the elderly from their regular and normal systems and institutions of social interaction (e.g., workplace).

Although research on most of these forms of intimate violence is scarce (the most research and policy is on elder abuse), any book on intimate violence and abuse would be incomplete without a discussion of violent relations other than parent-to-child and intimate partner violence.

Sibling Violence

Sibling violence is the most common form of intimate violence, the least studied, and the least likely to be viewed as an important social issue or social problem. Perhaps when we think of sibling violence, the narrative we imagine is two children in the back seat of a car slapping and pushing each other and arguing about whether one sibling crossed the imaginary line between the two. Yet sibling violence can go well beyond the nearly everyday squabbles and pushing and shoving. According to the U.S. Department of Justice (Durose et al., 2005), more than 100 murders in 2002 involved a sibling killing a brother or sister. Similarly, as long ago as 1980, sociologist David Finkelhor (Finkelhor, 1980) reported that 15% of the females surveyed and 10% of the males reported some type of sexual experience involving a sibling.[1]

As common as sibling violence may be, there are also harmful effects of such intimate violence and abuse. So why, almost 50 years after the transformation of child maltreatment into a significant social problem, is violence and abuse by siblings still marked by selective inattention? Perhaps one answer is that sibling conflict, aggression, and hitting are so common that parents and observers view it as a normal part of growing up and expected sibling rivalry—and inevitable.

The handful of social scientists who examine sibling violence generally find that parents feel it is important for their children to learn how to handle themselves in violent situations (Steinmetz, 1977b). Many parents do not actively discourage their children from becoming involved in disputes with their siblings. In fact, parents may try to ignore aggressive interactions and only become involved when minor situations are perceived as escalating into major confrontations. Sibling rivalry is considered a "normal" part of relations between siblings, and many parents believe that such rivalry provides a good training ground for the successful management of aggressive behavior in the real world. American parents generally feel that some exposure to aggression is a positive experience that should occur early in life, although over the years, support for exposure to aggression has declined. Whereas in the late 1960s seven out of ten Americans agreed with the statement, "When a boy is growing up it is important for him to have a few fist fights" (Stark & McEvoy, 1970), by 1995, only one in five of those surveyed agreed with this statement (Gallup, 1995).

Sociologist Suzanne Steinmetz (1977b) was one of the first social scientists to examine violence between siblings. In her study of sibling conflict in a representative sample of 57 intact families in Delaware, she found that it was sometimes difficult to get parents to discuss sibling violence, not because they were ashamed or embarrassed to admit such behavior, but because the parents often did not view their children's actions as abusive and worthy of mention. When questioned further about particular incidents, parents said that they found their children's conduct annoying but they did not perceive the situation as one of conflict. When prompted, most parents will freely discuss or admit to the existence of sibling violence in their homes. Parents willingly tell friends, neighbors, and researchers, without embarrassment or restraint, how their children are constantly involved in argumentative and abusive behavior toward one another. When Steinmetz asked the parents in her study, "How do your children get along?" she received such statements as:

"Terrible! They fight all the time."
"Oh, it's just constant, but I understand that this is normal."
"I talk to other people and their children are the same way."

Steinmetz, 1977b, p. 43

From these typical comments, it becomes obvious that parents view such frequent and violent confrontations as inevitable. Perhaps parents may be somewhat justified in their assessment of the inevitability of sibling violence. As we mentioned in the opening chapter of this book, the existence of sibling rivalry is documented throughout history, beginning with the biblical story of Cain and Abel, in which Cain kills his brother. This is perhaps the earliest, although certainly not the only, recorded account of sibling violence. Evidence of violence among siblings can also be found in more contemporary sources. However, what is lacking in the recorded accounts of sibling violence is information from controlled, scientific research projects. In the early 1970s, Suzanne Steinmetz and Murray Straus (1974) reported that, prior to their own investigations into the causes, frequency, and patterns of sibling violence, information on non-infant, nonfatal sibling violence was almost nonexistent. The research articles that appeared in the scientific literature dealt almost exclusively with sibling murders

(Adelson, 1972; Bender, 1959; Sargent, 1962; Smith, 1965). Society appears to take notice only of the most extreme expressions of sibling violence. Levels of violence among siblings that do not exceed the levels defined as socially acceptable or "normal" generally go unnoticed by both researchers and society in general (Pagelow, 1989).

THE EXTENT OF VIOLENCE BETWEEN SIBLINGS

There are scattered studies that examine sibling violence and abuse. The First National Family Violence Survey (Straus, Gelles, & Steinmetz, 1980) included a measure of the extent of sibling violence. Slightly more than four out of five (82%) children between the ages of three and seventeen, residing in the United States, and having one or more siblings living at home, engaged in at least one violent act toward a sibling during a one-year period. This translated into approximately 36.3 million children being violent toward a sibling within a year's time. Of course, much of the violence that siblings engage in includes pushing, slapping, shoving, and throwing things. Some people argue that these behaviors are not really serious and serve to overestimate the real rates of sibling violence. Therefore, when these "lesser" forms of violence were excluded and the researchers examined only the more severe forms of violence (such as kicking, biting, pushing, hitting with an object, and "beating up"), the rates were still alarmingly high. Straus and his colleagues estimated that over 19 million children a year engage in acts of abusive violence against a sibling. More than 2 in 100 children (2.6%) threatened a sibling with a gun or knife.

The National Crime Victimization Survey includes data on victim–offender relationships, but these data tend to under-report sibling violence, first because the survey is limited to individuals 12 years of age or older, and second because respondents are asked to report on criminal victimization. As noted earlier, violence at the hands of a brother or sister is rarely viewed as criminal behavior. Between 2002 and 2012, the average rate of sibling victimization was .04 per 1,000 (Truman & Morgan, 2014).

A third source of data on the extent of sibling violence is also criminal justice data. Jessie Krienert and Jeffrey Walsh (2011) examined the Federal Bureau of Investigation's National Incident-Based Reporting System (NIBRS). The NIBRS system provides incident-based data on all crimes reported to the FBI as part of the Uniform Crime Reporting Program. The researchers examined six years of NIBRS data. The advantage of the NIBRS data is that it enables researchers to examine all the characteristics of the offender and victim involved in a crime. The weakness, in terms of examining the extent of sibling violence, is that an event must be reported and responded to by the police as a crime to become part of the NIBRS data set. Obviously, a great deal of sibling violence is never reported or responded to as a criminal act.

Between 2000 and 2005, there were 33,066 reported cases of single-victim single-perpetrator incidents of sibling violence (Krienert & Walsh, 2011). The incidents included cases of aggravated assault, simple assault, and intimidation. Males were the most common offenders (73.4%). Female offenders were most likely to offend against sisters (69%), as were male offenders (54%).

Data on sibling violence are also available from self-report surveys. David Finkelhor and his colleagues (2005) conducted the Developmental Victimization Survey, which interviewed a nationally representative sample of 2,030 children aged 2–17 living in the United States. The survey was conducted between December 2002 and February 2003. One-third of those sampled reported that they had been hit or attacked by a sibling in the year prior to the study. Children 6–9 years of age reported the highest rates of sibling violence. Of the children who reported they were victimized by brothers or sisters, 15% reported they had suffered an injury from one or more attacks (Finkelhor, Turner, & Ormrod, 2006). As Finkelhor and his colleagues (2006) conclude, there is no basis to assume that sibling violence is more benign than other forms of violent victimization, even when the victim is young.

SEXUAL VICTIMIZATION

Sibling sexual abuse is also common and overlooked. Here again, there is a reluctance to view sibling sexual abuse as deviant. In one of the first studies of sibling sexual abuse, David Finkelhor (1979) found that, of 796 undergraduates, 15% of the women and 10% of the men reported some type of sexual experience involving a sibling. Based on this, Finkelhor speculated that sibling sexual abuse may be the most prevalent form of sexual abuse and incest, but his respondents were equally split in terms of viewing such sexual experiences positively or negatively. Females who reported sexual victimization at the hands of siblings were more likely to view the experiences negatively, largely because of the physical coercion that was part of the sexual experience. The actual extent of sibling sexual abuse depends on the definition of what constitutes "abuse." In another early study, Diane Russell (1986) used a narrower definition of sexual abuse (she asked whether subjects had experienced "at least one sexually abusive experience with a brother before the age of 18") and found that 2% of her 930 female subjects reported sexual abuse with a sibling. Clearly, some of the sexual interaction between siblings is sexual exploration or what may be called "sex play." But some sexual interaction is physically or psychologically coercive and exploitative, and is abusive.

FACTORS RELATED TO SIBLING VIOLENCE

Gender

Given that sibling violence occurs with alarming frequency, one important question is whether all children engage in these violent acts with the same frequency, or whether these aggressive actions are being carried out by a particular category of children. While children of all ages and both sexes engage in violence and abuse against a brother or sister, there appears to be some difference in the rates at which they are violent. A commonly held belief in our society is that boys are more physically aggressive and girls are more verbally aggressive. One would expect, then, that sibling violence is initiated primarily by brothers. Although the research on sibling violence tends to support this commonsense belief, the support is not so overwhelming as one might expect (Straus et al., 1980). Some studies do find that boys are more violent towards siblings than girls, while other studies find essentially that boys are about as aggressive as girls (Krienert & Walsh, 2011).

Age

Research into sibling violence generally confirms the belief that, as children grow older, the rates of using violence to resolve conflicts between siblings decrease (DeKeserdy & Ellis, 1997; Eriksen & Jensen, 2006, 2008; Steinmetz, 1977b; Straus et al., 1980). Some studies, however, find no difference in the rates of sibling violence across age groups (Abramovitch et al. 1982). David Finkelhor and his colleagues' national survey of child victimization (2006) reported that the most common age for sibling violence was 6–9 years old, but that sibling violence that involved a weapon or resulted in an injury was most common among adolescents (14–17 years of age).

Steinmetz (1977b) found that the factors precipitating conflicts varied with age. Younger children were more likely to have conflicts centered on possessions, especially toys. One family in Steinmetz's sample reported that, during a one-week period, their young children fought over "the use of a glider, sharing a truck, sharing a tricycle, knocking down one child's building blocks and taking them." Young adolescent conflicts focus on territory, with adolescents becoming very upset if a sibling invades their personal space. "They fuss. They say, 'He's sitting in my seat,' or 'He has got an inch of his pants on the line where I am supposed to be'" (Steinmetz, 1977b, p. 53). One father, driven to the breaking point by his children constantly fighting in the back seat of the car, took a can of red paint and painted boundary lines on the back seat and floor in an attempt to end disputes over personal space. Teenage conflicts, although less in number, still exist. These conflicts center around responsibilities, obligations, and social awareness. Teenagers are more likely to be verbally aggressive and find that hollering is usually effective in conflict situations, especially when the siblings differ in opinions.

Other Factors

Little is known about the factors that may be potentially associated with sibling violence. Those who have studied sibling murder often attribute the cause of such extreme aggression to jealousy. Adelson (1977), after examining several children who had committed murder, concluded that preschoolers are capable of homicidal rage when they are threatened regarding their sense of security in the family unit. Kay Tooley's (1977) investigation of "murderously aggressive children" suggests that younger victims of sibling violence may sometimes be the family scapegoats. However, it has not yet been established if lesser forms of sibling aggression can be attributed to the same factors believed to be associated with murder.

Research on violent adolescents generally concludes that the factors associated with intimate adult violence (child abuse and spouse abuse) are of little use in helping to explain violence among children (Cornell & Gelles, 1982). In other words, children are not committing acts of violence for the same reasons as adults.

Finally, some researchers have postulated that sibling violence is a learned response. Although it is commonly believed that children will resort to violence as a natural way to resolve conflicts, sociologists Straus, Gelles, and Steinmetz (1980) believe that siblings learn from their parents that physical punishment is an appropriate technique for resolving conflicts. Children raised in nonviolent environments learn that there is a variety of nonviolent techniques available for resolving conflicts with brothers and sisters, and later, with their spouses and children.

CONSEQUENCES OF SIBLING VIOLENCE AND ABUSE

The selective inattention to sibling violence and the view that violence and aggression between siblings is normal and inevitable blinds us to the fact that sibling violence produces the same kind of harmful consequences for victims as other forms of intimate and family violence. Children who experience violence and abuse at the hands of brothers and sisters are more likely to experience behavioral and psychological problems, including antisocial behavior and bullying (Eriksen & Jensen, 2008). Eating disorders, substance use and abuse, and intimate partner violence are also associated with sibling victimization (Eriksen & Jensen, 2008).

Adolescent Victims

The typical portrait and narrative of child maltreatment is that of a helpless infant or toddler brutally abused or neglected. Homicide data support both the portrait and the narrative, as more than half of all child maltreatment fatality victims are under five years of age. Apart from the prevailing narrative, however, adolescents are surprisingly common victims of child abuse and neglect. According to the NCANDS data on reported child abuse and neglect, the rate of child victimization for adolescents ranged from 7.0 per 1,000 for 13-year-olds to 3.5 per 1,000 for 17-year-olds. This compares to rates of 11.6 per 1,000 for 2-year-olds—see Figure 6.1 (U.S. Department of Health and Human Services, 2016).

In terms of the type of maltreatment adolescents' experience, the most common forms are physical and sexual abuse; while for children who are newborn to five years of age, the vast majority of maltreatment is neglect (U.S. Department of Health and Human Services, 2016).

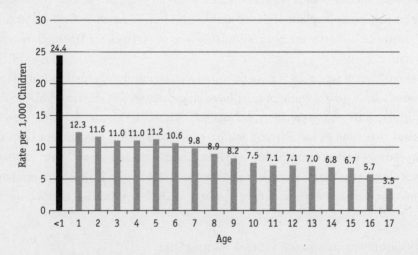

FIGURE 6.1 Child maltreatment victims by age: rate per 1,000 children.

Source: U.S. Department of Health and Human Services, Administration for Children and Families, Administration on Children, Youth and Families, Children's Bureau. (2016). *Child Maltreatment 2014.* Chapter 3, page 22. Available from http://www.acf.bhs.gov/programs/cb/research-data-technology/statistics-research/childmaltreatment

A second window into the extent of adolescent maltreatment is the number of teenagers who are removed from abusive and neglectful caregivers and placed in out-of-home care. Of the more than one-quarter million children (254,904) who entered some form of out-of-home care in fiscal year 2013 (October 1, 2012, to September 30, 2013), 64,341 were aged 13–18.[2] One caution—not all of the reasons for entry into foster care were a consequence of abusive or neglectful parenting or caregiving. Some adolescents are placed due to their own behavior or because parents have asked for the child's removal.

Even with the high numbers of adolescent victims and placement into care, adolescent victims of intra-family violence are generally ignored. As noted in the previous section, adolescent victims of sibling violence and sexual assault are generally overlooked because of the inattention to sibling violence as a social problem. In addition, societal attitudes perpetuate the myth that parents rarely abuse adolescents. Some observers believe the adolescents themselves are more likely to be a threat than the parents. As teenagers acquire greater physical strength with age, parents may begin to fear retaliation at the hands of children whose physical strength may surpass their own. For those children who are being struck, many people believe they precipitate or deserve being hit. Common sense sometimes suggests that teenagers frustrate their parents to such an extent that they deserve what they get!

The status of adolescents in our society is much the same as that of younger children. Both are considered the property and responsibility of their parents. Parents are granted societal permission to engage in a wide range of behaviors when disciplining their offspring. Although parents are expected to practice restraint when disciplining, the use of physical punishment is sanctioned as an acceptable behavior, even for teenage children. Both young children and adolescents are relegated to a subordinate position within the family structure, with parents being granted the right to bestow rewards and punishments as they see fit (Gil, 1970). Both preschoolers and teenagers are known for their difficult stages of development. Frustration in parents is often generated from young children going through the "terrible two's" stage. The "terrible two's" may be revisited as teenagers go through a stage of rebellion and independence. Preschool children are too young to be reasoned with, and teenagers do not wish to be reasoned with. It is this ability to frustrate their parents and create stress in the family unit as a whole that places young children and teenagers in the vulnerable position of being victimized. Adolescents have reached a point in their development in being able to make effective use of the verbal skills they have acquired through years of conflict resolutions with family members. The biggest complaint among parents of adolescents in Steinmetz's study on parent–child conflict was the "smart-talk mouthiness" used by adolescents in both sibling and parent–child interactions. Steinmetz describes the adolescents in her sample as being "verbally aggressive" and frequently engaging in yelling, threatening, and arguing (Steinmetz, 1977b).

If the position of young children and teenagers is so similar in our society, why has society become so deeply concerned with protecting the rights of younger children while ignoring the plight of adolescents? The answer to this question can again be traced to the differing expectations parents have for their younger children versus their older children. Parents expect their adolescents to begin acting in a more mature and responsible manner as they approach adulthood. They expect adolescents to be able to follow orders and to begin internalizing the parents' system of values. Parents do not hold the same expectations for their preschoolers. Therefore, when adolescents fail to live up to their parents' expectations of them, parents sometimes use physical force as a way of asserting their parental control. Society is more likely to condone the use of physical force directed at an adolescent due to the belief that adolescents deserve such treatment.

Adolescents are also perceived as being better able to fend for themselves in disputes with their parents. Adolescents are larger, stronger, and therefore, better able to protect themselves or avoid confrontations altogether. While this may be true, Mulligan (1977), in her sample of over 250 college students attending an eastern university, found that 8 in 100 students in her sample had been physically injured by a parent while they lived at home during their senior year of high school.

EXTENT OF VIOLENCE TOWARD ADOLESCENTS

Although researchers are not in total agreement about the exact extent of adolescent abuse, they do agree that violence toward adolescents is a legitimate and significant form of family violence that occurs more frequently than is generally assumed. In fact, researchers are generally surprised at the rate at which parents are physically abusing their adolescent and teenage children.

The NCANDS data and data on entry into foster care provide evidence of how much maltreatment of adolescents is officially recognized and for which there is an official response. The national survey of officially recognized and reported child maltreatment provides even more compelling data on how much more maltreatment of adolescents is recognized but for which there is rarely an official response.

The most recent National Incidence Study of Child Abuse and Neglect (NIS-4) reported that the lowest rates for overall abuse and neglect—using both the study's "endangerment standard" and "harm standard" measures[3]—occurred among the youngest children. Applying the "endangerment standard" of neglect, teens aged 15–17 had the lowest rates (Sedlak et al., 2010).

In terms of the overall "harm standard," the highest rates were for adolescents aged 12–14. The rate of physical abuse and neglect of 12–14-year-olds was also the highest for all children. Lastly, in terms of the rate of harm produced by maltreatment, the highest rate was again for children 12–14 years of age.

In terms of self-report survey data, David Finkelhor and Jennifer Dziuba-Leatherman (1994) surveyed a nationally representative sample of children aged 10–16. More than one in four (28.5%) of the children reported experiencing corporal punishment the year prior to the survey; 2.1% reported an attempted assault; while about 1 in 100 (.9%) reported a completed assault by a parent in the previous year.

SUMMARY

While there is not an abundance of research on adolescent victims of child maltreatment, there is enough for us to conclude that, at least in terms of prevalence, the problem is large enough to be considered a legitimate social problem. Carolyn Smith and her colleagues (2005), summarizing all the various sources of data, conclude that adolescent victims make up somewhere between 25% and 45% of all child maltreatment cases.

EXPLAINING VIOLENCE TOWARDS ADOLESCENTS

Why are parents violent toward their adolescents and teenage children? One explanation is that they are violent and abusive toward their older children for the same reasons they are violent and abusive toward their younger children. In some instances, abuse of adolescents is an extension of violence that began when the teenager was a younger child. Ira Lourie (1977) provides a second explanation and points out that, as children grow physically stronger and seek independence, parents may resort to more violent means of control. Another possible factor might be the struggle for independence between adolescents and their parents. Adolescence is a stressful period for children and parents. Lastly, parents see in their adolescent offspring the consequences of their parenting and may feel upset or guilty about their parental roles. Obviously, we need much more research on this issue in order to draw any kind of informed conclusion.

THE CONSEQUENCES OF ADOLESCENT ABUSE AND NEGLECT

One criterion of whether a personal trouble should be considered a social problem is the level of harm caused by the trouble. While there is not an abundance of research on the impact of adolescent maltreatment, there is sufficient research to document the harmful consequences of the abuse and neglect of adolescents. Melissa Jonson-Reid and Richard Barth (2000) examined data collected by child welfare agencies. The children whose first report of child maltreatment occurred after age 14 were more likely to be jailed than victims of maltreatment whose first report occurred before they were 14 years old. John Eckenrode and his colleagues (2001) compared a sample of children and their mothers when the children were 15 years old. There was no difference in outcome for the children first maltreated before adolescence compared to those whose first abuse or neglect occurred when they were teenagers. In other words, the consequences of the maltreatment were the same—irrespective of when it first occurred. Compared to children who were never maltreated, the children whose first abuse or neglect began in adolescence demonstrated earlier-onset negative behaviors.

Carolyn Smith and her colleagues (Smith, Ireland, & Thornberry, 2005) carried out a comprehensive analysis of data collected from 1,000 urban youths as part of the Rochester Youth Development Study. Of the 884 subjects analyzed for the study, slightly less than one in 10 (9.3%) had substantiated reports of abuse in adolescence. The most common form of maltreatment was physical abuse. Being maltreated as a teenager increases the odds of arrest, general and violent criminal offending, and illicit drug use.

Overall, it is clear that the maltreatment of adolescents is extensive and has significant harmful consequences. The harmful consequences extend across the lifespan.

Adolescent to Parent Violence and Abuse

It should come as no surprise that some adolescents direct violence and abuse toward their parents and caregivers. First, given what we know about the intergenerational transmission of maltreatment, we can assume that a significant number of children who are maltreated will direct violence back toward the maltreators. As children grow in size and strength, it is likely they will retaliate against offenders. Moreover, adolescents will use violence for the same reason parents and partners employ violence—to coerce and control other family members.

What is modestly surprising is the paucity of research, publication, and conversation about adolescent-to-parent violence and abuse. Even 50 years after the social transformation of child maltreatment into a social problem, we have very little reliable data on the extent of adolescent-to-parent violence. The few surveys that examined the incidence of adolescent violence using representative samples report rates ranging from 5–10% (Agnew & Huguley, 1989; Cornell & Gelles, 1982; Straus, Steinmetz, & Gelles, 1980).

Jeffrey Walsh and Jessie Krienert (2007) analyzed crime data from NIBRS. These data are based on crimes known to the police, and thus undercount the full extent of adolescent-to-parent violence. Based on what one can assume are the most serious cases of adolescent-to-parent violence, the profile indicates that the likeliest victims are mothers older than 40. The most likely offender is a male 14–17 years of age. Given that these events are reported to the police, the likeliest attack involves a personal weapon and results in either no injury or a minor injury. Barbara Cottrell and Peter Monk (2004) concur with Walsh and Krienert's analysis of crime data. Cottrell and Monk's summary of the literature on adolescent-to-parent violence concludes that mothers, especially single mothers, are the most common victims of adolescent violence. Boys are the most frequent offenders, and as would be expected, the rate of offending increases along with their age, size, and strength. There are no consistent findings that indicate differences in terms of socioeconomic status, race, or ethnicity.

Like other forms of hidden intimate violence, adolescent-to-parent violence is extensive enough and produces sufficient harm to be considered a social problem. And yet, there continues to be virtually no public or policy attention paid to adolescent offenders, and only limited research and scholarship.

Elder Abuse and Neglect

Elderly victims of intimate violence are also largely hidden from public view, but this form of intimate violence does receive much more attention from scholars, practitioners, and policy makers. There is an academic journal devoted to the topic of elder abuse—*Journal of Elder Abuse and Neglect*. The National Academy of Sciences carried out a review and prepared an overview report on elder abuse and mistreatment entitled *Elder Mistreatment: Abuse, Neglect, and Exploitation in an Aging America* (Bonnie & Wallace, 2002). The Elder Justice Act (EJA) was included in the 2010 Patient Protection and Affordable Care Act (PPACA)—Public Law 111-148 as amended.[4] While the intention of the Elder Justice Act was to coordinate a federal response to elder abuse and neglect, by the end of the 2014 legislative session, no funding was yet appropriated to fund the intended activities.

Some activities are being carried out using mandatory funding from the PPACA (Colello, 2014).

We do have a body of research that addresses some of the key questions concerning the nature and extent of elder abuse and neglect. The National Elder Mistreatment Study surveyed a nationally representative sample of 5,777 older adults and proxy responses from an additional 813 respondents (Acierno, Hernandez, Amstadter, et al., 2010).[5] In terms of the extent of elder mistreatment, the study reports that, in the year prior to the survey:

- 4.6% of respondents reported experiencing emotional mistreatment,
- 1.6% reported physical mistreatment,
- 0.6% reported sexual mistreatment,
- 5.1% reported potential neglect, and
- 5.2% reported financial exploitation.

Overall, more than one in ten of the elders or elder caretakers surveyed reported some form of mistreatment in the 12 months prior to the survey. The results are primarily based on reports by the elders themselves, as the proxy reports turned out to be not particularly useful in identifying mistreatment.

The stereotype of elder abuse and neglect is that the perpetrator is the elder's child, and the victim is a dependent elder (Pillemer, 2005). Indeed, adult children are the most likely to perpetrate elder mistreatment. However, a somewhat surprising 28% of the offenders are partners or spouses of the victims. Partners and spouses are the most frequent users of emotional maltreatment toward elder partners (see Figure 6.2).

Edward Laumann (Laumann, Leitsch, & Waite, 2008) and his colleagues provided a second estimate of the extent of elder abuse. Laumann and

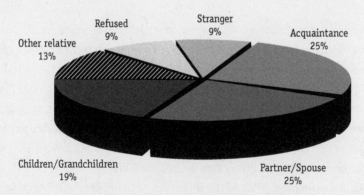

FIGURE 6.2 Perpetrators of most recent emotional mistreatment event.

Source: Acierno, R., Hernandez-Tejada, M., Muzzy, W., & Steve, K. (2009). Final Report: National Elder Mistreatment Study. Submitted to the National Institute of Justice October 26, 2015. Reproduced with permission.

his colleagues based their estimate on the National Social Life, Health and Aging Project. The researchers collected data from a nationally representative sample of 3,005 community-residing adults 57–85 years of age. Overall, 9% of older adults reported verbal mistreatment, 3.5% financial mistreatment, and 0.2% physical mistreatment by a family member. Women and those with physical disabilities are the likeliest victims of verbal mistreatment. Whites and Latinos reported the lowest rates of mistreatment. The rate of financial mistreatment is highest for African Americans and lower for Latinos than for whites, and lower for those with a spouse or romantic partner than for those without partners.

For an examination of elder abuse in Korea, see Global Perspectives 6.1.

GLOBAL PERSPECTIVES BOX 6.1
ELDER ABUSE IN SOUTH KOREA

Since the end of World War II, South Korea has undergone significant demographic changes. With its increasing life expectancy, South Korea is becoming an "aging society." At the same time, family structure has changed from the extended family to the nuclear form. These changes raise the question of who will be caring for the ageing population and whether there is a risk that elders will become victims of abuse and neglect.

Jinjoo Oh and her colleagues (2006) carried out the first major study of elder abuse in South Korea. The researchers surveyed the entire population of older adults, aged 65 and older, in a single *Gu*, or district, in Seoul. The research team completed interviews with about 15,700 elders, or roughly 53% of the entire elderly population in the district. While the sample is large, it is not representative of the district, city, or nation. Nonetheless, the results provide the first comprehensive look at elder abuse in South Korea.

Between 1.6% and 3.7% of elders experienced one form of abuse or another. The rates for specific forms of maltreatment were as follows:

Physical abuse, 1.9%
Emotional abuse, 4.2%
Economic abuse, 4.1%
Verbal abuse, 3.6%
Neglect, 2.4%
Any form, 6.3%

Overall, the rate of elder maltreatment reported by the Korean elders is lower than the rate of elder abuse in the United States (see Acierno et al., 2010). However, the rates for individual forms of maltreatment, including physical abuse and emotional maltreatment, are quite similar.

The risk of maltreatment was higher for older men than for older women. The oldest respondents, 80 years of age and older, reported lower rates of mistreatment than those less than 80 years of age. Those with the lowest education had the highest rates of mistreatment. In terms of living arrangements, elders who lived with married children reported higher rates of maltreatment than those not living with married children. Lastly, low income was a risk factor for maltreatment. In terms of perpetrators, sons were the most frequent offenders, followed by daughters-in-law.

Source: Oh, J., Kim, H. S., Martins, D., & Kim, H. (2006). A study of elder abuse in Korea. *International Journal of Nursing Studies*, 43, 203–214.

Keep in mind that surveys of community-dwelling elders will certainly produce underestimates of the extent of maltreatment. The surveys are confined to those who are able to respond to telephone calls and questions. The oldest, the most infirm, and those living in nursing homes or assisted-living facilities are not included in national surveys of elder mistreatment.

The stereotype regarding adult children who maltreat their parents is that the adult children are overwhelmed by their dependent parents' medical conditions, deteriorating mental health and cognitive abilities, and personal demands. The members of the so-called sandwich generation find themselves approaching middle age and having to meet the caregiving demands of their own children and the increasing caregiving needs of their aging parents. The stress of such caregiving demands outstrips their resources, and mistreatment—physical, emotional, neglect, and financial—follow.

As it turns out, victim dependency is one factor that leads to elder mistreatment, but offender dependency is also an important factor. Pillemer (2005) presents research evidence demonstrating that the offender's social, psychological, and economic dependence is a driving force behind much elder mistreatment.

THE CONSEQUENCES OF ELDER MISTREATMENT

Marks Lachs and his colleagues (Lachs et al., 1998) followed a cohort of community-dwelling elderly subjects in New Haven, Connecticut. The sample included a subset of elders who were referred to protective services for the elderly. Over the 13 years of the study, those members of the study cohort who experienced elder mistreatment had poorer survival outcomes than the subjects who had not been served by protective services. The risk of death was also elevated for elders who were categorized as "self-neglecting."

SUMMARY

As with the abuse and neglect of children—especially infants and toddlers, the abuse and mistreatment of the elderly exists in the shadows. The most dependent elderly victims are the most difficult to identify. As with child maltreatment, the healthcare and social service systems take on the majority of the responsibility for identifying and responding to elder mistreatment. While certain forms of elder abuse—physical abuse and sexual abuse—are clearly crimes, the criminal justice system plays only a minor role in responding to elder abuse.

While we have two relatively recent national surveys of the extent of elder abuse and neglect, the research knowledge base is still relatively small and immature. Karl Pillemer and his colleagues (2007) point out the difficulty in establishing the risk factors for elder abuse because so much of the research is based on clinical samples that do not include comparison groups. Pillemer and his colleagues also point out that the knowledge base is constrained by the lack of comparability of research studies. The lack of comparability is due to varying definitions of "elder" and "abuse and neglect." The results of research will vary greatly if one study defines "elder" as anyone over 60 years of age, while another study sets the floor at 65 or 70 years old. Results will also vary depending on the definition of abuse and neglect. As with child abuse, lumping financial exploitation in with sexual exploitation as part of a general definition of elder abuse will greatly distort findings of extent, risk factors, and consequences. The factors that cause each type of abuse and neglect are likely to be different, as would be the consequences.

The policy response to elder abuse and neglect has been diverse. There are adult protective services programs in all 50 states, the District of Columbia, Guam, Puerto Rico, and the U.S. Virgin islands (Colello, 2014). As with child maltreatment, there is considerable variation in state laws pertaining to adult protective services, including the age of those eligible for services, the definition of abuse and neglect, mandatory reporting requirements, and intervention strategies.

While the Elder Justice Act is an important initial step in coordinating services, research, and policy, the lack of appropriated funding for the act relegates elder abuse to a back seat in overall federal efforts to respond to the full range of intimate and family violence.

Summary

It is quite clear that the rates of the "hidden" forms of intimate violence are as high as or higher than the better-known types of violence. It is also evident that the harm caused by such violence and abuse is comparable to that experienced by children and women in intimate relationships. The big difference is that there are very few effective social movements that are pushing to move the hidden forms of intimate victimization into the public and policy spotlights. Elder-abuse advocates have had some success in pushing for the enactment of federal legislation and local adult protective service laws. Nonetheless, the vast majority of attention, funding, and policy focuses on children and female victims. Siblings, adolescents, and adult victims of child-to-parent violence are at best viewed as interesting curiosities by media talk shows and some magazines.

Our examination of the hidden forms of intimate violence underscores the reality that social problems are not *prima facie* obvious. Social movements and social advocacy are necessary to move private issues from behind closed doors into the public arena.

Discussion Questions

1. Why have the "hidden forms" of intimate violence been overlooked? How does blaming the victim contribute to keeping certain forms of intimate violence hidden? How do cultural norms and values concerning children, parents, or the elderly contribute to keeping certain forms of intimate violence hidden?
2. Why has elder abuse received more attention than the other forms of hidden violence?
3. What are some of the factors related to hidden forms of violence? How do the factors related to hidden violence compare to factors related to the abuse of young children or violence between spouses?

Suggested Assignments

1. Find out if your state has mandatory reporting laws for cases of elder abuse. Who is required to report? How many cases are reported each year? Has there been an increase in reporting in the last few years? What services are available in your community, city, or state for victims of elder abuse?

2. Conduct a survey and measure people's awareness of and attitudes toward the known forms of family violence (child abuse or wife abuse) and the hidden forms. Be sure to ask parallel questions so that you can compare the results.

Notes

1. The results are based on surveys of college students and were not then, and are not now, generalizable to any larger population.

2. See http://www.acf.hhs.gov/programs/cb/resource/afcars-report-21

3. The NIS applies two definitional standards in parallel: the Harm Standard and the Endangerment Standard. The Harm Standard has been in use since the NIS-1. It is relatively stringent in that it generally requires that an act or omission result in demonstrable harm in order to be classified as abuse or neglect. The Endangerment Standard has been in use since the NIS-2. It includes all children who meet the Harm Standard but adds others as well. The central feature of the Endangerment Standard is that it counts children who were not yet harmed by abuse or neglect if a sentinel thought that the maltreatment endangered the children, or if a CPS investigation substantiated or indicated their maltreatment.

4. The Patient Protection and Affordable Care Act of 2010 is frequently referred to as "Obamacare."

5. Proxy responses were provided by individuals who lived with or cared for older adults.

7 Explaining Intimate Violence and Abuse

WHEN IT COMES to explaining intimate violence and abuse, we are tasked with explaining the inexplicable. At some level, we can all understand violence that emerges out of pure hatred. We can comprehend revenge violence. We know that some individuals' violence arises out of mental illness and internal demons. But violence directed toward a defenseless child or a partner one professes to love is much more difficult to grapple with and understand.

Journalist George Lardner, an investigative reporter for the *Washington Post*, confronted a parent's worst nightmare. On Saturday evening, May 20, 1992, Casey Kristen Lardner, known as Kristen to her parents and friends, was hurrying to meet her roommate in the Brookline section near Boston. Kristen was a 21-year-old art student in Boston. Before she could get to the corner where her roommate awaited, her former boyfriend, Michael Cartier, confronted Kristen. Cartier had struck and abused Kristen while they were dating. Kristen had sought and received a restraining order, and Cartier was required to attend a counseling program for men. On the warm Saturday evening in Brookline, Cartier confronted Kristen and asked her to go out with him again. When Kristen refused, Cartier shot her in the head and fled. He actually returned and shot her twice more. Cartier went back to his apartment and killed himself.

By the time I met George Lardner, he had already won the 1993 Pulitzer Prize for his feature writing about the stalking and killing of his daughter Kristen. He was in the process of turning the article into a book, *The Stalking of Kristen: A Father Investigates the Murder of His Daughter* (1995). Lardner's investigation of his daughter's death uncovered a volume of disturbing information about her killer.

Michael Cartier had an extensive criminal record, including recent convictions for beating up a previous girlfriend and torturing and killing a kitten he had given her. Cartier stalked and harassed Kristin, which was a violation of both his probation and the restraining order Kristen had taken out against him. Although Kristin reported to the police that Cartier violated the restraining order, the information never reached the judge who made the decision to keep Cartier free just 11 days before he murdered Kristen. A warrant for Cartier's arrest remained outstanding six months after his suicide.

After the book was published, I had dinner with George and his wife, Rosemary. Four years after Kristen's death, her artwork leaned against the wall in the dining room. Lardner's training as an investigative reporter helped him crystallize three main questions that arise when we try to "explain" intimate violence and abuse. The first, and most obvious, question is, "Why did this man kill my daughter?" What are the characteristics—psychological, social, and even cultural—that would lead Michael Cartier to assassinate Kristen Lardner? The second half of the question is a bit more uncomfortable—"Was there anything about Kristen that made her a likely victim?" A less obvious question, but equally important to Lardner and those who study and try to explain intimate violence is: "What is it about intimate relationships that makes them so violence-prone?" Just reexamining the data on the extent of violence and abuse among intimates and comparing the data to violence between strangers, it is clear that intimate violence is vastly more common than stranger violence. A second part of the question, about the frequency of intimate violence, is more complicated. Why was the judicial system so lenient with a known offender? Michael Cartier was not a stranger to the criminal justice system, and many who dealt with him knew his violent tendencies, including animal cruelty. And yet he was allowed to continue to walk the streets after he had abused another girlfriend and then Kristen. The last question Lardner and scholars wrestle with is whether or not there are patterns—social and psychological—that would allow us not only to explain intimate and family violence and abuse, but also to effectively intervene and prevent deaths such as Kristen's.

Trying to understand the murder of his daughter, George Lardner dug as deeply as he could into Michael Cartier's past. Michael's father abandoned the family soon after Michael's birth. His mother placed him in a boarding school when he was eight years old. The director of the boarding school believed Michael was abused at a very early age. Lardner tried to track as much of Michael's childhood and adolescence as he could, looking for clues and signs for why this young man would end up murdering Kristen and then taking his own life.

Lardner's quest is not uncommon. When a case of child maltreatment, intimate partner violence, elder abuse, or for that matter, any form of intimate abuse comes to public attention, reporters and readers mine all the data they can obtain to try to understand the motives and explanations behind the behavior.

Levels of Theoretical Explanation

Before we explain both the factors that increase the overall risk of violence in intimate relationships compared to other social interactions, and before we inventory the various theoretical explanations that are applied to explaining intimate violence and abuse, it is important to point out that there are various "levels" of theoretical explanations: (1) Intra-Individual; (2) Social-Psychological; (3) and Socio-Cultural.

INTRA-INDIVIDUAL

Intra-individual levels of explanation look for factors within the individual that lead to violent behavior. As noted throughout this book, the most common means of explaining violent and abusive behavior is to look for a personality or character factor that leads to violence. In addition, factors such as alcohol and drug use and misuse are considered intra-individual factors.

SOCIAL-PSYCHOLOGICAL

Social-psychological levels of explanation examine the interaction between individuals or between individuals and groups. Perhaps the most common social-psychological explanation is that violent behavior is learned behavior—that observing others use and justify the use of violence increases the likelihood of violent behavior.

SOCIO-CULTURAL

Socio-cultural levels of explanation are generally the province of sociologists and anthropologists. Rather than search for individual personality defects, socio-cultural explanations examine factors such as cultural values and norms. A socio-cultural explanation will not necessarily explain why one individual is violent, but rather why one nation or culture is more violent than another. In terms of explaining intimate partner violence, a socio-cultural explanation will not focus on antisocial tendencies of offenders, but rather on why male violence is so commonly used against females across time and cultures.

Intimacy, Family Relations, and Violence

Following from the last section's discussion of socio-cultural levels of explanation, one intriguing question that arises in the study of intimate violence and abuse is, "Why are intimate and family relationships so much more violent than other social interactions, social settings, and social groups?" When looking at the data on the extent of child maltreatment, intimate partner violence, and all of the other forms of intimate violence and sexual offending, the rates are expressed in terms of incidents per 100 or per 1,000 individuals. On the other hand, crime statistics, including homicide and assault, are expressed in terms of the rate per 100,000. Statistically, an individual is considerably more likely to be struck, injured, or killed by an intimate or family relation than by a stranger. The chances of injury or death at the hands of an intimate are much greater for women and children than for men.

So why are intimate and family relations so much more violence-prone compared to other social interactions and settings? The answer lies in the nature of intimacy and the social organization of family and intimate relationships. Murray Straus and I (Gelles & Straus, 1979) identified the unique characteristics of the family as a social group that contribute to making the family a violence-prone institution. Later, Straus, with his colleague Gerald Hotaling (1979), noted the irony that these same characteristics we saw as making the family violence-prone also serve to make the family and intimate relations warm, supportive, and desirable. The key factors are:

1. *Time at Risk.* The ratio of time we spend interacting with family members and intimates far exceeds the ratio of time spent interacting with others, although the ratio will vary depending on stages in the family lifecycle. Young children spend much of their time with their parents. As teens, children spend less time with family and more time with peers, including intimate relations with peers.
2. *Range of Activities and Interests.* Not only do family members and intimates spend a great deal of time with one another, the interactions

range over a much wider spectrum of activities than non-familial interaction. We eat with, sleep with, and socialize with family members and intimates; make significant life-course decisions; and experience joys and tragedies together. We are share and allocate money and other economic resources.

3. *Intensity of Involvement.* The quality of family and intimate interaction is also unique. The degree of commitment to intimate relationships and family interaction is greater than for almost all of our social engagements, including, for most people, work. A cutting remark or criticism made by a family member or an intimate partner is likely to have a much larger impact than the same remark in another setting.

4. *Impinging Activities.* Many interactions in the family and intimate relationships are inherently conflict-structured and have a "zero sum" aspect. Whether it involves deciding what television show to watch or what car to buy, what vacation to take, or whether to spend the remaining family money on food or medical care, there will be both winners and losers in intimate relations.

5. *Right to Influence.* Belonging to a family and, to a somewhat lesser extent, being in an intimate relationship, carries with it the implicit right to influence the values, attitudes, and behaviors of other family members. Friends or co-workers may comment on my choice of dress or hygiene, and may criticize me behind my back, but they do not generally feel they can tell me to change my clothing or brush my teeth. Friends *advise us* what may be best for us, family members *tell and often coerce us* as to what is best.

6. *Age and Sex Differences.* The family is unique in that it is made up of different ages and sexes. Thus there is the potential for a battle between both the generations *and* the sexes.

7. *Ascribed Roles.* In addition to the age and sex differences is the fact that the family is perhaps the only social institution that assigns roles and responsibilities based on age and sex rather than on interest or competence. Even decades after the feminist movement, family roles as "breadwinner," "homemaker," "child carer" are still based on gender. Children are "children" as long as there are living parents.

8. *Privacy.* Perhaps the most important structural feature of family and intimate relationships is privacy. The modern family is a private institution, insulated from the eyes, ears, and often rules of the wider society. The same is true for most intimate interactions. The whole

notion of teasing friends for "PDA" (public displays of affection) reminds us that intimacy and privacy go hand-in-hand—but the real intimacy goes on behind closed doors. Where privacy is high, the degree of social control will be low.

9. *Involuntary Membership.* You may choose with whom you have an intimate relationship, but family membership is mostly involuntary (with the exception of adoption). Families are exclusive organizations. Birth relationships are involuntary and cannot be terminated except by a court of law, and even then, the parent–child social bond may remain. While there can be ex-wives and ex-husbands, there are very few "ex-children" or "ex- parents." Being in a family involves personal, social, material, and legal commitment and entrapment. When conflict arises, it is not easy to break off the conflict by fleeing the scene or resigning from the group.

10. *Stress.* Families are prone to stress. This is due in part to the theoretical notion that dyadic two-person relationships are unstable (Simmel, 1950). Moreover, families are constantly undergoing changes and transitions. The birth of children, maturation of children, aging, retirement, and death are all significant life stressors. Moreover, stress felt by one family member (such as unemployment, illness, bad grades at school) is transmitted to other family members.

11. *Extensive Knowledge of Social Biographies.* The very definition of intimacy implies that we know a great deal about those with whom we have intimate relationships. The intimacy and emotional involvement of family and intimate relations reveals a full range of identities to members of a family. Strengths and vulnerabilities, likes and dislikes, loves and fears are all known to family members. While this knowledge can help support a relationship, the information can also be used to attack intimates and lead to conflict.

It is one thing to say that the social organization of the family and intimate relationships make them conflict-prone institutions. However, the eleven characteristics we have listed are necessary but not sufficient factors. That the social organization of the family and intimacy exist within a cultural context where violence is tolerated, accepted, and even mandated is a critical factor that helps us understand why intimacy and families as currently structured can be loving, supportive, *and* violent. The widespread acceptability of physical punishment to rear children creates a situation where a conflict-prone institution serves as a training ground to teach children that it is acceptable: (1) to hit people you love;

(2) for powerful people to hit less powerful people; (3) to use hitting to achieve some end or goal; and (4) to hit as an end in itself (Straus, 1994).

Theories That Explain Intimate Violence and Abuse

INTRA-INDIVIDUAL THEORIES

As noted multiple times throughout this book, models and theories that locate the causes of violent and abusive behavior within the individual are both popular and resonate easily with those looking to explain intimate violence. At the same time, for more than 40 years, psychiatric explanations have been quickly dismissed by social scientists and replaced by sociological or social-psychological theories (Raine, 2013).

The conventional-wisdom genesis of psychiatric or individual-level explanations often arises out of the tragic portrayal of a defenseless child, woman, or grandparent subjected to abuse and neglect. Such portrayals arouse the strongest emotions among clinicians and others who see and/or treat the problem of intimate violence. There frequently seems to be no rational explanation for harming a loved one. It is not surprising, therefore, that a psychiatric model of intimate and family violence was the first applied to the problem, nor that it has endured for years. Even sociologists can find themselves using such a model. Once I was working in a clinic at Children's Hospital of Boston. We were examining and doing a psycho-social-medical evaluation of a young child who had suffered a severe immersion burn (she had been forced into a bathtub filled with scalding hot water). It was obvious that she had been purposely burned, since she had been pressed against the tub with such force that neither the soles of her feet nor her bottom had been burned. After the scalding, she had apparently been tied to the bed, and this resulted in lacerations of her wrists and ankles. After our examination, we returned to our offices and wrote up our clinic notes. My colleague Eli Newberger came by and asked me what I thought about the case. I responded, "Anyone who would do that is crazy!" Eli looked puzzled. "Aren't you the person who wrote in 1973 that the psychopathological model of abuse was a myth?" he asked me. "I don't care what I wrote," I responded, "I know what I saw!"

The psychiatric model focuses on the abuser's personality characteristics as the chief determinants of violence and abuse. A psychiatric model links factors such as mental illness, personality defects, psychopathology, sociopathology, alcohol and drug misuse, or other intra-individual abnormalities to family violence. Many studies report a high incidence of psychopathology among abusive individuals

(Hamberger & Hastings, 1986, 1991; Hart, Dutton & Newlove, 1993; Hastings & Hamberger, 1988).

Psychologist Donald Dutton (Dutton & Golant, 1995; Dutton & Starzomski, 1993) developed a psychological profile and explanation of men who batter their wives. Dutton's psychological profile applies to what he calls "cyclical batterers" (see Chapter 1 and 4 of this book), whose cyclical moods ebb and flow, as does their violent behavior. Dutton argues that cyclical abusers are characterized by having borderline personalities—that is, their personality type is on the border between psychotic and neurotic. Dutton explains that this personality is developed early in life. Abusive men have deep-seated feelings of powerlessness that have their origins in the man's early development. Abusive men tend to have shaming, emotionally rejecting, or absent fathers and are left in the arms of a mother who is only intermittently available but whom the boy perceives as all-powerful. According to Dutton, these boys never recover from early traumas (Dutton & Golant, 1995, p. 121).

While Donald Dutton believes that there is a common psychological profile of batterers, other researchers argue that less than 10% of instances of family violence are attributable solely to personality traits, mental illness, or psychopathology (Steele, 1978; Straus, 1980). We cannot, however, dismiss intra-individual explanations of violence too quickly. Over the past few decades, pioneer criminologist Adrian Raine built an impressive program of research looking at brain and behavior explanations for violence (2013). In his most recent book, *The Anatomy of Violence: The Biological Roots of Crime,* Raine explains how advances in brain imaging technology and the application of high-quality case/control research led him to conclude that "the brains of some offenders are physically different from the rest of us" (Raine, 2013, p. 136). Raine concludes from his examination of extremely violent individuals compared to matched controls that poor prefrontal-lobe functioning predisposes individuals to violent behavior. Poor prefrontal-lobe functioning can lead to: (1) loss of control over the more primitive parts of the brain; (2) risk-taking, irresponsibility, and rule-breaking; and (3) impulsivity and loss of self-control. The origins of poor prefrontal-lobe functioning can be genetic, or the result of a disease or an injury, including abusive violence experienced as a child.

Raine does not include much information on violence toward, and abuse of children in his analysis of the anatomy of violence, and it is unlikely his findings on prefrontal-lobe functioning apply to the use of corporal punishment of children. He does, however, devote a small section of the book to wife abuse. Raine and his colleagues, based on experimental research with 23 men who had been referred to the police for physically abusing their wives, concluded that spouse abuse can be caused by a lack of prefrontal-lobe regulatory control over the limbic regions of the brain. Such lack of control can "result in reactive aggression in the face of emotionally provocative stimuli" (Raine, 2013, p. 136).

Raine and other's research on brain functioning and violent behavior does not provide an answer for every form of violence, nor is it likely that every violent individual will demonstrate a similar form of brain function or dysfunction. Moreover, this very brief review does not do justice to the full extent of the research on the biological roots of violent behavior. Given the rapid advancements in technology that allow extensive and sophisticated studies of the human brain, it is likely that more and more attention will be paid to the biology of violence in the coming years.

SOCIAL-PSYCHOLOGICAL THEORIES

Social Learning Theory

By far the most common social-psychological explanation for violence and aggression in and outside of intimate relationships is social learning theory. Social learning theorists (e.g., Bandura, 1973) posit that most behavior is learned through individuals' experience and observation of their own and others' behaviors. According to this theory, individuals who have experienced or witnessed violence are more likely to use violence than those who have experienced little or no violence. Social learning theory provides support for the belief that family and intimate violence is learned. The family is the institution and social group in which people learn the roles of husband, wife, parent, and child. The home is the prime location where people learn how to deal with various stressors, crises, and frustrations. In many instances, the home is also the place where individuals first experience violence. Not only do people learn violent behavior, but they also learn how to justify being violent. For example, when a child hears a father say, "This will hurt me more than it will hurt you," or a mother say, "You have been bad, so you deserve to be spanked," this contributes to the child's learning how to justify violent behavior.

Attachment Theory

A second widely applied social-psychological theory of violence is attachment theory. Most often applied to explanations of child maltreatment, attachment theory describes the propensity of each individual to form a strong emotional bond with a primary caregiver who functions as a source of security and safety (Bowlby, 1973). The theory proposes that there is a clear association between a person's early attachment experiences and the pattern of affectionate bonds the individual makes throughout his or her lifetime. If an individual forms a strong and secure attachment with an early caregiver, the adult relationships he or she forms later will also have secure attachments. On the other hand, if an individual forms only insecure, anxious, or ambivalent attachments early on, his or her adult attachments will be similarly unsatisfactory. Therefore, according to the theory, attachment difficulties underlie adulthood relational problems. Bowlby (1988) posits that anxiety and anger go hand-in-hand as responses to risk of loss, and that anger is often functional. For certain individuals who have weak and insecure attachments, the functional reaction to anger becomes distorted and is manifested through violent acts against intimates.

General Strain/Self Esteem Theories

Sociologist Robert Agnew (1992) asserts that violent behavior may be related to the frustration and anger that result when an individual is treated poorly in social relationships. Agnew outlines three types of strains that increase an individual's feelings of anger and fear. The first is the strain associated with the failure to achieve positively valued goals. This type of strain may result in an individual's using illegitimate means to get what he or she wants. Another type of strain is that caused by the presentation of negative stimuli. Stressful life situations of this type may include such adverse events as criminal victimization, child maltreatment, and interpersonal violence. An individual confronted with such stressors may engage in criminal acts to seek revenge. The third type of strain that Agnew describes is caused by the anticipated or actual loss of positively valued stimuli, such as loss of a loved one or the experience of a major life transition. Difficulties arise when an individual attempts to seek revenge for a loss or tries to prevent major life changes through illegal methods. According to Agnew, the most critical response to strain is anger, which can result in increased aggression and possibly violent criminal behavior.

Another way of expressing general strain theory is proposed by Leonard Berkowitz (1993). Berkowitz examined a wide range of violence and aggression, including emotional or psychological aggression. In addition, he identified various types of violent offenders. Looking for a link across types and forms of aggression, Berkowitz, in what he admits is an oversimplification, notes that people who feel bad about themselves are the ones most likely to engage in aggressive behavior as a means of allaying, at least temporarily, a poor self-image. James Gilligan (1992) focused on the most violent and deadly perpetrators of violence. His model revolves around the concept of "shame." Individuals who experience shaming events or experiences are more prone to violent behavior.

Thus, at the social-psychological level of analysis, self-esteem and self-concept are significant factors. Individuals who experience devaluing or shaming experiences tend to use violent behavior to compensate for devaluing experiences. And, in a society that values violence to a certain degree, exhibiting violent behaviors can enhance self-esteem.

Resource Theory

Resource theory (Goode 1971) is one of the first theoretical explanations developed to explain intimate partner violence. Resource theory is a more sociological version of the self-concept explanations. The theory assumes that all social systems (including the family) rest to some degree on force or the threat of force. The more resources—social, personal, and economic—a person can command, the more force he or she can muster. However, according to William Goode (1971), the author of the theory, the more resources a person actually has, the less he or she will actually use force in an open manner. Thus, a husband who wants to be the dominant person in the family, but has little education, has a job low in prestige and income, and lacks interpersonal skills, may choose to use violence to maintain the dominant position. In addition, family members (including children) may use violence to redress a grievance when they have few alternative resources available.

Social Exchange Theory

Many scholars use exchange theory to explain the complex dynamics inherent in intimate violence (Gelles, 1983, 1997). The theory proposes that both partner abuse and child abuse are governed by the principle of costs and benefits. Individuals use violence when the rewards of doing so are greater than the costs (Gelles, 1983). Exchange theorists assert that inflicting costs on someone who has hurt you is rewarding (e.g., Homans, 1967). The notion of "sweet revenge" is useful for explaining why victims may respond with extreme forms of violence after having been victimized. There is a gain to using violence, and that gain is the achievement of dominance and control over another. The private nature of the family, the reluctance of social institutions and agencies to intervene in intimate relationships—in spite of mandatory child-abuse reporting laws and mandatory-arrest laws for partner violence—and the low risk of other interventions reduce the costs that abusers face for using violence. In addition, the cultural approval of violence as both expressive and instrumental behavior raises the potential rewards for using violence—the most significant reward being social and interpersonal control and power.

Social-Situational/Stress and Coping Theory

That personality problems and psychopathology do not fully explain acts of family violence does not mean that personal problems are unrelated to intimate abuse.

Many personal problems, however, tend to arise from social antecedents, such as marital conflict, unemployment, isolation, unwanted pregnancy, and stress.

A social situational/stress and coping theory of violence proposes that abuse and violence arise out of two main factors. The first is structural stress. The association between low income and intimate violence, for instance, indicates that a central factor in violence and abuse is inadequate financial resources. The second main factor is the cultural norm concerning force and violence in the home (see Chapter 2). "Spare the rod and spoil the child." "The marriage license is a hitting license." These are phrases that underscore the widespread social approval for the use of force and violence at home.

The social-situational/stress and coping theory notes that such structural stresses as low income, unemployment, limited educational resources, illness, and the like are unevenly distributed in society. While we are told that we should be loving parents, adoring husbands, and caring wives, only some individuals get sufficient resources to meet these demands. Others fall considerably short of being able to have the psychological, social, and economic resources to meet the expectations of society, friends, neighbors, loved ones, and themselves. Combined with the cultural approval for violence, these shortfalls lead many intimates to adopt violence and abuse as a means of coping with structural stress.

The Ecological Conceptual Framework

The "ecological conceptual framework" is a bridge between individual and socio-cultural levels of explanation. In addition, the ecological framework is more of a conceptual model than a true theory. Rather than offer a set of testable theoretical propositions, the ecological model provides a cognitive lens through which to see the individual, social-psychological, and socio-cultural levels of analysis. James Garbarino (1977) and Jay Belsky (1980, 1993) proposed an "ecological model" to explain the complex nature of child maltreatment. The same model is applicable to every form of intimate and family violence and abuse. The model rests on three levels of analysis: (1) The relationship between the organism and its environment; (2) the interacting and overlapping systems in which human development occurs; and, (3) environmental quality (Figure 7.1).

The ecological model proposes that violence and abuse toward children arise out of a mismatch of parent to child and family to neighborhood and community. The risk of abuse and violence is greatest when the functioning of the children and parents is limited and constrained by developmental problems. Children with learning

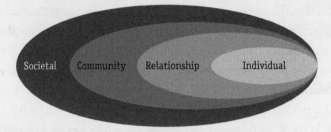

FIGURE 7.1 Levels of analysis of the ecological model.
Source: http://www.cdc.gov/violenceprevention/overview/social-ecologicalmodel.html (retrieved April 14, 2016).

disabilities and social or emotional handicaps are at increased risk for abuse. Parents under considerable stress, or who have personality problems, are at increased risk for abusing their children. These conditions are worsened when social interactions between the spouses or the parents and children heighten the stress or make the personal problems worse. Finally, if there are few institutions and agencies in the community to support troubled families, then the risk of abuse is further raised. Garbarino (1977) identifies two necessary conditions for child maltreatment. First, there must be cultural justification for the use of force against children. Secondly, the maltreating family is isolated from potent family or community support systems.

The ecological model has served as a perspective to examine other forms of family and intimate violence. Linda Dahlberg and Etienne Krug (2002) use both an ecological conceptual framework and a public health perspective to examine intimate partner violence. At the *individual* level, the key variables are biological and personal history factors that increase the likelihood of becoming a victim or perpetrator of violence. As discussed in Chapter 4, some of the key factors are age, education, income, substance use, or history of abuse. Prevention strategies at this level are often designed to promote attitudes, beliefs, and behaviors that ultimately prevent violence. Specific approaches may include education and life-skills training.

The second level of analysis, *relationships*, examines close relationships that may increase the risk of experiencing violence as a victim or perpetrator. Individuals' closest social circle—peers, partners, and family members—influence their behavior and contribute to their range of experience. Prevention strategies at this level may include mentoring and peer programs designed to reduce conflict, foster problem-solving skills, and promote healthy relationships.

The *community* level explores the settings, such as schools, workplaces, and neighborhoods, in which social relationships occur and seeks to identify the characteristics of these settings that are associated with becoming victims or perpetrators of violence. Prevention strategies at this level are typically designed to mold the climate, processes, and policies in a given system. Social norm and social marketing campaigns are often used to foster community climates that promote healthy relationships.

Lastly, the *societal* level looks at the broad societal factors that help create a climate in which violence is encouraged or inhibited. These factors include social and cultural norms. Other larger societal factors include the health, economic, educational, and social policies that help maintain economic or social inequalities between groups in society.

Socio-Cultural Theories

SOCIOBIOLOGY THEORY

A sociobiological, or evolutionary, perspective on child maltreatment suggests that violence toward human or non-human primate offspring is the result of the reproductive success potential of children and parental investment in them. The theory's central assumption is that natural selection is the process of differential reproduction and reproductive success (Daly & Wilson, 1980). Males can be expected to invest in offspring when there is some degree of parental certainty (i.e., how confident the father is that the child is his own genetic offspring), while females are also inclined to invest under conditions of parental certainty. Parents recognize their offspring and avoid squandering valuable reproductive effort on someone else's offspring. Children not genetically related to the parent (e.g., step-children, adopted, or foster children) or children with low reproductive potential (e.g., handicapped or disabled children) are at the highest risk for infanticide and abuse (Burgess & Garbarino, 1983; Daly & Wilson, 1980; Hrdy, 1979). Large families can dilute parental energy and lower attachment to children, thus increasing the risk of child abuse and neglect (Burgess, 1979).

Barbara Smuts (1992) applied an evolutionary perspective to male aggression against females. Smuts explains that male aggression against females often reflects male reproductive striving. Both human and non-human male primates are believed to use aggression against females to intimidate females so that they will not resist future male efforts to mate with them, and to reduce the likelihood that females will mate with other males. Thus males use aggression to control female sexuality, to males' reproductive advantage. The frequency of male aggression varies across societies and situations depending on the strength of female alliances, the support women can receive from their families, the strength and importance of male alliances, the degree of equality in male–female relationships, and the degree to which males control the economic resources within a society. Male aggression towards females, both physical violence and rape, is high when female alliances are weak, when females lack kin support, when male alliances are strong, when male–female relationships are unbalanced, and when males control societal resources.

FEMINIST THEORY

The single most widely used theory to explain intimate partner violence is feminist theory. The key explanatory concept is "coercive control." Feminist theorists and researchers (e.g., Loseke & Kurz, 2005; Dobash & Dobash, 1979; Pagelow, 1984; Smith, 1991a, 1991b; Yllo, 1983, 1988, 1993, 2005) see violence against women as a unique phenomenon more closely aligned with other forms of violence against women (such as rape and sexual assault) than with child abuse and non-marital forms of elder abuse. The central thesis of the theory is that economic, social, and historical processes operate directly and indirectly to support a patriarchal (male-dominated) social order and family structure. Patriarchy leads to the subordination of women, and violence and abuse are mechanisms for maintaining subordination. As with all forms of oppression, patriarchal means of control are often subtle and deeply entrenched, with the most violent forms not emerging until and unless patriarchal control is threatened—as when individual women leave or threaten to leave relationships or groups of women assert their rights (Counts, Brown, & Campbell, 1992; Campbell, 1992; Stark & Flitcraft, 1996). For a test of Feminist Theory on a Global population, see Global Perspectives 7.1.

The main tenets of feminist theory are presented in the form of a wheel, often referred to as the "Duluth Power and Control Wheel" (Figure 7.2).

The Power and Control Wheel was developed in 1984 by the staff at the Domestic Abuse Intervention Project (DAIP) in Duluth, Minnesota. The wheel presents the pattern of actions that an individual uses to intentionally control or dominate his intimate partner. The wheel is applicable only to the victimization of women and is not applicable to other forms of intimate violence and victimization.

A Model of Sexual Abuse

As pointed out in Chapter 3, the risk factors associated with the sexual victimization of children are not the same as risk factors for other forms of child maltreatment. As a result, the theories derived from assessing risk factors will not be applicable to the special case of the sexual victimization of children. David Finkelhor (1984) reviewed research on the factors proposed as contributing to sexual abuse of children and developed what he calls a "Four Precondition Model

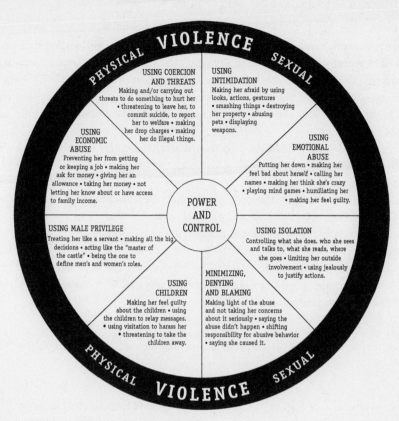

FIGURE 7.2 Duluth Power and Control Wheel.

Source: http://www.theduluthmodel.org/training/wheels.htmlPermission: Domestic Abuse Intervention Project (DAIP) in Duluth, Minnesota

GLOBAL PERSPECTIVES BOX 7.1
TESTING THE FEMINIST THEORY OF VIOLENCE AGAINST WOMEN, USING GLOBAL DATA

Feminist theory is the dominant theoretical model of the causes of violence against women. However, the theory is rarely tested. The difficulty of testing feminist theory applies to other socio-cultural models of intimate violence. Since the main concepts of socio-cultural theories are cultural variables, collecting individual-level data, such as individual social class, social isolation, or experience with violence, cannot test the theories.

Carrie Yodanis (2004) created a data set that allowed her to test the feminist theory of violence against women. Using data from the International Crime Victims Survey (ICVS), Yodanis operationalized her dependent variable, violence against women. The ICVS is an internationally comparative survey of experience with, and response to victimization, including crimes, theft, robbery, and assault. The samples in each nation are representative, and data are collected mostly by telephone contact (some nations employ face-to-face data collection). Women were asked to report whether they were sexually victimized in the previous five years. A second question asked whether, apart from the sexual victimization, the women had experienced a physical attack. Although the question did not specify who the assailant was, Yodanis assumed that the majority of the assailants were intimate male partners.

For her explanatory variables, Yodanis created an index of the status of women in each country covered by the survey. Yodanis also included the measure of fear from the ICVS.

Drawing from feminist theory, Yodanis' main hypothesis was that the higher the educational, occupational, and political status of women in a country, the lower the rates of physical and sexual assault. The hypothesis was confirmed for sexual assault. On the other hand, the hypothesis was not confirmed for violence against women. There was no relationship between the status of women and the violence rates. Apparently, sexual violence and physical violence are, at a socio-cultural level, very different behaviors.

Source: Yodanis, C. L. (2004). Gender inequality, violence against women, and fear: A cross-national test of the feminist theory of violence against women. *Journal of Interpersonal Violence, 19*, 655–675.

of Sexual Abuse" (see Figure 7.3). His review suggests that all the factors relating to sexual abuse can be grouped into one of four preconditions that need to be met before sexual abuse can occur. The preconditions are:

1. A potential offender needs to have some motivation to abuse a child sexually.
2. The potential offender has to overcome internal inhibitions against acting on that motivation.
3. The potential offender has to overcome external impediments to committing sexual abuse.
4. The potential offender or some other factor has to undermine or overcome a child's possible resistance to sexual abuse.

Summary

There is no "correct" theory or level of analysis that must be applied to the study of intimate violence and abuse. Some of the theories presented in this chapter have been tested in research; for example, William's (1992) test of exchange theory found

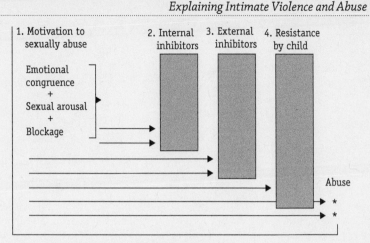

FIGURE 7.3 Four Preconditions: A model of sexual abuse.
Source: Finkelhor, D. (1984). *Child Sexual Abuse: New Theory and Research* (p. 55). New York: Free Press. Reproduced with permission.

that the data support the core propositions of the theory. Other theories, such as feminist theory, form the foundation of social policy approaches to intervening in and preventing intimate partner violence. Which theory is appropriate and useful depends in large part on who will be using and applying the theory. A psychiatrist, for example, will find intra-individual theories more useful than socio-evolutionary theory. Theories provide a cognitive lens and means to organize one's thinking about how to explain, understand, and predict intimate violence and abuse.

Discussion Questions

1. How does the private nature of the family contribute to both love and violence within families?
2. What are some of the "rewards" of being violent?

Suggested Assignments

1. Design model legislation for either child abuse or intimate partner violence that would raise the costs of violence.
2. Assume that you have been asked to testify before a state legislature or Congress on the topic of preventing family violence. Based on the theories that attempt to explain intimate violence, what would you recommend? Prepare your testimony.

8 Policy, Intervention, and Prevention
SOCIETY'S RESPONSE TO INTIMATE VIOLENCE AND ABUSE

ADVOCACY, RESEARCH, POLICY, AND PRACTICE in the broad field of intimate violence and abuse generally focus on a single aspect of the problem—for example, IPV, child maltreatment, or elder abuse. Thus, when we turn to examine society's efforts to prevent and treat intimate violence, we find that policies and practices focus on only a single form of violence and abuse. There are no overarching laws and interventions designed to ameliorate or prevent every form of intimate violence.

A second important facet of examining policies, interventions, and prevention efforts is to consider how each policy and practice initiative balances compassion and control. Physicians Alvin Rosenfeld and Eli Newberger (1977) note that there are two competing philosophies applied to treating child abuse, and the same is true for all forms of intimate violence. On one hand is the compassionate approach. Human service professionals who treat violence and abuse from this perspective approach it with an abundance of human kindness and a non-punitive outlook on intervention. The compassionate approach views abusers as victims themselves. The cause of abuse may be seen in social and developmental origins and not in the abuser. Abusers and offenders, rather than being viewed as cold and cruel monsters, are seen as deprived and needy human beings. Compassionate intervention involves supporting the offender and his or her family. Homemaking services, parenting classes, health services, childcare, substance-abuse treatment, and counseling are the typical interventions brought to bear in the compassionate approach.

On the other hand is the control model. The control model involves the aggressive use of interventions to limit, and if necessary, punish and incapacitate the offender. The control approach places full responsibility for actions with the abuser. Control interventions include arrest, prosecution, and expedited termination of parental rights.

Child maltreatment, with the exception of sexual abuse and exploitation of children, takes a decidedly compassionate approach to policy and practice. When the first mandatory reporting laws were enacted in the late 1960s, advocates and lawmakers agreed that reports would be made to human service branches of government rather than to the police. The narrative supporting the choice of having reports go to social service agencies was that those who maltreat their children have either psychological deficits or social deficits that, if remedied or addressed, would allow parents to successfully and safely provide for their children. As discussed later, there is also a legal foundation for taking a compassionate approach to child maltreatment.

On the other hand, the policy and practice approach to intimate partner violence (IPV) takes a strong control approach for offenders and a compassionate approach for the victims. IPV is viewed simply and straightforwardly as a crime. In the 1970s, women's advocacy groups brought lawsuits against police departments and prosecutors for failing to adequately protect victims of IPV. Advocates pushed for strong control responses to intimate violence and sexual assault. Here, too, legal and constitutional precedents supported calls for a control, as opposed to a compassionate, approach to IPV.

Child Maltreatment: Policy and Practice

How we go about responding to child maltreatment and the very philosophy of our interventions is guided by policy—laws pertaining to the rights of parents and the role of the state in protecting children. As noted in the last section, the response to child maltreatment in the United States draws largely from the compassion model. This follows directly from legal precedents derived from United States Supreme Court rulings regarding parent's and children's rights.

The development of parental rights and responsibilities stems from English common law and American case law. Parental rights, while not specifically articulated in the United States Constitution, are embodied in precedents set by rulings of the United States Supreme Court and are heavily influenced by the privacy rights of citizens. Parental rights include the right to custody, control, and decision-making for children. With these rights are reciprocal parental responsibilities to protect, educate, support, and care for the child. Children's rights are also developed in case law, in which the doctrine of the *best interest of the child* and *parens patria* (the state as ultimate parent) were crafted (Davidson, 1997). The rights of children have been slow to develop, but have been advanced by various advocacy groups seeking to assure that children are protected from acts of omission or commission that threaten their safety and well-being.

There were two major Supreme Court rulings in the 1970s and 1980s that established guiding precedents for the American child welfare system. In issues of child protection and custody, the Supreme Court has been the arbiter of the relationship between parents, children, and the state. U.S. law and tradition grant parents broad discretion as to how they rear their children. In *Smith v. Organization of Foster Families for Equality and Reform*,[1] the U.S. Supreme Court held that the Fourteenth Amendment gave parents a "constitutionally recognized liberty interest" in maintaining the custody of their children "that derives from blood relationship, state law sanction, and basic human right." This interest is not absolute, however, because of the state's power and authority to exercise *parens patriae* duties to protect citizens who cannot fend for themselves. The state may attempt to limit or end parent–child contact and make children eligible for temporary or permanent placement or adoption when parents:

1. Abuse, neglect, or abandon their children;
2. Become incapacitated in their ability to be a parent;
3. Refuse or are unable to remedy serious identified problems in caring for their children; or,
4. Experience an extraordinarily severe breakdown in their relationship with their children (e.g., owing to a long prison sentence).

Cognizant that severing the parent–child relationship is an extremely drastic measure, the U.S. Supreme Court held in *Santosky v. Kramer*[2] that a court may only terminate parental rights if the state can demonstrate with clear and convincing evidence that a parent has failed in one of the aforementioned four ways. Most state statutes also contain provisions for parents to voluntarily relinquish their rights. In addition, the state also has the authority to return a child to his or her parents. Ideally, this occurs once a determination is made that it would be safe to return a child to his or her home and that the child's parents would be able to provide appropriate care.

A second important aspect of child welfare policy and law is that the states retain all powers that are not specifically reserved for the federal government. The federal powers include monetary policy, foreign policy, interstate commerce and transactions, and national taxation policy. Child protection is the responsibility of the states. Thus, there is no single, national child welfare system, nor is there one set of policies in the United States. Because states have the authority to define child abuse and neglect and to develop their own policy responses, there are in fact no fewer than 300 child welfare systems—some state-operated, some county-based, and some hybrid models. There are 51 sets of child welfare policies—one for each state and one for the District of Columbia. Most other nations—with the exception of Australia, which has an even stronger federalist system of government, concentrate child welfare policies and programs under a single national policy. In the United States, federal policy formation has followed the development of state policies. Today, however, there is a federal statutory framework that shapes and is influenced by state policies through the establishment of standards and funding mechanisms.

There are six key pieces of federal legislation that structure child welfare interventions in the United States:

1. The Child Abuse Prevention and Treatment Act of 1974 (CAPTA—Public Law 93-247);
2. The Adoption Assistance and Child Welfare Act of 1980 (AACWA—Public Law 96-272;
3. The Indian Child Welfare Act of 1978 (ICWA—Public Law 95-608);
4. The Multiethnic Placement Act of 1994 (MEPA—Public Law 103-382, Title V, Part E);
5. The Adoption and Safe Families Act of 1997 (ASFA—Public Law 105-89); and
6. The Foster Care Independence Act of 1999 (Public Law 106-169).

CHILD ABUSE PREVENTION AND TREATMENT ACT OF 1974

By 1967, all 50 states and the District of Columbia had enacted mandatory reporting laws based on the United States Children's Bureau's model reporting law. In 1974, Congress enacted the Child Abuse Prevention and Treatment Act (CAPTA) and created the National Center on Child Abuse and Neglect (Nelson, 1984). CAPTA provided a federal definition of child maltreatment, funds for states to implement prevention and treatment efforts, and a mandate to carry out a national incidence study of child maltreatment. State definitions of child maltreatment had to conform to requirements articulated in CAPTA in order for states to receive federal funds. The requirements include enforcing mandatory child-abuse and neglect-reporting laws, investigating reports of abuse and neglect, and educating the public about abuse and neglect. CAPTA has been re-authorized numerous times, with major modifications to the definition of child maltreatment and enhancing service delivery. The main practice implication of CAPTA is enforcing and funding state mandatory reporting laws.

ADOPTION ASSISTANCE AND CHILD WELFARE ACT OF 1980

As a result of a 1961 amendment to the Social Security Act of 1935 (Public Law 74-271), children who were removed from their homes for abuse and neglect could have the costs of their placement funded from the Aid to Families with Dependent Children (AFDC, "welfare") program of the Social Security Act if they would have been eligible for the program had they remained at home (O'Neil & Gesiriech, 2005). The funds covered the cost of foster care, but provided no funds for services to parents. The composition of the foster care population was shifting to a system that was disproportionately populated by single-parent families, children of color, as well as children removed from homes with incomes significantly below the poverty level (Pecora et al., 2000).

The actual number of children in foster care did not increase dramatically during the 1960s and into the early 1970s, but the prevailing professional view of foster care shifted during the two decades. By the late 1950s, serious questions were raised about the role and function of the foster care system. Until this time, the system was focused on the removal of children from high-risk situations, and the focus of casework practice was on the placement process. Little attention was paid to what happened to children after they entered care. A landmark study, Children in Need of Parents (Maas & Engler, 1959), documented the status of children in foster care as "orphans of the living," not belonging to their own parents nor to any other set of parents. This work and other research indicated that foster care was far from temporary (Fanshel & Shinn, 1978). By the late 1970s, foster care had become a permanent status for many children who had entered the child welfare system. Children placed in foster care did not reside in a single foster home; rather they *drifted* from one placement to another with little stability or continuity of care. The view of foster care began to shift toward that of a temporary service whose purpose was to reunite children with their families or place them in another family if necessary (Pecora, Whittaker, Maluccio, & Barth, 2000).

In addition to concern over "foster care drift," the paradigm of child abuse and neglect changed in the 1970s. At the time of Kempe and his colleague's (1962) first publication on the "battered child syndrome," the prevailing causal model was that child abuse was caused by the psychopathology of the caregivers. This model explained abuse and neglect as a function of individual psychopathy. Other models proposed that maltreatment arose out of mental illness or the use and abuse of alcohol and illicit drugs.

By the mid-1970s, the psychopathological model of child abuse and neglect was being replaced with conceptual models that placed greater emphasis on social factors such as income, education, age, marital conflict, stress, and child-produced stressors (see Gil, 1970; Gelles, 1973). Such models were more consistent with an intervention approach that envisioned foster care as a temporary placement, while services and resources are directed toward parents to provide them the means to adequately care for their children. The key assumption behind social-psychological stress models is that all caregivers want to be adequate parents, but there are structural and economic barriers that impede that desire. Children should be kept safe in temporary foster care while the barriers are addressed and removed, or at least lowered.

As early as 1962, there were more than 270,000 children in out-of-home care. The number peaked at 330,000 in 1971, and the next available formal estimate was 302,000 children in foster care in 1980. The Adoption Assistance and Child Welfare Amendments[3] of 1980 (AACWA) were the result of expanded recognition that children in foster care were in social and legal limbo. The Act called for demonstrated permanency-planning programs that documented the ability to move children in foster care back to their own families or on to adoptions, and declared the need to clearly shift the purpose and operation of the child welfare system.

There were *three* major components of AACWA aimed at reducing foster care drift and assuring the right of children to have permanent homes. The first major provision of the legislation was the requirement that states make "reasonable efforts to maintain a family" before they remove a child from the child's birth parent(s), and "reasonable efforts to reunify a family" before establishing a permanent plan of adoption. The reasonable efforts requirement mandated states to provide appropriate services prior to placement, and/or services that would allow a safe family reunification for a child who had been removed. The legislation, however, provided no additional funds for such services.

A second provision of the legislation was the requirement that states engage in permanency planning. In brief, permanency planning required each state to have a plan developed within 18 months of a child's being placed into foster care that would assure that the child would have a permanent home, either through a safe return to her/his birth parents or through an adoption. In order to facilitate permanency planning, the law established a set of procedural requirements that included the development of case plans, periodic judicial reviews, and dispositional hearings at which the child's permanent plan was established.

The legislation created Title IV-E of the Social Security Act, which provided un capped entitlement funding[4] for foster care and adoption assistance for children who were eligible for AFDC. The foster care funding was an extension of the old AFDC provision that allowed for payment of foster care costs for poor children. In addition to permanency planning, the major policy innovation was the provision of funds to subsidize the adoption of special-needs foster children. Federal funds could be used to support the cost of operating adoption and foster care programs. The funding continued to be linked to placement services—adoption and foster care—with no targeted funding for services to the families of children in need of protection. Furthermore, states were expected to adhere to the spirit of the reasonable efforts provision and to meet the procedural and temporal requirements of the legislation in order to qualify for Title IV-E federal funds for foster care and adoption.

The available data on foster care[5] (see Figure 8.1) indicate that in the first few years after AACWA was enacted, there was a decline in the number of children in foster care. From an estimated 302,000 children in foster care the year AACWA was enacted, the number of children in foster care dropped to 274,000 in 1981 and to 262,000 in 1982, the lowest on record. The number of children in foster

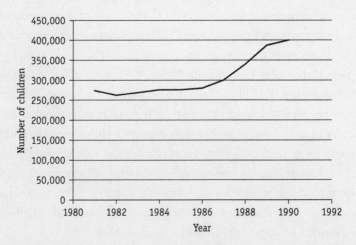

FIGURE 8.1 Number of children in foster care, 1981–1990.

Source: Adapted from Gelles, R. J., & Spigner, C. W. (2008). Child welfare policy. In I. C. Colby, K. M. Sowers, & C. N. Dulmus, Eds., *Comprehensive Handbook of Social Work and Social Welfare, Volume 4: Social Policy and Policy Practice* (pp. 295–317). Hoboken, NJ: John Wiley & Sons; 2008. Reproduced with permission.

care remained under 300,000 until 1987, and then the number began a significant increase, reaching 400,000 in 1990.

The emphasis on permanency led to the freeing of children for adoption and the subsequent adoption of some of the children. Over 50,000 children were freed for adoption in 1982 as a result of state court action (Maza, 1983). Of the children available for adoption, 17,000 had a specific permanency plan for adoption (Maximus, 1984). Of this number, 14,400 children were placed for adoption in 1982 (Maximus, 1984).[6]

INDIAN CHILD WELFARE ACT OF 1978

During the period between the enactment of CAPTA and the year AACWA became law, a disproportionate number of Native American children were removed from their parents and placed in the foster care system. Some states placed as many as 25–35% of Native American children in the foster care system between 1974 and 1978 (Myers, 2006). The vast majority of the children were placed outside of their tribe with non-Indian families. In response to a multi-year study of the placement of Indian children (Fanshel, 1972), tribal advocacy groups challenged such practices. The Indian Child Welfare Act (ICWA) of 1978 (Public Law 95-608) established standards for child custody proceedings related to foster care, termination of parental rights, and adoption for Indian children. The standards included: tribal court jurisdiction over children who reside on the reservations; the requirement of notification to the tribe of state or local proceedings involving the placement of an Indian child living off of the reservation, along with tribal rights to intervene and request transfer of the proceeding to tribal court; an increased standard of proof—clear and convincing evidence; and placement preferences for the extended family or tribe (Pecora et al., 2000).

The intent of ICWA was to limit the placement of Native American children into non–Native American homes. However, ICWA had numerous ambiguities, including the definition of an "Indian child," as well as interpretation of key clauses and terms in the Act (e.g., what is "good cause?"). The Act also challenged the tribes to develop or expand their protective services and tribal court capacities.

THE MULTI-ETHNIC PLACEMENT ACT OF 1994 AND THE INTER-ETHNIC ADOPTION PROVISIONS OF THE SMALL BUSINESS JOB PROTECTION ACT OF 1996

Between the 1950s and the 1980s, the foster care population became disproportionately children of color (Pecora at al., 2000). One impact of the civil rights era was to move adoption away from the traditional practice of physically matching infant placement, and to increase the acceptance of adoption across racial lines. Prior to the successes of the civil rights movement, some southern states, including Louisiana and Texas, legally banned transracial adoption (Myers, 2006). Such laws were struck down in the 1960s. Subsequently, African American children began to be placed transracially, as Native American children had been in earlier decades. In the early 1970s, however, advocates raised concerns over the adoption of African American children by white families. The National Association of Black Social Workers (NABSW) led a campaign against transracial adoption. The NABSW issued a position paper in 1972 (NABSW, 1974) that stated that black children should only be placed with black families—either in foster care or by adoption. A measure of the depth of concern of the Association was reflected in the statement "We have committed ourselves to go back to our communities and work to end this particular form of genocide."

The year prior to the NACSW resolution, there were 2,500 black-white adoptions (Silverman, 1993). In the aftermath of the NABSW resolution, the number of transracial adoptions dropped by more than 50%. In 1976, black-white placements were 1,076 (Silverman, 1993). In 1987, black-white transracial adoptions were estimated to be 1,169, while adoptions of children of other racial, ethnic groups, or cultural groups—mainly Asian and Hispanic—were estimated to be 5,850. It is difficult to ascertain how the preference for within-race adoptions and the racial preferences of adoptive parents who are willing to adopt across racial and cultural lines have interacted to produce this result.

Although they are only a small proportion of adoptions, the decline in the number of transracial adoptions contributed to the persistent findings that children of color stayed in foster care longer and were less likely to be adopted (Barth, 1997). In addition, a growing body of social science research (Simon & Alstein, 1977, 1987) found no developmental disadvantages among children who were transracially adopted.

The Multiethnic Placement Act of 1994 (MEPA: Public Law 103-382, Title V, Part E) had three major goals: (1) Decrease the length of time that children wait to be adopted; (2) facilitate the recruitment and retention of foster and adoptive parents who can meet the distinctive needs of children awaiting placement; and, (3) eliminate discrimination on the basis of the race, color, or national origin of the child or the prospective parent.

The statutory language of the law included two prohibitions and one affirmative obligation for state agencies and other agencies that were involved in foster care. First, state and private agencies (i.e., those who received funds under

Title IV-E of the Social Security Act) were prohibited from delaying or deny-ing a child's foster care or adoptive placement on the basis of the child's or the prospective parent's race, color, or national origin. Second, agencies were pro-hibited from denying any individual the opportunity to become a foster or adop-tive parent on the basis of the child's race, color, or national origin. Finally, in order to remain eligible for funding for state child welfare programs, states were required to make diligent efforts to recruit foster and adoptive parents who re-flected the racial and ethnic diversity of children in the state who needed foster and adoptive homes.

Congress revisited MEPA in 1996 in order to address what were perceived to be loopholes in the original law. The Inter-ethnic Provisions of the Small Business Protection Act of 1996 (Public Law 104-188) repealed allowable exceptions under MEPA and replaced them with specific prohibitions against *any* actions that de-layed or denied placements on the basis of race, color, or national origin. The law also protected children in placements from racial or ethnic discrimination under Title VI of the Civil Rights Act of 1964 by creating a right to sue. State and/or private foster care agencies could be sued by children, prospective parents, or the federal government for delaying or denying placements. States that delayed or denied placements based on race, color, or national origin would also be penal-ized by a reduction in their federally allocated child welfare funding. MEPA and the Inter-ethnic Provisions did not require transracial adoptions, nor did they prohibit same-race adoptions. What the two laws accomplished was to place the foster care and adoption system under the provisions and protections of the Civil Rights Act of 1964.

THE ADOPTION AND SAFE FAMILIES ACT OF 1997

The Adoption Assistance and Child Welfare Act of 1980 (AACWA) required states to make "reasonable efforts" to keep a child in his or her home or reunite the child with his or her caregivers as soon as possible and practical. AACWA also required states to make timely permanency decisions for children in out-of-home care that would move the child back to his or her own family, or forward to adop-tion. The balance between reasonable efforts and decision-making for children was difficult to establish.

State and local child welfare systems worked hard to meet the goal of family preservation. The majority of children removed from their homes were ulti-mately reunited with their parents. Unfortunately, between 20% and 40% of chil-dren reunited with their parents were returned to out-of-home placement within 18 months of the reunification (Barth, Courtney, Berrick, & Albert, 1994). Nearly half of the children killed by parents or caregivers are killed after the children come to the attention of the child welfare system (Gelles, 1996; U.S. Advisory Board on Child Abuse and Neglect, 1995). Some children are killed when they remain in their homes, others are killed after a reunification, and an even smaller number die in foster care.

Employing a compassionate approach to child maltreatment, AACWA encouraged states to focus on helping families and working toward reunification. The unintended consequence of the mandate of reasonable efforts and the compassion approach is that children spend long spells in foster care. Prior to 1997, the median length of stay for a child in foster care was 21 months (Child Welfare League of America, 1999). Approximately 18% of children in foster care stayed longer than five years. They remained in foster care while child welfare workers worked towards family reunification, or they remained in foster care because a reunification was not possible, and adoption was not achieved for the child. Approximately 100,000 children had a goal of adoption in 1996, but only 27,761 were adopted that year (Child Welfare League of America, 1999). At the same time, approximately 20,000 children "aged out" of the child welfare system each year not having secured a permanent family. That is, they reach the age of majority in their state and they are no longer eligible for foster care or payment to a foster parent on their behalf.

An important statistic influencing the enactment of the Adoption and Safe Families Act of 1997 (ASFA) was that the number of adoptions of children from the foster care system was about 20,000, and the number of adoptions was in decline—See Figure 8.2 (Bevan et al., 1996). The main adverse consequence for children in out-of-home care was that while they might spend years awaiting reunification, a reunification might never occur. The longer children waited, the less the likelihood that they would secure permanency through adoption.

The Adoption and Safe Families Act of 1997 revised the legal mandate for child welfare by making the child's safety and permanency the paramount goals of the child welfare system. The mandate for reasonable efforts was modified to identify circumstances in which the reasonable-efforts requirement was not mandatory. The circumstances included "aggravated circumstances," such as when a parent had committed a murder of another child, when a parent committed or aided in voluntary manslaughter of another child of the parent, when a parent committed an assault that resulted in serious injury to a child or another child of the parent, or when a parent had had his or her parental rights involuntarily terminated for a sibling of the child. In addition, shorter timelines were established for reunification efforts and permanency decisions,

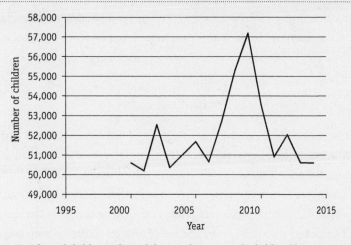

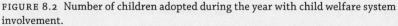

FIGURE 8.2 Number of children adopted during the year with child welfare system involvement.

Source: Adapted from Gelles, R. J., & Spigner, C. W. (2008). Child welfare policy. In I. C. Colby, K. M. Sowers, & C. N. Dulmus, Eds., *Comprehensive Handbook of Social Work and Social Welfare, Volume 4: Social Policy and Policy Practice* (pp. 295–317). Hoboken, NJ: John Wiley & Sons; 2008. Reproduced with permission.

in order to remove barriers to adoption and reduce the time children would stay in foster care awaiting an improbable or questionable reunification. The law required states to seek termination of parental rights in the instance of children being in out-of-home care for 15 of the previous 22 months. The exceptions to this timeline were if children were in the care of relatives, or if there was a compelling reason for not terminating parental rights that was in the best interests of the child. Thirdly, states were required to develop a permanency plan for children in out-of-home care within 12 months of the children's being placed in care (AACWA required a permanency plan within 18 months of a child's being placed in care). Permanency plans could no longer be "long-term foster care." Lastly, states were encouraged to engage in concurrent planning that considered permanency plans that would be used if a safe reunification could not be accomplished.

By defining the safety of the child as the paramount goal of the child welfare system, the Adoption and Safe Families Act of 1997 changed family preservation from *the* goal of child welfare systems to *a* goal, albeit one of the central and primary goals. The legislation also required states to make reasonable efforts to secure a permanent family for children who could not safely return home and created incentives for states to increase adoptions. The initial impact of the Adoption and Safe Families Act of 1997 has been an increase in yearly adoptions, from 20,000 per year to more than 50,000 in 2013. The median length of time children stay in foster care declined to 13.5 months in 2013, while the percentage of children remaining on foster care for five years or longer declined to 5%. The number of children of children in foster care dropped from 552,000 in 2000 to 402,378 in 2013.[7]

FOSTER CARE INDEPENDENCE ACT OF 1999

Each year, approximately 20,000 youths age out of foster care without a permanent family of their own (U.S. Department of Health and Human Services, 2015). The children who age out are young adults who spent a substantial part of their lives in foster care and consequently are ill-prepared for independent living (Cook, 1991; Kerman, Wildfire, & Barth, 2002). Upon leaving foster care, many of the youths raised in care have not completed their education and are unable to secure or keep employment. The thousands of "graduates" of the public child welfare system often experience homelessness, depression, arrest, and early parenthood. In 1999, Congress enacted legislation to better meet the needs of those aging out of foster care. The Foster Care Independence Act extended the age of eligibility for federal funding to 21. The law allowed youths to save up to $10,000 without losing their Title IV-E eligibility and created an option for states to enroll former foster children in the state medical assistance program until age 21. In a continued effort to create opportunities for former foster children, Congress modified the law in 2001 to provide $50 million additional funds for education and training vouchers (Public Law 107-133),

Interventions for Child Abuse and Neglect

IDENTIFICATION AND REPORTING

The first step in treating child abuse is to identify children in need of services. As noted above, by the 1970s, all states enacted mandatory child-maltreatment reporting laws. Each year, millions of children are reported as suspected victims of maltreatment. Consequently, considerable effort is devoted to improving the techniques of identifying and reporting cases of child abuse to the proper human service agencies. Such steps involve a variety of efforts, which are coordinated among numerous public and private agencies. Public and private agencies engage in training programs to educate potential reporters about the signs of abuse. During the 1980s and 1990s, public education and awareness programs greatly increased the number of child abuse and neglect reports. For an example of another country manages reports of suspected child maltreatment without requiring reporting see Global Perspectives 8.1.

GLOBAL PERSPECTIVES BOX 8.1
MANAGING CHILD ABUSE AND NEGLECT

Only the United States and a few other nations manage child maltreatment through the use of mandatory reporting laws and investigations by child protective service investigators. In Europe, only France enacted mandatory reporting codes that require physicians to report cases of child abuse to child protective services.

The Netherlands employs a unique system for managing child maltreatment. Rather than require mandatory reporting, the Dutch employ a system of "confidential doctors." Anyone suspecting that a child is being maltreated can (voluntarily) contact a "confidential doctor." The contact can include a request for advice for handling the matter or a referral to other professionals for assistance. The confidential doctor is the point person and the responsible professional for organizing assistance and contacting and arranging for appropriate services (Doek, 1991). Belgium and Germany have also adopted the confidential doctor approach.

Absent mandatory reporting of child maltreatment in Europe, most European nations employ the criminal justice system to respond to instances of child sexual abuse.

Source: Doek, J. E. (1991). Management of child abuse and neglect at the International Level: Trends and Perspectives. *Child Abuse & Neglect: The International Journal*, 15, 51–56.

CHILD WELFARE SERVICES: PRESERVE AND PROTECT

State, county, and local agencies (and their contracted agencies) investigate the majority of reports of suspected child maltreatment. There were an estimated 3.6 million reports of suspected child maltreatment in 2014, of which 1.8 million were screened in as being appropriate for investigation (U.S. Department of Health and Human Services, 2016). The 1.8 million "screened-in" reports generated the same number of investigations and dispositions. Of the 1.8 million investigations, 702,208 children were identified as victims of some form of child maltreatment.

In cases of substantiated child maltreatment, agencies must decide whether to close the case, keep the case open for voluntary services, allow the child to remain in the home, or seek court-ordered removal of the child. Of the 644,561 individual victims of child maltreatment in 2014, 410,000 received post-investigation services and 147,462 children were placed into out-of-home care (U.S. Department of Health and Human Services, 2016).

FAMILY PRESERVATION AND SUPPORT

The child welfare system's main resources consist of casework services; plans to find permanent placements for children; and using foster care, termination of parental rights, and adoption as a last resort. Some observers see the attempt to find a balance between these approaches as a pendulum that swings from control to compassion and back, depending on current theories about the causes of maltreatment, the development of new interventions, and publicity about sensational cases (Lindsey, 1994). Although child welfare policy does tend to swing back and forth between compassion and control like a pendulum, the essential philosophy of the child welfare system remains one of compassion. Ideally, the system aims at supporting and preserving families as a means of protecting children from maltreatment.

Family preservation programs are not new. They go back at least to the settlement house movement created at Hull House in Chicago by Jane Addams in 1910. Family preservation programs are designed to help children and families (including extended and adoptive families) that are at risk or in crisis. A slightly newer version of family preservation programs is Homebuilders, developed by David Haapala and Jill Kinney (Barthel, 1991). The goal of Homebuilders and all intensive family-preservation services (IFPS) is to safely maintain children in their homes or to facilitate a safe and lasting reunification. The essential feature is intensive, short-term, crisis intervention. Services are provided in the client's home. The length of session is variable—it is not confined to a 30–60-minute home visit. Services are available seven days a week, 24 hours a day, not just during business hours Monday through Friday. Caseloads are small—two or three families per worker. Services are both "soft," such as counseling, parent education, and advocacy; and "hard," such as housing assistance, homemaker services, or daycare. But the most important difference between Homebuilders and traditional family-reunification programs is the intensive, short-term nature of the program. Although services can be provided daily, Homebuilders was designed to be "short-term." Finally, whereas traditional child welfare programs are based on a deficit model that assumes that abusive parents do not have the personal, social, or economic resources to cope with rearing children, intensive family-preservation programs are designed to identify and work with families around their strengths. Thus, if a family has a strong network of relatives, the work focuses on using this network to help with family stressors or crises.

The initial evaluations of intensive family-preservation programs were uniformly enthusiastic. The programs were claimed to have reduced the placement of children while still assuring the safety of those children. Foundation program officers and program administrators claimed that the families involved in intensive family preservation programs had low rates of placement and "100% safety records" (Barthel, 1991; Forsythe, 1992).

The empirical case that abusive and neglectful families can be preserved using IFPS has yet to be made, however. Amid the claims and counter-claims about intensive family preservation, and following the funding of the Family Preservation and Support Act of 1993, the Department of Health and Human Services funded a national evaluation of family preservation and support services. This evaluation, conducted by Westat, the Chapin Hall Center for Children, and James Bell Associates, examined a full range of family preservation and support programs at a number of sites across the country. The study used a randomized clinical trial design with a variety of outcome measures, including placement, cost, and family functioning. More important, the study evaluated IFPS that rigorously followed the Homebuilders model. The multi-year project concluded that intensive family-preservation programs do not reduce placement, do not reduce cost, do not improve family functioning and, most important, do not improve child safety. It is not that such programs serve no useful purpose; it is that they offer no broadly effective solution to the vexing problems confronting those in the child welfare system (U.S. Department of Health and Human Services, 2001).

The child protective service system employs a variety of other promising but yet-unproven interventions. Family Group Decision-Making employs a group conferencing model that brings together the immediate family, relatives, friends, and other close supports for the purpose of making decisions about how to stop maltreatment (Pennel & Buford, 2000). Family Group Decision-Making, initially developed in New Zealand, is now widely implemented in the United States and Canada. While viewed as a promising approach, there is not yet a body of research that supports Family Group Decision-Making as a means of preserving families and protecting children.

DIFFERENTIAL RESPONSE

Another newer approach in child protective services is Differential Response. Differential response is a means of eliminating the "one-size-fits-all" approach to child maltreatment investigations. In addition, differential response brings a more compassionate approach to the response to a report of child maltreatment. As implied by its name, differential response involves employing more than one method to respond to reports of suspected abuse and neglect. "Dual track," "multiple track," or "alternative response" approaches begin with the assumption that there are different kinds of reports of child maltreatment (Schene, 2005). The goal is to divert a large percentage of the cases that traditionally are under Child Protective Services (CPS) jurisdiction to the new, voluntary "alternative response" or AR track. Differential response is a means of employing a less adversarial approach to suspected child maltreatment. While some reports of suspected abuse—serious physical abuse and sexual abuse—are investigated in the traditional way, other reports, such as neglect, are approached from a service point of view. Children are viewed as members of the community, and families are offered services (Schene, 2005).

The alterative response track is entirely voluntary for parents. At the outset, they can accept or reject the offer to participate in the program, with no adverse consequence for rejecting it. They can also start down the track but get off it at any point they choose, again with no consequence.

Differential response is mainly a means of responding to the demands on resources of carrying out hundreds of thousands of investigations of suspected child maltreatment—most of which are ruled "unsubstantiated." Second, differential response is a way of responding to community dissatisfaction with the traditional forms of investigations. Thirdly, differential response is a response to concerns about differential reporting of minority families.

Differential response, like intensive family preservation and family group conferencing, expanded quickly, even in the absence of data supporting its effectiveness. Local child protective service agencies may save resources by not fielding a full-scale investigation, but there still is a question about whether agencies can accurately determine which cases involve children at dire risk of harm prior to an actual investigation. Law professor Elizabeth Bartholet (2014) is even more critical of differential response, labeling it another fad designed to prioritize the preservation of families over the safety, well-being, and permanence of children.

NURSE-FAMILY PARTNERSHIP

The singular success in child maltreatment intervention is David Old's Nurse-Family Partnership (Eckenrode et al., 2010). The Nurse-Family Partnership involves having trained nurses make home visits to low-income mothers who have had no previous live births (Olds, 2006). The visiting nurses have three goals: (1) to improve the outcomes of pregnancies by helping women with prenatal health; (2) to improve the child's health and development by helping parents provide more sensitive and competent child care; and (3) to improve the parental life course by helping them plan future pregnancies. Olds and his colleagues have spent nearly three decades evaluating the effectiveness of the Nurse-Family Partnership program, including three separate random clinical trials with different populations. In terms of child maltreatment, the programs demonstrate positive effects, with the treatment groups having fewer childhood injuries and ingestions that may be associated with child abuse. Specifically focusing on child abuse, program participants had fewer substantiated reports of child maltreatment (Kitzman et al., 2010; Eckenrode et al., 2010).

While not a silver bullet, Nurse-Family Partnership is effective enough that the Patient Protection and Affordable Care Act of 2010 (Public Law 111-148)[8] included $1.4 billion in funding under the Maternal, Infant, and Early Childhood Home Visiting Program to establish home visiting programs across the nation.

Intimate Partner Violence: Control and Empowerment

The approach to preventing and treating IPV—specifically male-to-female violence—takes a decidedly "control" approach with offenders. In the initial years of advocacy for treating violence against women as a social problem, advocates focused on the perceived reluctance of police and prosecutors to respond to IPV with the same level of control as in their responses to violence between strangers. There were numerous class action lawsuits filed in the 1970s against police departments and prosecutors, claiming that police and prosecutor indifference to violence against women violated women's constitutional rights to equal treatment.

The watershed lawsuit occurred in the 1980s in Torrington, Connecticut. Tracy Thurman sued the City of Torrington.[9] Her estranged husband had battered Thurman, and when he tracked her down at the home of a friend, she called the police for help. The police response to the call was delayed, and when the officer arrived, he did not intervene, even when he witnessed Thurman being struck and beaten by her husband. Thurman was left permanently injured by the attack and filed a civil suit against the City of Torrington and 29 police officers.[10] Thurman ultimately settled out of court for $1.9 million, and police departments across the country were put on notice that an indifferent approach to violence against women could be very costly.

VIOLENCE AGAINST WOMEN ACT OF 1994

The Violence Against Women Act of 1994 (VAWA; Public Law 103-322) is the single most important piece of federal legislation related to IPV. In brief, the legislation aims to provide funding for programs that protect victims of IPV and enhance local jurisdiction's ability to prosecute offenders. The United States Supreme Court struck down one provision of the initial bill—the right for victims to sue their attackers in federal court.

The control approach of federal policy is evident in the fact that the funding and programs authorized under VAWA are under the United States Department of Justice. Congress reauthorized VAWA multiple times since its initial enactment. The most recent reauthorization, in 2013, added a non-discrimination provision that prohibits organizations that receive VAWA funding from discriminating on the basis of sex. The non-discrimination provision was a minor attempt to address arguments from men's rights groups that VAWA omitted any consideration of the hundreds of thousands of male victims of IPV.

MANDATORY ARREST AND SHELTERS

Many options are available to women who want to escape or be protected from partner violence. One option is to call the police. The most well-known assessment of intervention in IPV is the Minneapolis Police Experiment, which was designed to examine whether arresting men for violent attacks on their partners would decrease the risk of further violence (Sherman & Berk, 1984). In the study, the police randomly assigned incidents of misdemeanor family assaults to one of three treatments: arrest, separation, or advice/mediation. The households that received the arrest intervention had the lowest rate (10%) of recidivism (relapse into violent behavior), and those in which the abuser and victim were only separated had the highest (24%).

Replications of the Minneapolis study, however, found that arrest is no more effective in deterring future arrests or complaints of violence than are separation or counseling (Berk, Campbell, Klap, & Western, 1992; Dunford, Huizinga, & Elliott, 1990; Pate & Hamilton, 1992; Sherman, Smith, Schmidt, & Rogan, 1992). The replications did find that employed men who were arrested were less likely to be violent after the intervention than were men who were not arrested. However, unemployed men who were arrested were actually more likely to be violent after the intervention than were unemployed men who were not arrested.

Although the evaluations of mandatory arrest do not uniformly demonstrate the effectiveness of arrest as a means of preventing future violence, mandatory arrest is consistent with the control approach to IPV, and, without any compelling theory or data to implement other strategies, mandatory arrest continues to be a major tool in the efforts to intervene and prevent IPV. However, an unanticipated consequence of mandatory arrest policies is the fact that in numerous instances, police arrest the woman in the household, if the evidence indicates she is the primary offender. When police cannot identify a primary offender, they employ a dual arrest policy (Dichter & Gelles, 2012).

A second option for a woman who wants to escape an abuser is to go to a shelter or safe house. *If* a shelter is nearby, *if* the woman knows how to get to it, and *if* the shelter has room for her, this is a good option. Shelters provide physical protection, social support, counseling, legal aid, and even occupational counseling. Shelters are the most cost-efficient form of intervention in domestic violence.

Researchers report that the effectiveness of shelters depends on the attributes of the victims. When a victim is actively engaged in taking control of her life, a shelter stay can dramatically reduce the likelihood of her being the victim of new violence. For some victims, though, a shelter stay may have no impact, while for others it may actually lead to an escalation of violence when they return home (Berk, Newton, & Berk, 1986).

Bowker (1983) interviewed women who had been physically abused and who managed to get their partners to stop being violent. These women utilized a number of different interventions, including talking to friends and relatives, threatening their partners, aggressively defending themselves, going to shelters, calling social service agencies, and calling the police. No single action worked best, and Bowker concluded that, ultimately, the crucial factor was a woman's taking a stand and showing her determination that the violence had to stop.

It is important to point out that most of the services we have in place for victims of IPV are designed for the prototypical case of a heterosexual women abused by a heterosexual man. These are also the services for which there is the greatest amount of evaluation research. We have little in place and little knowledge of the effectiveness of services for other types of victims of IPV.

The prevailing control response to IPV in the United States has produced an escalating number of male batterers who have found their way into the criminal justice system, and then often into court-mandated treatment. The approach most frequently used in programs for batterers is based on the group intervention model (Austin & Dankwort, 1999; Gondolf, 2002). Some of the earliest studies of such programs appeared to demonstrate that group counseling for batterers is effective in reducing subsequent violence (Dutton, 1986; Gondolf, 1987; Pirog-Good & Stets, 1986). However, the quality of these programs is uneven at best, and no particular modality, length, or type of program is more effective than any other in reducing men's violence (Babcock et al., 2004; Holtzworth-Munroe, 2001; Levesque, 1998). Research suggests that batterer treatment programs may be able to increase their effectiveness by tailoring interventions to specific types of batterers (Cavanaugh & Gelles, 2005; Saunders, 2008).

Many states do not allow court-mandated programs to use alternative interventions for IPV, such as couples counseling, individual treatment, family counseling, and group couples counseling, in spite of a lack of empirical support for that stance

(Babcock et al., 2004; Holtzworth-Munroe, 2001). In addition, given the high rate of co-occurrence of spouse abuse and physical child abuse (Appel & Holden, 1998), some researchers suggest that more integrated interventions are needed to address family violence, such as interventions based on a family-level model (Slep & Heyman, 2001).

Interventions for Hidden Forms of Intimate Violence and Abuse

As noted in Chapter 6, violent intimate relations other than parent-to-child and IPV have long been hidden from public attention. Thus, with only rare exceptions, there are no treatment programs for offenders or victims of sibling violence and violence toward parents (with the exception of violence toward the elderly). If these forms of violence are recognized and treated at all, they typically are dealt with through traditional individual and family counseling. If the violence leads to significant injury or death, only then does the criminal justice system become involved.

Mandatory elder-abuse reporting laws exist in the District of Columbia, Puerto Rico, and all states with the exception of South Dakota. The laws vary from state to state, and the results are mixed. Funding and staffing for mandatory adult protective service laws is often quite limited. Adult protective service workers find that elderly victims of violence are extremely reluctant to leave violent and abusive homes. The fear of being institutionalized seems to outweigh the pain and suffering some elderly experience. Thus, adult protective service workers often invest countless hours investigating reports of elder abuse, only to find the victims reluctant to accept any form of treatment.

There is a limited number of self-help groups for victims of elder abuse. Most victims of violence toward parents, irrespective of the parents' age, still seem to be suffering in silence and shame. Violent siblings, unless they maim or kill a brother or sister, are not even recognized as violent, let alone attended to with treatment or intervention.

Conclusion

The nearly five-decade effort to identify, intervene in, and prevent intimate violence and abuse is a qualified success. What was once a private trouble sequestered behind closed doors is now a very public social problem. Policy makers turned from selective inattention and indifference, to consistent efforts to enact legislation and channel appropriate funds to assist victims and control offenders. Varied new services and programs are now in place—some promising, a few proven, and many just innovative.

The results, at least for the forms of intimate violence and abuse that are tracked, are impressive. Both the rates and absolute number of victims of child maltreatment and violence toward women are now substantially lower than the rates and numbers in the mid-1990s. This means that there are hundreds of thousands fewer victims today than just 20 years ago.

I use the term "qualified success" because there are a few caveats about the claim of success of less violent homes and intimate relationships. The most obvious caution is that the basis for claiming success is the trend data collected on self-reported IPV and recognized and reported child maltreatment. There still is not a definitive and uniformly accepted mechanism to measure and track intimate violence and abuse. There is a variety of alternative plausible explanations for the decline in rates of intimate violence and child maltreatment. Perhaps victims are more reluctant to report. Perhaps, because of budgetary cutbacks, child welfare agencies are less able to receive and investigate reports of abuse and neglect. Perhaps the methods of data collection are less accurate.

On the other hand, there are arguments that can counter the plausible rival explanations. The decline in intimate violence and child maltreatment mirrors the decline in homicide and criminal assault since 1994 (Truman & Langton, Bureau of Justice Statistics, 2014; Federal Bureau of Investigation, 2015). Second, the declines are consistent with the forms of intimate violence and abuse that receive the greatest public and policy attention. The pessimists may continue to doubt that the declines are real, but there are good reasons to believe intervention and prevention efforts succeed.

A second qualification is that the greatest declines are in terms of non-fatal intimate violence. Although there is a nearly 50% decline in the number of men murdered by their intimate partners, the number of women killed by male intimates and the number and rate of child fatalities have declined only modestly. Our prevention and intervention efforts seem less robust in terms of preventing fatal assaults.

The third qualification raises an interesting paradox. Assuming we accept the accuracy of the trend data and accept the fact that key types of intimate violence and abuse are declining, the fact remains: We do not really know how to explain the decline. While we have implemented many different interventions and programs, we only have data to support two interventions as evidence-based and evidence-proven—Nurse- Family Partnership, and, under certain circumstances, arrest of domestic violence offenders. Of the hundreds of other efforts, including public awareness campaigns, the best we can say is that they are innovative and perhaps promising.

So, what seems to be working? I use exchange theory in my research on all forms of intimate violence and abuse, and my theory-based explanation is that the combination of public awareness and implementation of both control and compassion interventions has raised the cost of offending and increased the rewards of taking action against abuse. The rather dramatic decrease in female-to-male intimate homicide seems to be a consequence of creating shelters and avenues of support and escape for battered women. Whereas women were forced to use deadly violence to defend their lives in the 1970s and 1980s, the increase in public awareness of IPV and the plethora of programs for battered women means women do not have to remain in harm's way as did Francine Hughes (see Chapter 4).

As public awareness about intimate violence and child maltreatment increased and the certainty of intervention increased, there has been a small but significant change in the culture regarding the acceptance and appropriateness of violence behind closed doors. While we see a payoff in terms of the two most-discussed forms of intimate violence and abuse, it is certainly appropriate to believe that the same approaches would be successful for the forms of intimate violence that still are shrouded in secrecy and responded to with a shrug of indifference.

Discussion Questions

1. How do police expectations about battered women's being prone to drop charges against their abusive husbands create a self-fulfilling prophecy and deny women their proper legal rights of protection?
2. What legal remedies could be enacted to deal with the problems of hidden family violence—elderly abuse, sibling violence, parent abuse, abuse of adolescents?
3. Give an example of how compassion and control could be used to intervene in cases of child abuse, intimate partner violence, and abuse of the elderly.
4. Should the criminal justice system be given more responsibility for child maltreatment cases?

Suggested Assignments

1. Create a resource guide that lists the community services (names, addresses, telephone numbers, websites) of agencies and organizations that deal with various aspects of family violence.

2. Find out what the local laws are about domestic violence and see how they are implemented by observing cases in a courtroom.

Notes

1. 431 U.S. 816 (1977).

2. 455 US 745 (1982).

3. Amendments to the Social Security Act of 1935.

4. In an uncapped, open-ended entitlement program, the state receives a certain level of reimbursement from the federal government for every eligible claim submitted. There is no budgetary cap on the funding. The amount allocated is dependent on the number of eligible children and the reimbursement rate per child.

5. In the 1980s, there was still no official federal effort to collect data on foster care; therefore, the numbers cited in the text and table are from unofficial tabulations.

6. The remaining proportion of the 50,000 children whose plan was not adoption had permanency plans of long-term foster care or emancipation—(reaching the age of a legal adult).

7. See https://www.acf.hhs.gov/sites/default/files/cb/afcarsreport21.pdf

8. Commonly referred to as "Obamacare."

9. A movie, *A Cry for Help*, dramatized this case.

10. *Thurman v. City of Torrington*. UDC No. H-84120, June 25, 1985.

Appendix

Child Welfare Information Gateway

https://www.childwelfare.gov
The Child Welfare Information Gateway is a website of the Children's Bureau of the U.S. Department of Health and Human Services. The Information Gateway is a resource for child welfare professionals, families, and youth. The annual results of the National Child Abuse and Neglect Data System (NCANDS), the Adoption and Foster Care Reporting System (AFCARS), are posted on the website, as are the results of the National Incidence Surveys of reported and recognized child maltreatment. There is also a link that allows users to search state statutes related to child welfare.

BUREAU OF JUSTICE STATISTICS

http://www.bjs.gov
The Bureau of Justice Statistics is a branch of the U.S. Department of Justice. The BJS periodically publishes reports on the extent and trends in intimate partner violence.

National Center for Elder Abuse

http://www.ncea.aoa.gov/
The National Center for Elder Abuse is located within the Administration on Aging, U.S. Department of Health and Human Services. The website provides resources for educators, policy makers, advocates, and researchers.

The Campbell Collaboration

http://www.campbellcollaboration.org/
The Campbell Collaboration conducts and publishes systematic reviews of social interventions. In the field of intimate violence and abuse, the Campbell Collaboration has published systematic reviews of Multisystemic Therapy intensive family-preservation services (http://www.campbellcollaboration.org/lib/project/5/) and advocacy interventions designed to eliminate intimate partner violence (http://www.campbellcollaboration.org/lib/project/84/).

Prevent Child Abuse America

http://www.preventchildabuse.org/
Prevent Child Abuse America is a nationwide advocacy organization with many state chapters. The website contains numerous resources for advocates.

Futures Without Violence

http://www.futureswithoutviolence.org/
Futures Without Violence is a national advocacy organization focusing on violence against women, sexual assault, and teen dating violence. The website includes training, educational, and advocacy resources.

Intimate Partner Violence Against Men

There is a variety of websites focusing on men's rights and men's health that include information and advocacy materials pertaining to male victims of intimate partner violence. Among the websites are:
National Coalition for Men: http://ncfm.org/
National Center for Men: http://www.nationalcenterformen.org/

SCHOLARLY JOURNALS

The following are the leading scholarly journals that publish articles on intimate violence and abuse:

Journal of Interpersonal Violence (Sage Publications)
Journal of Family Violence (Springer)
Violence and Victims (Springer)
Partner Abuse (Springer)
Trauma, Violence, and Abuse (Sage Publications)
Child Abuse and Neglect: The International Journal (Elsevier)
Child Maltreatment (Sage Publications)
Journal of Elder Abuse and Neglect (Taylor & Francis)
Journal of Child Sexual Abuse (Taylor & Francis)
Sexual Abuse: A Journal of Research and Treatment (Sage Publications)

References

Aber, J. L., Allen, J. P., Carlson, V., & Cicchetti, D. (1990). The effects of maltreatment on development during early childhood: Recent studies and their theoretical, clinical, and policy implications. In D. Cicchetti & V. Carlson, Eds., *Child Maltreatment: Theory and Research on Causes and Consequences* (pp. 579–619). New York: Cambridge University Press.

Acierno, R., Hernandez, M. A., Amstadter, A. B., Resnick, H. S., Steve, K., Muzzy, W., & Kilpatrick, D. G. (2010). Prevalence and correlates of emotional, physical, sexual, and financial abuse and potential neglect in the United States: The National Elder Mistreatment Study. *American Journal of Public Health, 100*, 292–297.

Adelson, L. (1972). The battering child. *Journal of the American Medical Association, 222*, 159–161.

Agnew, R., & Huguley, S. (1989). Adolescent violence towards parents. *Journal of Marriage and the Family, 51*, 699–711.

American Association for Protecting Children. (1989). *Highlights of Official Child Neglect and Abuse Reporting, 1987*. Denver, CO: American Humane Association.

Appel, A. E., & Holden, G. W. (1998). The co-occurrence of spouse and physical child abuse: A review and appraisal. *Journal of Family Psychology, 12*, 578.

Aries, P. (1962). *Centuries of Childhood*. New York: Alfred Knopf.

Austin, J. B., & Dankwort, J. (1999). Standards for batterer programs: A review and analysis. *Journal of Interpersonal Violence, 14*, 152–168.

Babcock, J. C., Green, C. E., & Robie, C. (2004). Does batterers' treatment work? A meta-analytic review of domestic violence treatment. *Clinical Psychology Review, 23*, 1023–1053.

Babu, G. R., & Babu, B. V. (2011). Dowry deaths: A neglected public health issue in India. *International Health, 3*(1), 35–43.

Bandura, A. (1973). *Aggression: A Social Learning Analysis*. Englewood Cliffs, NJ: Prentice-Hall.

Barnett, O. W., & LaViolette, A. D. (1993). *It Could Happen to Anyone: Why Battered Women Stay*. Newbury Park, CA: Sage Publications.

Barth, R. P. (1997). Effects of age and race on the odds of adoption versus remaining in long-term out-of-home care. *Child Welfare*, 76, 285–308.

Barth, R. P., Courtney, M., Berrick, J. D., & Albert, V. (1994). *From Child Abuse to Permanency Planning: Child Welfare Services Pathways and Placements*. New York: Aldine De Gruyter.

Barthel, J. (1991). *For Children's Sake: The Promise of Family Preservation*. New York: Edna McConnell Clark Foundation.

Bartholet, E. (2009). Racial disproportionality movement in child welfare: False facts and dangerous directions. *The Arizona Law Review*, 51, 871–932.

Bartholet, E. (2014). Differential Response: A Dangerous Experiment in Child Welfare. Harvard Public Law Working Paper No. 14-31. Available at SSRN: http://ssrn.com/abstract=2477089. (Accessed April 15, 2016).

Basile, K. C., Chen, J., Black, M. C., & Saltzman, L. E. (2007). Prevalence and characteristics of sexual violence victimization among US adults, 2001–2003. *Violence and Victims*, 22, 437–448.

Bassis, M. S., Gelles, R. J., & Levine, A. (1980). *Sociology: An Introduction*. New York; Random House.

Bellamy, C. (Ed.). (2004). *The State of the World's Children 2004*. New York: United Nations Children's Fund.

Belsky, J. (1980). Child maltreatment: An ecological integration. *American Psychologist*, 35, 320–335.

Belsky, J. (1993). Etiology of child maltreatment: A developmental-ecological analysis. *Psychological Bulletin*, 114, 413–434.

Belsky, J., & Vondra, J. (1989). Lessons from child abuse: The determinants of parenting. In D. Cicchetti & C. Carlson, Eds., *Child Maltreatment: Theory and Research on the Causes and Consequences of Child Abuse and Neglect* (pp. 153–202). New York, New York: Cambridge University Press.

Ben-Arieh, A., & Haj-Yahia, M. M. (2006). The "geography" of child maltreatment in Israel: Findings from a national data set of cases reported to the social services. *Child Abuse and Neglect*, 30, 991–1003.

Bender, L. (1959). Children and adolescents who have killed. *American Journal of Psychiatry*, 116, 510–513.

Bennie, E. H., & Sclare, A. B. (1969). The battered child syndrome. *American Journal of Psychiatry*, 125, 975–979.

Berk, R. A., Campbell, A., Klap, R., & Western, B. (1992). The deterrent effect of arrest incidents of domestic violence: A Bayesian analysis of four field experiments. *American Sociological Review*, 57, 698–708.

Berk, R., Newton, P., & Berk, S. F. (1986). What a difference a day makes: An empirical study of the impact of shelters for battered women. *Journal of Marriage and the Family*, 48, 481–490.

Berkowitz, A. D. (2004). Working with men to prevent violence against women: An overview. http://www.alanberkowitz.com/articles/VAWNET.pdf. (Accessed April 15, 2016).

Berkowitz, L. (1993). *Aggression: Its Causes, Consequences, and Control*. New York: McGraw-Hill Book Company.

Bevan, C. S., Bosnick, A. J., & Mainwaring, D. S. (1996). *Foster Care: Too Much, Too Little, Too Early, Too Late: Final Report: Child Protection, Old Problem, New Paradigm*. Washington, DC: National Council for Adoption.

Bishop, S. J., & Leadbeater, B. J. (1999). Maternal social support patterns and child maltreatment: Comparison of maltreating and non-maltreating mothers. *American Journal of Orthopsychiatry*, 69, 172–181.

Black, D. A., Heyman, R. E., & Slep, A. M. S. (2001). Risk factors for child physical abuse. *Aggression and Violent Behavior*, 6, 121–188.

Black, M. C. (2011). Intimate partner violence and adverse health consequences: Implications for clinicians. *American Journal of Lifestyle Medicine*, 5, 428–439.

Black, M. C., Basile, K. C., Breiding, M. J., Smith, S. G., Walters, M. L., Merrick, M. T., et al. (2011). The National Intimate Partner and Sexual Violence Survey (NISVS): 2010 Summary Report. Atlanta, GA: National Center for Injury Prevention and Control, Centers for Disease Control and Prevention.

Blumberg, M. (1964). When parents hit out. *Twentieth Century*, 173, 39–44.

Bonnie, R. J., & Wallace, R. B., Eds. (2002). *Elder Mistreatment: Abuse, Neglect, and Exploitation in an Aging America*. Washington, DC: National Academy Press.

Bowker, L. H. (1983). *Beating Wife-Beating*. Lexington, MA: Lexington Books.

Bowker, L. H. (1993). A battered woman's problems are social, not psychological. In R. J. Gelles & D. Loseke, Eds., *Current Controversies on Family Violence* (pp. 154–165). Newbury Park, CA: Sage Publications.

Bowlby, J. (1973). *Attachment and Loss; Vol. II: Separation*. New York: Basic Books.

Bowlby, J. (1988). *A Secure Base: Parent-Child Attachment and Healthy Human Development*. New York: Basic Books.

Bronfembrenner, U. (1958). Socialization and social class through time and space. In. E. C. Maccoby, T. M. Newcomb, & E. L. Hartley, Eds., *Readings in Social Psychology* (3rd ed., pp. 400–425). New York: Holt, Reinhart, and Winston.

Brown, J., Cohen, P., Johnson, J. G., & Smailes, E. M. (1999). Childhood abuse and neglect: Specificity of effects on adolescent and young adult depression and suicidality. *Journal of the American Academy of Child and Adolescent Psychiatry*, 38, 1490–1496.

Burgdorf, K. (1980). *Recognition and Reporting of Child Maltreatment*. Rockville, MD: Westat.

Burgess, A. W., & Crowell, N. A., Eds. (1996). *Understanding Violence Against Women*. Washington, DC: National Academies Press.

Burgess, R. L. (1979). Family violence: Some implications from evolutionary biology. Paper presented at the *annual meetings of the American Society of Criminology, Philadelphia*.

Burgess, R. L., & Garbarino, J. (1983). Doing what comes naturally? An evolutionary perspective on child abuse. In D. Finkelhor, R. Gelles, M. Straus, & G. Hotaling, Eds., *The Dark Side of the Families: Current Family Violence Research* (pp. 88–101). Beverly Hills, CA.: Sage Publications.

Caetano, R., Ramisetty-Mikler, S., & Field, C. A. (2005). Unidirectional and bidirectional intimate partner violence among white, black, and Hispanic couples in the United States. *Violence and Victims*, 20(4), 393–406.

Caetano, R., Schafer, J., & Cunradi, C. B. (2001). Alcohol-related intimate partner violence among white, black, and Hispanic couples in the United States. *Alcohol Research and Health*, 25, 58–65.

Caetano, R., Vaeth, P. A. C., & Ranisetty-Mikler, S. (2008). Intimate partner violence victim and perpetrator characteristics among couples in the United States. *Journal of Family Violence*, 23, 507–518.

Caffey, J. (1946). Multiple fractures in the long bones of infants suffering from chronic subdural hematoma. *American Journal of Roentgenology, Radium Therapy, and Nuclear Medicine*, 58, 163–173.

Campbell, J. C. (1992). "If I can't have you, no one can": Issues of power and control in domestic homicide. In J. Radford & D. Russell, Eds., *Femicide: The Politics of Woman Killing* (pp. 99–113). New York: Twayne.

Campbell, J. C. (2002). Health consequences of intimate partner violence. *The Lancet*, 359, 1331–1336.

Capaldi, D. M., & Stoolmiller, M. (1999). Co-occurrence of conduct problems and depressive symptoms in early adolescent boys: III. Prediction to young-adult adjustment. *Development and Psychopathology*, 11, 59–84.

Capaldi, D. M., Knoble, N. B., Shortt, J. W., & Kim, H. K. (2012). A systematic review of risk factors for intimate partner violence. *Partner Abuse*, 3, 231–280.

Catalano, S. M. (2012). *Intimate Partner Violence, 1993–2010.* Washington, DC: US Department of Justice, Office of Justice Programs, Bureau of Justice Statistics.

Catalano, S. M. (2013). *Intimate Partner Violence: Attributes of Victimization, 1993–2011.* Washington, DC: US Bureau of Justice Statistics (NCJ243300).

Cavanaugh, M. M., & Gelles, R. J. (2005). The utility of male domestic violence offender typologies: New directions for research, policy, and practice. *Journal of Interpersonal Violence*, 20, 155–166.

Centers for Disease Control and Prevention. (2006). Physical dating violence among high school students—United States, 2003. *MMWR: Morbidity and Mortality Weekly Report*, 55, 532–535.

Centers for Disease Control and Prevention. (2003). Costs of intimate partner violence against women in the United States. Available at http://www.cdc.gov/violenceprevention/pub/ipv_cost.html (retrieved May 20, 2015).

Centers for Disease Control and Prevention. (2014). Intimate partner violence: Risk and protective factors. Available at http://www.cdc.gov/violenceprevention/intimatepartnerviolence/riskprotectivefactors.html (retrieved May 20, 2015).

Chaffin, M., Kelleher, K., & Hollenberg, J. (1996). Onset of physical abuse and neglect: Psychiatric, substance abuse, and social risk factors from prospective community data. *Child Abuse and Neglect*, 20, 191–203.

Child Trends, C. (2002). *Charting Parenthood: A Statistical Portrait of Fathers and Mothers in America.* Washington, DC: Child Trends.

Child Trends. (2013). Attitudes towards spanking. Retrieved May 15, 2015.

Child Welfare League of America. (1999). *Child Abuse and Neglect: A Look at the States: 1999 CWLA Stat Book.* Washington, DC: CWLA Press.

Coker, A. L., Smith, P. H., Thompson, M. P., McKeown, R. E., Bethea, L., & Davis, K. E. (2002). Social support protects against the negative effects of partner violence on mental health. *Journal of Women's Health and Gender-Based Medicine*, 11, 465–476.

Colello, K. (2014). The Elder Justice Act: Background issues for Congress. Washington DC: Congressional Research Services (September 3). Retrieved May 21, 2015.

Conklin, J. E., & Jacobson, J. (2003). Why crime rates fell. *Crime and Justice International*, 19, 17–20.

Connelly, C. D., & Straus, M. A. (1992). Mother's age and risk for physical abuse. *Child Abuse and Neglect*, 16, 709–718.

Coohey, C., & Braun, N. (1997). Toward an integrated framework for understanding child physical abuse. *Child Abuse and Neglect*, 21, 1081–1094.

Cook, R. (1991). *A National Evaluation of Title IV-E Independent Living Programs for Youth*. Rockville, MD: Westat.

Cooper, A., & Smith, E. L. (2011). Homicide trends in the United States, 1980–2008. *Bureau of Justice Statistics (BJS). Department of Justice. Reports and Trends* (p. 36). Washington, DC: Bureau of Justice Statistics.

Cornell, C. P., & Gelles, R. J. (1982). Adolescent to parent violence. *Urban Social Change Review*, 15, 8–14.

Cottrell, B., & Monk, P. (2004). Adolescent-to-parent abuse: A qualitative overview of common themes. *Journal of Family Issues*, 25, 1072–1095.

Coulton, C. J., Crampton, D. S., Irwin, M., Spilsbury, J. C., & Korbin, J. E. (2007). How neighborhoods influence child maltreatment: A review of the literature and alternative pathways. *Child Abuse and Neglect*, 31, 1117–1142.

Counts, D., Brown, J., & Campbell, J. C. (1992). *Sanctions and Sanctuary: Cultural Perspectives on the Beating of Wives*. Boulder, CO: Westview Press.

Dahlberg, L. L., & Krug, E. G. (2002). Violence—a global public health problem. In E. G. Krug, L. L. Dahlberg, J. A. Mercy, A. B. Zwi, & R. Lozano, Eds., *World Report on Violence and Health* (pp. 1–21). Geneva: World Health Organization [WHO].

Daly, M., & Wilson, M. (1980). Discriminative parental solicitude: A biosocial perspective. *Journal of Marriage and the Family*, 42, 277–288.

Daro, D. (1995). *Public Opinion and Behaviors Regarding Child Abuse Prevention: The Results of NCPCA's 1995 Public Opinion Poll*. Chicago: National Committee to Prevent Child Abuse.

Daro, D., & Gelles, R. (1992). Public attitudes and behaviors with respect to child abuse prevention. *Journal of Interpersonal Violence*, 7, 517–531.

Davidson, H. (1997). The courts and child maltreatment. In M. Helfer, R. Kempe, & R. Krugman, Eds., *The Battered Child* (5th ed., pp. 482–499). Chicago: University of Chicago Press.

DeKeseredy, W. S., & Ellis, D. (1997). Sibling violence: A review of Canadian sociological research and suggestions for further empirical work. *Humanity and Society*, 21, 397–411.

DePanfilis, D. (1996). Social isolation of neglectful families: A review of social support assessment and intervention models. *Child Maltreatment*, 1, 37–52.

Dichter, M. E., & Gelles, R. J. (2012). Women's perceptions of safety and risk following police intervention for intimate partner violence. *Violence Against Women*, 18, 44–63.

Dobash, R. E., & Dobash, R. (1979). *Violence Against Wives*. New York: Free Press.

Dobash, R. E., & Dobash, R. P., Eds. (1998). *Rethinking Violence Against Women* (Vol. 9). Thousand Oaks, CA: Sage Publications.

Dodge, K. A., Bates, J. E., & Pettit, G. S. (1990). Mechanisms in the cycle of violence. *Science*, 250, 1678–1683.

Doek, J. E. (1991). Management of child abuse and neglect at the international level: Trends and perspectives. *Child Abuse and Neglect: The International Journal*, 15, 51–56.

Dubowitz, H. (2007). Understanding and addressing the "neglect of neglect": Digging into the molehill. *Child Abuse and Neglect*, 31, 603–606.

Dubowitz, H., Kim, J., Black, M. M., Weisbart, C., Semiatin, J., & Magder, L. S. (2011). Identifying children at high risk for a child maltreatment report. *Child Abuse and Neglect*, 35, 96–104.

Dunford, F. W., Huizinga, D., & Elliott, D. (1990). The role of arrest in domestic assault: The Omaha Police Experiment. *Criminology*, 28, 183–206.

Durose, M. R., Harlow, C. W., Langan, P. A., Motivans, M., Rantala, R. R., & Smith, E. L. (2005). Family violence statistics: Including statistics on strangers and acquaintances. NCJ 207846. Department of Justice, Office of Justice Programs, Bureau of Justice Statistics. Retrieved May 20, 2015.

Dutton, D. G. (1986). The outcome of court-mandated treatment for wife assault: A quasi-experimental evaluation. *Violence and Victims*, 1, 163–175.

Dutton, D. G., & Golant, S. K. (1995). *The Batterer: A Psychological Profile*. New York: Basic Books.

Dutton, D. G., & Starzomski, A. J. (1993). Borderline personality in perpetrators of psychological and physical violence. *Violence and Victims*, 8, 327–337.

Dutton, M. A., & Goodman, L. A. (2005). Coercion in intimate partner violence: Toward a new conceptualization. *Sex Roles*, 52, 743–756.

Eckenrode, J., Campa, M., Luckey, D. W., Henderson, C. R., Cole, R., Kitzman, H., et al. (2010). Long-term effects of prenatal and infancy nurse home visitation on the life course of youths: 19-year follow-up of a randomized trial. *Archives of Pediatrics and Adolescent Medicine*, 164, 9–15.

Eckenrode, J., Zielinski, D., Smith, E., Marcynyszyn, L. A., Henderson, J., Charles, R., et al. (2001). Child maltreatment and the early onset of problem behaviors: Can a program of nurse home visitation break the link? *Development and Psychopathology*, 13, 873–890.

Edleson, J. L. (1999). The overlap between child maltreatment and woman battering. *Violence Against Women*, 5, 134–154.

Edleson, J. L., & Graham-Bermann, S. A., Eds. (2001). *Domestic Violence in the Lives of Children: The Future of Research, Intervention, and Social Policy*. Washington, DC: American Psychological Association.

Egeland, B., & Sroufe, L. A. (1981). Attachment and early child maltreatment. *Child Development*, 52, 44–52.

Egeland, B., Jacobvitz, D., & Sroufe, L. A. (1988). Breaking the cycle of abuse. *Child Development*, 59, 1080–1088.

Elmer, E. (1967). *Children in Jeopardy: A Study of Abused Minors and Their Families*. Pittsburgh: University of Pittsburgh Press.

Eriksen, S., & Jensen, V. (2006). All in the family? Family environment factors in sibling violence. *Journal of Family Violence*, 21, 497–507.

Eriksen, S., & Jensen, V. (2008). A push or a punch: Distinguishing the severity of sibling violence. *Journal of Interpersonal Violence*, 24, 183–208.

Erlanger, H. (1974). Social class and corporal punishment in childrearing: A reassessment. *American Sociological Review*, 39, 68–85.

Family Violence Prevention Fund. (1995). Poll finds rising concern about abuse. *Speaking Up*, 1, 1ff.

Fanshel, D. (1972). *Far from the Reservation: The Transracial Adoption of American Indian Children*. Metuchen, NJ: The Scarecrow Press.

Fanshel, D., & Shinn, E. B. (1978). *Children in Foster Care: a Longitudinal Investigation*. New York: Columbia University Press.

Federal Bureau of Investigation (2015). *Crime in the United States 2013*. Available at http://www.fbi.gov/about-us/cjis/ucr/crime-in-the-u.s/2013/crime-in-the-u.s.-2013. Retrieved May 25, 2015.

Feld, S. L., & Straus, M. A. (1989). Escalation and desistance of violence in marriage. *Criminology, 27*, 141–161.

Figgie, H. E. (1980). *The Figgie Report on Fear of Crime. America Afraid*. Willoughby, OH: Research & Forecasts.

Finkelhor, D. (1979). *Sexually Victimized Children*. New York: Simon & Schuster.

Finkelhor, D. (1980). Sex among siblings: A survey on prevalence, variety, and effects. *Archives of Sexual Behavior, 9*, 171–194.

Finkelhor, D. (1984). *Child Sexual Abuse: New Theory and Research*. New York: Free Press.

Finkelhor, D., & Dziuba-Leatherman, J. (1994). Children as victims of violence: A national survey. *Pediatrics, 94*, 413–420.

Finkelhor, D., & Jones, L. M. (2010). *Updated Trends in Child Maltreatment, 2007*. Durham, NH: Crimes Against Children Research Center.

Finkelhor, D., & Jones, L. M. (2012). *Have Sexual Abuse and Physical Abuse Declined Since the 1990s?* Crimes Against Children Research Center.

Finkelhor, D., & Korbin, J. (1988). Child abuse as an international issue. *Child Abuse and Neglect: The International Journal, 12*, 3–23.

Finkelhor, D., Moore, D., Hamby, S. L., & Straus, M. A. (1997). Sexually abused children in a national survey of parents: Methodological issues. *Child Abuse and Neglect, 21*, 1–9.

Finkelhor, D., Ormrod, R., Turner, H., & Hamby, S. L. (2005). The victimization of children and youth: A comprehensive, national survey. *Child Maltreatment, 10*, 5–25.

Finkelhor, D., Turner, H., & Ormrod, R. (2006). Kid's stuff: The nature and impact of peer and sibling violence on younger and older children. *Child Abuse and Neglect, 30*, 1401–1421.

Flanzer, J. P. (2004). Alcohol and other drugs are key causal agents of violence. In D. Loseke, R. J. Gelles, & M. C. Cavanaugh, Eds., *Current Controversies on Family Violence* (2nd ed., pp. 153–174). Thousand Oaks, CA: Sage Publications.

Forsythe, P. (1992). Homebuilders and family preservation. *Children and Youth Services Review, 14*, 37–47.

Fox, J. A. (2012). Intimate partner violence: Down but far from out. Available at http://www.corrections.com/news/article/32051-intimate-partner-violence-down-but-far-from-out. Retrieved October 9, 2015.

Freisthler, B., Gruenewald, P. J., Remer, L. G., Lery, B., & Needell, B. (2007). Exploring the spatial dynamics of alcohol outlets and child protective services referrals, substantiations, and foster care entries. *Child Maltreatment, 12*, 114–124.

Friederich, W. N., & Boriskin, J. A. (1976). The role of the child in abuse: A review of literature. *American Journal of Orthopsychiatry, 46*, 580–590.

Galdston, R. (1965). Observations on children who have been physically abused and their parents. *The American Journal of Psychiatry, 122*, 440–443.

Gallup Organization. (1995). *Disciplining Children in America: A Gallop Poll Report Survey (#765)*. Princeton, NJ: Gallup.

Garbarino, J. (1977). The human ecology of child maltreatment. *Journal of Marriage and the Family, 39*, 721–735.

García-Moreno, C., Jansen, H. A. F. M., Ellsberg, M., Heise, L., & Watts, C. (2005). *WHO Multi-Country Study on Women's Health and Domestic Violence Against Women*. Geneva: World Health Organization.

Gelles, R. J. (1973). Child abuse as psychopathology: A sociological critique and reformulation. *American Journal of Orthopsychiatry*, 43, 611–621.

Gelles, R. J. (1974). *The Violent Home*. Newbury Park, CA: Sage Publications.

Gelles, R. J. (1976). Abused wives: Why do they stay? *Journal of Marriage and the Family*, 38, 659–668.

Gelles, R. J. (1983). An exchange/social control theory. In D. Finkelhor, R. J. Gelles, G. T. Hotaling, & M. Straus, Eds., *The Dark Side of Families: Current Family Violence Research* (pp. 151–165). Thousand Oaks, CA: Sage Publications.

Gelles, R. J. (1987). The family and its role in the abuse of children. *Psychiatric Annals*, 17, 229–232.

Gelles, R. (1993). Through a sociological lens: Social structure and family violence. In D. Loseke & R. J. Gelles, Eds., *Current Controversies on Family Violence* (pp. 31–56). Thousand Oaks, CA: Sage Publications.

Gelles, R. J. (1996). *The Book of David: How Preserving Families Can Cost Children's Lives*. New York: Basic Books.

Gelles, R. J. (2000). Estimating the incidence and prevalence of violence against women: National data systems and sources. *Violence Against Women*, 6(7), 784–804.

Gelles, R. J. (2011). *The Third Lie: Why Government Programs Don't Work—and a Blueprint for Change*. Walnut Creek, CA: Left Coast Press.

Gelles, R. J., & Brigham, R. (2011). Child protection considerations in the United States. In M. Lamb, D. J. LaRooy, & L. C. Malloy, Eds., *Children's Testimony: A Handbook of Psychological Research and Forensic Practice* (2nd ed., pp. 403–421). New York: Wiley.

Gelles, R. J., & Cavanaugh, M. M. (2005). Association is not causation: Alcohol and other drugs do not cause violence. In. D. Loseke, R. J. Gelles, & M. C. Cavanaugh, Eds., *Current Controversies on Family Violence* (2nd ed., pp. 175–189). Thousand Oaks, CA: Sage Publications.

Gelles, R. J., & Cornell, C., Eds. (1983). *International Perspectives on Family Violence*. Lexington, Mass: Lexington Books.

Gelles, R. J., & Harrop, J. W. (1989). Violence, battering, and psychological distress among women. *Journal of Interpersonal Violence*, 4, 400–420.

Gelles, R. J., & Harrop, J. W. (1991). The risk of abusive violence among children with non-biological parents. *Family Relations*, 40, 78–83.

Gelles, R. J., & Perlman, S. (2012). *Estimated Annual Cost of Child Abuse and Neglect*. Chicago, IL: Prevent Child Abuse America.

Gelles, R. J., & Straus, M. A. (1979). Determinants of violence in the family: Toward a theoretical integration. In W. R. Burr, R. Hill, F. I. Nye, & I. L. Reiss, Eds., *Contemporary Theories About the Family* (Vol. 1, pp. 549–581). New York: Free Press.

Gelles, R. J., & Straus, M. A. (1987). Is violence towards children increasing? A comparison of 1975 and 1985 national survey rates. *Journal of Interpersonal Violence*, 2, 212–222.

Gelles, R. J., & Straus, M. A. (1988). *Intimate Violence*. New York: Simon and Schuster.

Gil, D. (1970). *Violence Against Children: Physical Child Abuse in the United States*. Cambridge, MA: Harvard University Press.

Gilligan, J. (1992). *Violence: Our Deadly Epidemic and Its Causes*. New York: Putnam.

Giovannoni, J. M., & Becerra, R. M. (1979). *Defining Child Abuse*. New York: Free Press.

Gondolf, E. W. (1987). Changing men who batter: A developmental model for integrated interventions. *Journal of Family Violence*, 2, 335–349.

Gondolf, E. W. (1988). Who are those guys? Toward a behavioral typology of batterers. *Violence and Victims*, 3, 187–203.

Gondolf, E. W. (2002). *Batterer Intervention Systems: Issues, Outcomes, and Recommendations.* Thousand Oaks: Sage Publications.

Goode, W. (1971). Force and violence in the family. *Journal of Marriage and the Family, 33,* 624–636.

Gottman, J. M., Jacobson, N. S., Rushe, R. H., & Shortt, J. W. (1995). The relationship between heart rate reactivity, emotionally aggressive behavior, and general violence in batterers. *Journal of Family Psychology, 9,* 227–248.

Govindshenoy, M., & Spencer, N. (2007). Abuse of the disabled child: A systematic review of population-based studies. *Child: Care, Health and Development, 33,* 552–558.

Gracia, E., & Musitu, G. (2003). Social isolation from communities and child maltreatment: A cross-cultural comparison. *Child Abuse and Neglect, 27,* 153–168.

Greven, P. (1990). *Spare the Child: The Religious Roots of Punishment and the Psychological Impact of Physical Abuse.* New York: Alfred Knopf.

Hamberger, L. K., & Hastings, J. E. (1986). Personality correlates of men who abuse their partners: A cross-validation study. *Journal of Family Violence, 1,* 232–346.

Hamberger, L. K., & Hastings, J. E. (1991). Personality correlates of men who batter and non-violent men. Some continuities and discontinuities. *Journal of Family Violence, 6,* 131–147.

Hamberger, L. K., Lohr, J. M., Bonge, D., & Tolin, D. F. (1996). A large sample empirical typology of male spouse abusers and its relationship to dimensions of abuse. *Violence and Victims, 11,* 277–292.

Hampton, R. L., & Newberger, E. H. (1985). Child abuse incidence and reporting by hospitals: The significance of severity, class, and race. *American Journal of Public Health, 75,* 56–60.

Harris Poll. (2013). Four out of five Americans believe spanking their children is sometimes appropriate. (September 26, 2013). Retrieved May 15, 2015.

Hart, S. D., Dutton, D. G., & Newlove, T. (1993). The prevalence of personality disorder among wife assaulters. *Journal of Personality Disorders, 7,* 328–340.

Hastings, J. E., & Hamberger, L. K. (1988). Personality characteristics of spouse abusers: A controlled study. *Violence and Victims, 3,* 31–48.

Hines, D. A., & Douglas, E. M. (2009). Women's use of intimate partner violence against men: Prevalence, implications, and consequences. *Journal of Aggression, Maltreatment and Trauma, 18,* 572–586.

Holtzworth-Munroe, A. (2001). Standards for batterer treatment programs: How can research inform our decisions? *Journal of Aggression, Maltreatment and Trauma, 5,* 165–180.

Holtzworth-Munroe, A., & Stuart, G. L. (1994). Typologies of male batterers: Three subtypes and the differences among them. *Psychological Bulletin, 116,* 476–497.

Homans, G. C. (1967). Fundamental social processes. In N. J. Smelser, Ed., *Sociology* (pp. 549–593). New York: Wiley.

Hrdy, S. B. (1979). Infanticide among animals: A review of classification, and examination of implications for reproductive strategies for females. *Ethology and Sociobiology, 1,* 13–40.

Johnson, M. P. (1995). Patriarchal terrorism and common couple violence: Two forms of violence against women. *Journal of Marriage and the Family, 57,* 283–294.

Johnson, M. P., & Ferraro, K. J. (2000). Research on domestic violence in the 1990s: Making distinctions. *Journal of Marriage and Family, 62*(4), 948–963.

Jonson-Reid, M., & Barth, R. P. (2000). From placement to prison: The path to adolescent incarceration from child welfare supervised foster or group care. *Children and Youth Services Review, 22*, 493–516.

Kaufman, J., & Zigler, E. (1987). Do abused children become abusive parents? *American Journal of Orthopsychiatry, 57*, 186–192.

Kaukinen, C. (2014). Dating violence among college students: The risk and protective factors. *Trauma, Violence, and Abuse, 15*, 283–296.

Kempe, C. H., Silverman, F. N., Steele, B. F., Droegemueller, W., & Silver, H. K. (1962). The battered child syndrome. *Journal of the American Medical Association, 181*, 107–112.

Kendall-Tackett, K. A., Williams, L., & Finkelhor, D. (1993). The impact of sexual abuse on children: A view and synthesis of recent empirical literature. *Psychological Bulletin, 113*, 164–180.

Kerman, B., Wildfire, J., & Barth, R. P. (2002). Outcomes for young adults who experienced foster care. *Children and Youth Services Review, 24*, 319–344.

King, P. A., & Chalk, R., Eds. (1998). *Violence in Families: Assessing Prevention and Treatment Programs*. Washington, DC: National Academies Press.

Kitzman, H. J., Olds, D. L., Cole, R. E., Hanks, C. A., Anson, E. A., Arcoleo, K. J., et al. (2010). Enduring effects of prenatal and infancy home visiting by nurses on children: Follow-up of a randomized trial among children at age 12 years. *Archives of Pediatrics and Adolescent Medicine, 164*, 412–418.

Klerman, L. V. (1993). The relationship between adolescent parenthood and inadequate parenting. *Children and Youth Services Review, 15*, 309–320.

Knickerbocker, L., Heyman, R. E., Smith Slep, A. M., Jouriles, E. N., & McDonald, R. (2007). Co-occurrence of child and partner maltreatment. *European Psychologist, 12*, 36–44.

Korbin, J., Ed. (1981). *Child Abuse and Neglect: Cross-Cultural Perspectives*. Berkeley, CA: University of California Press.

Koss, M. P., Gidycz, C. A., & Wisniewski, N. (1987). The scope of rape: Incidence and prevalence of sexual aggression and victimization in a national sample of higher education students. *Journal of Consulting and Clinical Psychology, 55*, 162–170.

Kosten, T. R., & Singha, A. K. (1999). Stimulants. *Textbook of Substance Abuse Treatment, 2*, 183–193.

Kotch, J. B., Browne, D. C., Dufort, V., Winsor, J., & Catellier, D. (1999). Predicting child maltreatment in the first 4 years of life from characteristics assessed in the neonatal period. *Child Abuse and Neglect, 23*, 305–319.

Krebs, C. P., Lindquist, C. H., Warner, T. D., Fisher, B. S., & Martin, S. L. (2007). *The Campus Sexual Assault (CSA) Study*. Washington, DC: National Institute of Justice, US Department of Justice.

Krienert, J. L., & Walsh, J. A. (2011). My brother's keeper: A contemporary examination of reported sibling violence using national level data, 2000–2005. *Journal of Family Violence, 26*, 331–342.

Kurz, D. (1993). Physical assaults by husbands: A major social problem. In R. J. Gelles & D. Loseke, Eds., *Current Controversies on Family Violence* (pp. 88–103). Thousand Oaks, CA: Sage Publications.

Lachs, M. S., Williams, C. S., O'Brien, S., Pillemer, K. A., & Charlson, M. E. (1998). The mortality of elder mistreatment. *Journal of the American Medical Association, 280*, 428–432.

Langhinrichsen-Rohling, J. (2010). Controversies involving gender and intimate partner violence in the United States. *Sex Roles, 62*, 179–193.

Langhinrichsen-Rohling, J., Misra, T. A., Selwyn, C., Robling, M. L. (2012). Rates of bidirectional versus unidirectional intimate partner violence across samples, sexual orientations and race/ethnicities: A comprehensive review. *Partner Abuse, 3*, 199–230.

Lardner, G. (1995). *The Stalking of Kristen: A Father Investigates the Murder of His Daughter.* New York: The Atlantic Monthly Press.

Laumann, E. O., Leitsch, S. A., & Waite, L. J. (2008). Elder mistreatment in the United States: Prevalence estimates from a nationally representative study. *The Journals of Gerontology Series B: Psychological Sciences and Social Sciences, 63*, S248–S254.

Letellier, P. (1994). Gay and lesbian male domestic violence victimization: Challenges to feminist theory and responses to violence. *Violence and Victims, 9*, 95–106.

Leventhal, J. M., & Gaither, J. R. (2012). Incidence of serious injuries due to physical abuse in the United States: 1997 to 2009. *Pediatrics, 130*, 847–852.

Levesque, D. A. (1998). Violence desistance among battering men: Existing interventions and the application of the transtheoretical model of change. Unpublished doctoral dissertation, Kingston, RI: University of Rhode Island.

Lindsey, D. (1994). *The Welfare of Children.* New York: Oxford University Press.

Lockhart, L. L., White, B. W., Causby, V., & Isaac, A. (1994). Letting out the secret: Violence in lesbian relationships. *Journal of Interpersonal Violence, 9*, 469–492.

Loseke, D. R., & Kurz, D. (2005). Men's violence toward women is the serious social problem. In. D. Loseke, R. J. Gelles, & M. C. Cavanaugh, Eds., *Current Controversies on Family Violence* (2nd ed., pp. 79–96). Thousand Oaks, CA: Sage Publications.

Lourie, I. (1977). The phenomenon of the abused adolescent: A clinical study. *Victimology, 2*, 268–276.

MacAndrew, C, & Edgerton, R. B. (1969). *Drunken Comportment: A Social Explanation.* Chicago: Aldine.

MacMillan, H. L., Tanaka, M., Duku, E., Vaillancourt, T., & Boyle, M. H. (2013). Child physical and sexual abuse in a community sample of young adults: Results from the Ontario Child Health Study. *Child Abuse and Neglect: The International Journal, 37*, 14–21.

Maier, S. F., & Seligman, M. E. (1976). Learned helplessness: Theory and evidence. *Journal of Experimental Psychology: General, 105*, 3–46.

Maximus Inc. (1984). *Child Welfare Statistical Factbook: 1984: Substitute Care and Adoption.* Washington, DC: Office of Human Development Services.

McNulty, F. (1980). *The Burning Bed: The True Story of Francine Hughes—A Beaten Wife Who Rebelled.* New York: Harcourt Brace Jovanovich.

Miller, K. M., Cahn, K., & Orellana, E. R. (2012). Dynamics that contribute to racial disproportionality and disparity: Perspectives from child welfare professionals, community partners, and families. *Children and Youth Services Review, 35*, 2201–2207.

Mills, C. W. (1959). *The Sociological Imagination.* New York: Oxford University Press.

Mulligan, M. (1977). An investigation of factors associated with violent modes of conflict resolution in the family. M. A. thesis. Kingston, RI: University of Rhode Island.

Myers, J. (2006). *Child Protection in America: Past, Present, And Future.* New York: Oxford University Press.

National Association of Black Social Workers. (1974). Position statement on transracial adoption. September 1972. In R. Bremner, Ed., *Children and Youth in*

America: A Documentary History (Vol. III, pp. 777–780). Cambridge, MA: Harvard University Press.

National Center for Injury Prevention and Control. (2003). *Costs of Intimate Partner Violence Against Women in the United States*. Atlanta, GA: Centers for Disease Control and Prevention.

National Center of Child Abuse and Neglect. (1988). *Study Findings: Study of National Incidence and Prevalence of Child Abuse and Neglect: 1988*. Washington, DC: U.S. Department of Health and Human Services.

National Center of Child Abuse and Neglect. (1996). *Study Findings: Study of National Incidence and Prevalence of Child Abuse and Neglect: 1993*. Washington, DC: U.S. Department of Health and Human Services.

National Research Council. (1993). *Understanding Child Abuse and Neglect*. Washington, DC: National Academy Press.

Nelson, B. J. (1984). *Making an Issue of Child Abuse: Political Agenda Setting for Social Problems*. Chicago: University Chicago Press.

Newberger, E., Reed, R., Daniel, J. H., Hyde, J., & Kotelchuck, M. (1977). Pediatrics social illness: Toward an etiologic classification. *Pediatrics, 60*, 178–185.

O' Neill, K., & Gesiriech, S. (2005). *A Brief Legislative History of the Child Welfare System*. Philadelphia, PA: Pew Commission on Children in Foster Care. Working paper.

O'Farrell, T. J., Hutton, V. V., & Murphy, C. M. (1999). Domestic violence before and after alcoholism treatment: A two-year longitudinal study. *Journal of Studies on Alcohol and Drugs, 60*, 317–321.

O'Leary, K. D. (1999). Psychological abuse: A variable deserving critical attention in domestic violence. *Violence and Victims, 14*, 3–23.

Oh, J., Kim, H. S., Martins, D., & Kim, H. (2006). A study of elder abuse in Korea. *International Journal of Nursing Studies, 43*, 203–214.

Olds, D. L. (2006). The nurse–family partnership: An evidence-based preventive intervention. *Infant Mental Health Journal, 27*, 5–25.

Oudekerk, B., Blachman-Demner, D., & Mulford, C. (2014). *Teen Dating Violence: How Peers Can Affect Risk and Protective Factors. National Institute of Justice Research In Brief*. Washington, DC: U.S. Department of Justice, Office of Justice Programs.

Pagelow, M. (1981). *Woman-Battering: Victims and Their experiences*. Newbury Park, CA: Sage.

Pagelow, M. (1984). *Family Violence*. New York: Praeger.

Parent, M. (1996). *Turning Stones: My Days and Nights with Children at Risk*. New York: Harcourt.

Parke, R. D., & Collmer, C. W. (1975). Child abuse: An interdisciplinary analysis. In M. Hetherington, Ed., *Review of Child Development Research* (Vol. 5, pp. 1–102). Chicago: University of Chicago Press.

Parrish, J. W., Young, M. B., Perham-Hester, K. A., & Gessner, B. D. (2011). Identifying risk factors for child maltreatment in Alaska: A population-based approach. *American Journal of Preventive Medicine, 40*, 666–673.

Pate, A. M., & Hamilton, E. E. (1992). Formal and informal social deterrents to domestic violence: The Dade County Spouse Assault Experiment. *American Sociological Review, 57*, 691–697.

Pecora, P. J., Whittaker, J. K., Maluccio, A. N., & Barth, R. P. (2000). *The Child Welfare Challenge: Policy, Practice, and Research*. New York: Aldine De Gruyter.

Pennell, J., & Burford, G. (2000). Family group decision making: Protecting children and women. *Child Welfare, 79,* 131–158.

Petersen, A., Joseph, J., & Feit, M., Eds. (2014). *New Directions in Child Abuse and Neglect Research.* Washington, DC: National Academies Press.

Pierotti, R. S. (2013). Increasing rejection of intimate partner violence evidence of global cultural diffusion. *American Sociological Review, 78,* 240–265.

Pillemer, K. (2005). Elder abuse is caused by the deviance and dependence of abusive caregivers. In. D. Loseke, R. J. Gelles, & M. C. Cavanaugh, Eds., *Current Controversies on Family Violence* (2nd ed., pp. 207–220). Thousand Oaks, CA: Sage Publications.

Pillemer, K., Suitor, J. J., Mock, S. E., Sabir, M., Pardo, T., Sechrist, J. (2007). Capturing the complexity of intergenerational relations: Exploring ambivalence within later-life families. *Journal of Social Issues, 63:* 775–791.

Pirog-Good, M. A., & J. Stets (1986). Programs for abusers: Who drops out and what can be done. *Response, 9,* 17–19.

Pizzey, E. (1974). *Scream Quietly or the Neighbors Will Hear.* Harmondsworth, Great Britain: Penguin.

Pleck, E. (1987). *Domestic Tyranny: The Making of American Social Policy Against Family Violence from Colonial Times to The Present.* New York: Oxford University Press.

Pleck, E., Pleck, J., Grossman, M., & Bart, P. (1977). The battered data syndrome: A comment on Steinmetz's article. *Victimology, 2,* 680–683.

Probst, J. C., Wang, J. Y., Martin, A. B., Moore, C. G., Paul, B. M., & Samuels, M. E. (2008). Potentially violent disagreements and parenting stress among American Indian/Alaska native families: Analysis across seven states. *Maternal and Child Health Journal, 12,* 91–102.

Putnam-Hornstein, E. (2011). Report of maltreatment as a risk factor for injury death: A prospective birth cohort study. *Child Maltreatment, 16,* 163–174.

Putnam-Hornstein, E., & Needell, B. (2011). Predictors of Child Protective Service contact between birth and age five: An examination of California's 2002 birth cohort. *Children and Youth Services Review, 33,* 1337–1344.

Quinsey, V. L. (1984). Sexual aggression: Studies of offenders against women. In D. N. Weisstub, Ed., *Law and Mental Health: International Perspectives* (Vol. I, pp. 84–121). New York: Pergamon.

Radbill, S. (1987). Children in a world of violence: A history of child abuse. In R. Helfer & R. Kempe, Eds., *The Battered Child* (4th ed., pp. 3–20). Chicago: University of Chicago Press.

Raine, A. (2013). *The Anatomy of Violence: The Biological Roots of Crime.* New York: Vintage.

Renner, L. M., & Slack, K. S. (2006). Intimate partner violence and child maltreatment: Understanding intra- and intergenerational connections. *Child Abuse and Neglect, 30,* 599–617.

Renner, L. M., & Whitney, S. D. (2012). Risk factors for unidirectional and bidirectional intimate partner violence among young adults. *Child Abuse and Neglect, 36,* 40–52.

Renzetti, C. (1992). *Intimate Betrayal: Partner Abuse in Lesbian Relationships.* Newbury Park, CA: Sage Publications.

Renzetti, C. (1995). Violence in gay and lesbian relationships. In R. Gelles, Ed., *Visions 2010: Families and Violence, Abuse, and Neglect* (pp. 6ff). Minneapolis, MN: National Council on Family Relations.

Rivara, F. P., Anderson, M. L., Fishman, P., Bonomi, A. E., Reid, R. J., Carrell, D., & Thompson, R. S. (2007). Healthcare utilization and costs for women with a history of intimate partner violence. *American Journal of Preventive Medicine*, 32, 89–98.

Roberts, A. L., Austin, S. B., Corliss, H. L., Vandermorris, A. K., & Koenen, K. C. (2010). Pervasive trauma exposure among US sexual orientation minority adults and risk of posttraumatic stress disorder. *American Journal of Public Health*, 100, 2433–2441.

Roberts, D. (2002). *Shattered Bonds: The Color of Welfare*. New York: Basic Books.

Robin, M. (1982). Historical introduction: Sheltering arms: The roots of child protection. In E. H. Newberger, Ed., *Child Abuse* (pp. 1–41). Boston: Little Brown.

Rosenfeld, A., & Newberger, E. H. (1977). Compassion vs. control: Conceptual and practical pitfalls in the broadened definition of child abuse. *Journal of the American Medical Association*, 237, 2086–2088.

Rudd, J. (2001). Dowry-murder: An example of violence against women. *Women's Studies International Forum*, 24, 513–522.

Russell, D. E. (1986). *The Secret Trauma: Incest in the Lives of Girls and Women*. New York: Basic Books.

Sargent, D. (1962). Children who kill—A family conspiracy. *Social Work*, 7, 35–42.

Saunders, D. G. (2008). Group interventions for men who batter: A summary of program descriptions and research. *Violence and Victims*, 23, 156–172.

Schechter, S. (1982). *Women and Male Violence: The Visions and Struggles of the Battered Women's Movement*. Boston, MA: South End.

Schene, P. (2005). The emergence of differential response. *Protecting Children*, 29, 4–20.

Scheuerman, D. (2007). Lost children: Riders on the Orphan Train. *Humanities*, 28, 44–47.

Schumacher, J. A., Feldbau-Kohn, S., Slep, A. M. S., & Heyman, R. E. (2001). Risk factors for male-to-female partner physical abuse. *Aggression and Violent Behavior*, 6, 281–352.

Sedlak, A. J. (1997). Risk factors for the occurrence of child abuse and neglect. *Journal of Aggression, Maltreatment and Trauma*, 1, 149–186.

Sedlak, A. J., Mettenburg, J., Basena, M., Peta, I., McPherson, K., & Greene, A. (2010). *Fourth National Incidence Study of Child Abuse and Neglect (NIS-4)*. Washington, DC: US Department of Health and Human Services. http://cap.law.harvard.edu/wp-content/uploads/2015/07/sedlaknis.pdf. Retrieved on July 9, 2010.

Shenk, M. K. (2007). Dowry and public policy in contemporary India. *Human Nature*, 18, 242–263.

Sherman, L. W., & Berk, R. (1984). The specific deterrent effects of arrest for domestic assault. *American Sociological Review*, 49, 261–272.

Sherman, L. W., Smith, D. A., Schmidt, J. D., & Rogan, D. P. (1992). Crime, punishment, and stake in conformity: Legal and informal control of domestic violence. *American Sociological Review*, 57, 680–690.

Silverman, A. R. (1993). Outcomes of transracial adoption. *The Future of Children*, 3, 104–118.

Simmel, G. (1950). *The Sociology of Georg Simmel* (K. Wolf, Ed.). New York: Free Press.

Simon, R., & Alstein, H. (1977). *Transracial Adoption*. New York: Wiley.

Simon, R., & Alstein, H. (1987). *Transracial Adoptees and Their Families: A Study of Identity and Commitment*. New York: Wiley Interscience.

Sinozich, S., & Langton, L. 2014 (December). *Rape and Sexual Victimization Among College-Age Females, 1995–2013. Special Report*. Washington, DC: U.S. Department of Justice, Office of Justice Programs, Bureau of Justice Studies.

Slep, A. M. S., & Heyman, R. E. (2001). Where do we go from here? Moving toward an integrated approach to family violence. *Aggression and Violent Behavior, 6,* 353–356.

Smith, C. A., Ireland, T. O., & Thornberry, T. P. (2005). Adolescent maltreatment and its impact on young adult antisocial behavior. *Child Abuse and Neglect, 29,* 1099–1119.

Smith, M. (1991a). Patriarchal ideology and wife beating: A test of a feminist hypothesis. *Violence and Victims, 5,* 257–273.

Smith, M. (1991b). Male peer support of wife abuse: An exploratory study. *Journal of Interpersonal Violence, 6,* 512–519.

Smith, S. (1965). The adolescent murderer. *Archives of General Psychiatry, 13,* 310–319.

Smuts, B. (1992). Male aggression against women: An evolutionary perspective. *Human Nature, 3,* 1–44.

Sommers, C. H. (1994). *Who Stole Feminism? How Women Have Betrayed Women.* New York: Simon and Schuster.

Sommers, C. H. (2014). Five feminist myths that will not die. *Time* (September 2). http://time.com/3222543/5-feminist-myths-that-will-not-die/. (Retrieved May 19, 2015).

Stark, E. (2007). *Coercive Control. The Entrapment of Women in Personal Life.* New York: Oxford University Press.

Stark, E., & Flitcraft, A. (1996). *Women at Risk: Domestic Violence and Women's Health.* Newbury Park, CA: Sage Publications.

Stark, R., & McEvoy, J. (1970). Middle class violence. *Psychology Today, 4,* 52–65.

Starr, R. H.Jr. (1988). Physical abuse of children. In V. B. Van Hasselt, R. L. Morrison, A. S. Bellack, & M. Hersen, Eds., *Handbook of Family Violence* (pp. 119–155) New York: Plenum.

Steele, B. F. (1978). The child abuser. In I. Kutash, S. B. Kutash, L. B. Schlesinger & Associates, Eds., *Violence: Perspectives on Murder and Aggression* (pp. 285–300). San Francisco: Jossey Bass.

Steele, B. F., & Pollock, C. B. (1974). A psychiatric study of parents who abuse infants and small children. In R. Helfer & C. Henry Kempe, Eds., *The Battered Child* (2nd ed., pp. 89–134). Chicago: University of Chicago Press.

Steinmetz, S. K. (1971). Occupation and physical punishment: A response to Straus. *Journal of Marriage and the Family, 33,* 664–666.

Steinmetz, S. K. (1977a). *The Cycle of Violence: Assertive, Aggressive, and Abusive Family Interaction.* New York: Praeger Publishers.

Steinmetz, S. K. (1977b). The battered husband syndrome. *Victimology, 2,* 499–509.

Steinmetz, S. K. (1978). Violence between family members. *Marriage and Family Review, 1,* 1–16.

Steinmetz, S. K., & Straus, M. A. (1974). *Violence in the Family.* New York: Dodd, Mead.

Stith, S. M., Liu, T., Davies, L. C., Boykin, E. L., Alder, M. C., Harris, J. M., et al. (2009). Risk factors in child maltreatment: A meta-analytic review of the literature. *Aggression and Violent Behavior, 14,* 13–29.

Stith, S. M., Smith, D. B., Penn, C. E., Ward, D. B., & Tritt, D. (2004). Intimate partner physical abuse perpetration and victimization risk factors: A meta-analytic review. *Aggression and Violent Behavior, 10,* 65–98.

Straus, M. (1971). Some social antecedents of physical punishment: A linkage theory interpretation. *Journal of Marriage and the Family, 33,* 658–663.

Straus, M. A. (1977). Wife beating: How common and why? *Victimology, 2,* 443–458.

Straus, M. A. (1979). Measuring intrafamily conflict and violence: The Conflict Tactics (CT) scales. *Journal of Marriage and the Family, 41,* 75–88.

Straus, M. A. (1980). A sociological perspective on the causes of family violence. In M. R. Green, Ed., *Violence and the Family* (pp. 7–31). Boulder, CO: Westview Press.

Straus. M. A. (1993). Physical assault by wives: A major social problem. In R. J. Gelles & D. Loseke, Eds., *Current Controversies on Family Violence* (pp. 67– 87). Thousand Oaks, CA: Sage Publications.

Straus, M. A. (1994). *Beating the Devil Out of Them: Corporal Punishment in American Families*. New York: Lexington Books.

Straus, M. A. (2004). Prevalence of violence against dating partners by male and female university students worldwide. *Violence Against Women, 10*, 790–811.

Straus, M. A. (2005). Women's violence toward men is a serious social problem. In. D. Loseke, R. J. Gelles, & M. C. Cavanaugh, Eds., *Current Controversies on Family Violence* (2nd ed., pp. 55–77). Thousand Oaks, CA: Sage Publications.

Straus, M. A. (2008). Dominance and symmetry in partner violence by male and female university students in 32 nations. *Children and Youth Services Review, 30*, 252–275.

Straus, M. A. (2011). Gender symmetry and mutuality in perpetration of clinical-level partner violence: Empirical evidence and implications for prevention and treatment. *Aggression and Violent Behavior, 16*(4), 279–288.

Straus, M. A., & Gelles, R. J. (1986). Societal change and family violence from 1975 to 1985 as revealed by two national surveys. *Journal of Marriage and the Family, 48*, 465–479.

Straus, M. A., & Hotaling, G. T. (1979). *The Social Causes of Husband–Wife Violence*. Minneapolis: University of Minnesota Press.

Straus, M. A., & Ramirez, I. L. (2007). Gender symmetry in prevalence, severity, and chronicity of physical aggression against dating partners by university students in Mexico and USA. *Aggressive Behavior, 33*, 281–290.

Straus, M. A., & Stewart, J. H. (1999). Corporal punishment by American parents: National data on prevalence, chronicity, severity, and duration, in relation to child and family characteristics. *Clinical Child and Family Psychology Review, 2*, 55–70.

Straus, M. A., & Sweet, S. (1992). Verbal aggression in couples: Incidence rates and relationships to personal characteristics. *Journal of Marriage and the Family, 54*, 346–357.

Straus, M. A., Douglas, E. M., & Medeiros, R. A. (2013). *The Primordial Violence: Spanking Children, Psychological Development, Violence, and Crime*. New York: Routledge.

Straus, M. A., Gelles, R. J., & Steinmetz, S. K. (1980). *Behind Closed Doors: Violence in the American Family*. Garden City, NY: Anchor Press.

Straus, M. A., Hamby, S. L., Boney-McCoy, S., & Sugarman, D. B. (1996). The revised Conflict Tactics Scales (CTS2) development and preliminary psychometric data. *Journal of Family Issues, 17*, 283–316.

Straus, M., Kaufman Kantor, G., & Moore, D. (1994). Change in cultural norms approving marital violence. Paper presented at the annual meeting of the American Sociological Association, Los Angeles, California, August 7.

Strube, M. J., & Barbour, L. S. (1983). The decision to leave an abusive relationship: Economic dependence and psychological commitment. *Journal of Marriage and the Family, 45*, 785–793.

Sugarman, D., & Hotaling, G. T. (1989). Dating violence: Prevalence, context, and risk markers. In M. A. Pirog-Good & J. E. Stets, Eds., *Violence in Dating Relationships: Emerging Issues* (pp. 3–32). New York: Praeger.

The battered-child syndrome. [Editorial]. (1962, July 7). *Journal of the American Medical Association*, 42.

Theodore, A. D., Chang, J. J., Runyon, D. K., Hunter, W,M., Bangdiwala, S. I., Agains, R. (2005). Epidemiologic features of physical and sexual mistreatment of children in the Carolinas. *Pediatrics*, 115, 331–337.

Thornberry, T. P., Knight, K. E., & Lovegrove, P. J. (2012). Does maltreatment beget maltreatment? A systematic review of the intergenerational literature. *Trauma, Violence, and Abuse*, 13, 135–152.

Tjaden, P. G., & Thoennes, N. (2000). *Extent, Nature, and Consequences of Intimate Partner violence: Findings from the National Violence Against Women Survey* (pp. 1–62). Washington, DC: National Institute of Justice.

Tooley, K. (1977). The young child as victim of sibling attack. *Social Casework*, 58, 25–28.

Truman, J. L., & Langton, L. Bureau of Justice Statistics, US Dept of Justice, Office of Justice Programs, & United States of America. (2014). *Criminal Victimization, 2013.* US Department of Justice, Office of Justice Programs, Bureau of Justice Statistics. Available at http://www.bjs.gov/content/pub/pdf/cv13.pdf. Retrieved May 25, 2015.

Truman, J. L., Morgan, R. E., Bureau of Justice Statistics, US Dept. of Justice, Office of Justice Programs, & United States of America. (2014). *Nonfatal Domestic Violence, 2003–2012.* US Department of Justice, Office of Justice Programs, Bureau of Justice Statistics. http://www. bjs. gov/content/pub/pdf/ndvo312. pdf. Retrieved April 16, 2016.

Turbett, J. P., & O'Toole, R. (1980). Physician's recognition of child abuse. Paper presented at the 1980 annual meeting of the American Sociological Association, New York.

U.S. Advisory Board on Child Abuse and Neglect. (1995). *A Nation's Shame: Fatal Child Abuse and Neglect in the United States.* Washington, DC: U.S. Department of Health and Human Services.

U.S. Bureau of the Census. (2014). *Statistical Abstract of the United States, 2014.* Available at http://www2.census.gov/library/publications/2011/compendia/statab/131ed/2012-statab.pdf. Retrieved April 16, 2016.

U.S. Department of Health and Human Services, Administration for Children and Families, Administration on Children, Youth, and Families. (2016). *Child Maltreatment 2014.* Washington, DC: US Department of Health and Human Services.

U.S. Department of Health and Human Services, National Center on Child Abuse and Neglect. (1995). *Child Maltreatment 1993: Reports from the States to the National Center on Child Abuse and Neglect.* Washington, DC: U.S. Government Printing Office.

U.S. Department of Health and Human Services. (2001). *Evaluation of Family Preservation and Reunification Programs.* Available at http://aspe.hhs.gov/hsp/fampres94/chapter1.htm. Retrieved April 16, 2016.

U.S. Department of Health and Human Services. (2015). *Adoption and Foster Care Analysis and Reporting System* (AFCARS). Available at http://www.acf.hhs.gov/programs/cb/resource/afcars-report-15. Retrieved October 15, 2015.

United Nations Children's Fund. (2006). *The State of the World's Children 2007: Women and Children: The Double Dividend of Gender Equality.* New York: UNICEF.

United Nations Children's Fund. (2014). *Hidden in Plain Sight: A Statistical Analysis of Violence Against Children.* New York: UNICEF.

United Nations. (1995). *The World's Women: Trend and Statistics.* New York: United Nations.

Vissing, Y. M., Straus, M. A., Gelles, R. J., & Harrop, J. W. (1991). Verbal aggression by parents and psychosocial problems of children. *Child Abuse and Neglect: The International Journal*, 15, 223–238.

Walker, L. (1979). *The Battered Woman*. New York: Harper & Row.

Walker, L. A. (1984). Battered women, psychology, and public policy. *American Psychologist*, 39, 1178–1182.

Walker, L. (1993). The battered woman syndrome is a psychological consequence of abuse. In R. J. Gelles & D. Loseke, Eds., *Current Controversies on Family Violence* (pp. 133–153). Newbury Park, CA: Sage Publications.

Walsh, J. A., & Krienert, J. L. (2007). Child–parent violence: An empirical analysis of offender, victim, and event characteristics in a national sample of reported incidents. *Journal of Family Violence*, 22, 563–574.

Walters, M. L., Chen, J., & Breiding, M. J. (2013). *The National Intimate Partner and Sexual Violence Survey (NISVS): 2010 Findings on Victimization by Sexual Orientation*. Atlanta, GA: National Center for Injury Prevention and Control, Centers for Disease Control and Prevention.

Wauchope, B., & Straus, M. A. (1990). Physical punishment and physical abuse of American children: Incidence rates by age, gender, and occupational status. In M. Straus & R. J. Gelles, Eds., *Physical Violence in American Families: Risk Factors and Adaptations to Violence in 8,145 Families* (pp. 113–148). New Brunswick, NJ: Transaction Books.

White, N., & Lauritsen, J. L. (2012). *Violent Crime Against Youth, 1994–2010. Report# NJC*, 240106. Washington, DC: U.S. Department of Justice.

Widom, C. S. (1989a). The cycle of violence. *Science*, 244, 160–166.

Widom, C. S. (1989b). Child abuse, neglect, and violent criminal behavior. *Criminology*, 27, 251–271.

Widom, C. S. (1991). The role of placement experiences in mediating the criminal consequences of early childhood victimization. *American Journal of Orthopsychiatry*, 61, 195–209.

Widom, C. S. (1995). Victims of childhood sexual abuse—later criminal consequences. *National Institute of Justice Research in Brief*. Washington, DC: U.S. Department of Justice, Office of Justice Programs.

Widom, C. S., Czaja, S. J., & DuMont, K. A. (2015). Intergeneration transmission of child abuse and neglect: Real or detection bias? *Science*, 347, 1480–1485.

Williams, K. (1992). Social sources of marital violence and deterrence: Testing an integrated theory of assaults between partners. *Journal of Marriage and the Family*, 54, 620–629.

Williams, L. (1994). Recall of childhood trauma: A prospective study of women's memories of child sexual abuse. *Journal of Consulting and Clinical Psychology*, 62, 1167–1176.

Wolfe, D. A. (1999). *Child Abuse: Implications for Child Development and Psychopathology* (Vol. 10). Thousand Oaks, CA: Sage.

Wolfner, G. (1996). Family functioning and physical child abuse: Are certain types more prone to abuse? Unpublished doctoral dissertation. Kingston, RI: University of Rhode Island.

Wooley, P., & Evans, W. (1955). Significance of skeletal lesions resembling those of traumatic origin. *Journal of the American Medical Association*, 158, 539–543.

World Health Organization. (2013). *Responding to Intimate Partner Violence and Sexual Violence Against Women: WHO Clinical and Policy Guidelines*. Geneva: World Health Organization.

Wulczyn, F., Barth, R. P., Yuan, Y. Y., Jones-Harden, B., & Landsverk, J. (2005). *Evidence for Child Welfare Policy Reform*. New York: Transaction De Gruyter.

Yampolskaya, S., & Banks, S. M. (2006). An assessment of the extent of child maltreatment using administrative databases. *Assessment, 13*, 342–355.

Yllo, K. (1983). Using a feminist approach in quantitative research. In D. Finkelhor, R. Gelles, M. Straus, & G. Hotaling, Eds., *The Dark Side of Families: Current Family Violence Research* (pp. 277–288). Beverly Hills, CA.: Sage Publications.

Yllo, K. (1988). Political and methodological debates in wife abuse research. In K. Yllo & M. Bograd, Eds., *Feminist Perspectives on Wife Abuse* (pp. 28–50). Newbury Park, CA.: Sage Publications.

Yllo, K. (1993). Through a feminist lens: Gender, power, and violence. In R. Gelles & D. Loseke, Eds., *Current Controversies on Family Violence* (pp. 47–62). Newbury Park, CA: Sage Publications.

Yllo, K. (2005). Through a feminist lens: Gender, diversity, and violence: Extending the feminist framework. In In. D. Loseke, R. J. Gelles, & M. C. Cavanaugh, Eds., *Current Controversies on Family Violence* (2nd ed., pp. 19–34). Thousand Oaks, CA: Sage Publications.

Yodanis, C. L. (2004). Gender inequality, violence against women, and fear: A cross-national test of the feminist theory of violence against women. *Journal of Interpersonal Violence, 19*, 655–675.

Zellman, G. (1990). Child abuse reporting and failure to report among mandated reporters. *Journal of Interpersonal Violence, 5*, 3–22.

Zolotor, A. J., Theodore, A. D., Coyne-Beasley, T., & Runyan, D. K. (2007). Intimate partner violence and child maltreatment: Overlapping risk. *Brief Treatment and Crisis Intervention, 7*, 305–321.

Zolotor, A. J., Theodore, A. D., Runyan, D. K., Chang, J. J., & Laskey, A. L. (2011). Corporal punishment and physical abuse: Population-based trends for three-to-11-year-old children in the United States. *Child Abuse Review, 20*, 57–66.

Author Index

Page numbers followed by *b, f,* and *t* refer to boxes, figures, and tables, respectively.

Subject Index

Page numbers followed by *b, f,* and *t* refer to boxes, figures, and tables, respectively.